A PLUME BOOK

TO CATCH A PREDATOR

CHRIS HANSEN is the correspondent for the successful "To Catch a Predator" series. For the last twelve years, he has been an on-air correspondent for NBC's *Dateline*. Since the *Dateline* specials have aired, Chris Hansen has testified before Congress on this issue as a nationally known authority on protecting children from child predators.

To Catch a
Predator

Protecting Your Kids
from Online Enemies
Already in Your Home

CHRIS HANSEN

A PLUME BOOK

PLUME
Published by the Penguin Group
Penguin Group (USA) Inc., 375 Hudson Street, New York, New York 10014, U.S.A. • Penguin Group (Canada), 90 Eglinton Avenue East, Suite 700, Toronto, Ontario, Canada M4P 2Y3 (a division of Pearson Penguin Canada Inc.) • Penguin Books Ltd., 80 Strand, London WC2R 0RL, England • Penguin Ireland, 25 St. Stephen's Green, Dublin 2, Ireland (a division of Penguin Books Ltd.) • Penguin Group (Australia), 250 Camberwell Road, Camberwell, Victoria 3124, Australia (a division of Pearson Australia Group Pty. Ltd.) • Penguin Books India Pvt. Ltd., 11 Community Centre, Panchsheel Park, New Delhi – 110 017, India • Penguin Group (NZ), 67 Apollo Drive, Rosedale, North Shore 0632, New Zealand (a division of Pearson New Zealand Ltd.) • Penguin Books (South Africa) (Pty.) Ltd., 24 Sturdee Avenue, Rosebank, Johannesburg 2196, South Africa

Penguin Books Ltd., Registered Offices: 80 Strand, London WC2R 0RL, England

Published by Plume, a member of Penguin Group (USA) Inc. Previously published in a Dutton edition.

First Plume Printing, March 2008
10   9   8   7   6   5   4   3   2   1

Ⓡ REGISTERED TRADEMARK—MARCA REGISTRADA

The Library of Congress has catalogued the Dutton edition as follows:
Hansen, Chris.
   To catch a predator : protecting your kids from online enemies already in your home / Chris Hansen.
     p. cm.
   ISBN 978-0-525-95009-7 (hc.)
   ISBN 978-0-452-28927-7 (pbk.)
   1. Computer crimes—Investigation—United States. 2. Child sexual abuse—United States—Prevention. 3. Child molesters—United States—Identification. 4. Undercover operations—United States. 5. Online chat groups. I. Title.
   HV6773.2.H36 2007
   363.25'953—dc22   2007007927

Printed in the United States of America

To my sons, whom I love and admire; a father could not ask for better boys. And to the millions of other children who use the Internet every day: although you may think you are smarter than your parents and that we worry about you too much, every once in a while just listen; you may be surprised what you can learn and how it can make you smarter and safer.

Contents

Introduction

There was a time not long ago when stories about Internet crimes were a tough sell for TV newsmagazines. Executive producers were wary because images of people typing on keyboards and video of computer monitors did not make especially compelling television, even when combined with emotional interviews with victims. We were not the first news show to discover that predators pursued kids online. But we did figure out how to expose it in an enterprising way.

A lot of people had been banging the drum on the issue before *Dateline NBC* arrived on the scene. Advocacy groups, victims of computer predators, and even so-called vigilante groups had been trying to expose this years before the first "To Catch a Predator" investigation aired.

Local law enforcement and the FBI had been doing stings in chat rooms before we started. On average, the FBI caught one "traveler" every single day. "Traveler" is the term the bureau uses for someone who seduces a child online, makes a date, and then travels for the liaison. Police and sheriff's departments around the country have made occasional headlines about the teacher, businessman, or clergyman caught in one of their stings.

The controversial online watchdog group Perverted Justice had received attention in some local news markets for its stings before working with *Dateline NBC*. Perverted Justice was started by a twenty-something computer enthusiast named Xavier Von Erck. Von Erck got tired of hearing stories of adults harassing children online in his home-town of Portland, Oregon, and decided to do something about it. He went online posing as a teenager. If he was solicited by an adult who then set up a meeting, Von Erck would post the man's identity on the Perverted Justice Web site. Perverted Justice caught the attention of an-other Web site called Cruel.com. Cruel.com would feature a link to a Web site that embarrassed or "punked" someone every day. On Au-gust 7, 2003, a thirty-eight-year-old Redondo Beach, California, man named Dennis Kerr, whom we'd come to know as Frag, was perusing the site and was captivated by the Perverted Justice mission. Frag owned his own company creating computer programs that helped other com-panies train their employees.

Frag contacted Xavier and they instantly became collaborators. Now Perverted Justice (PJ) has more than sixty contributors across the country. But, when *Dateline* first contacted PJ in early 2004, it was still a small operation that was not widely accepted by law enforcement. "Del Harvey," the now twenty-four-year-old woman who has received so much notoriety on *Dateline NBC* for her work as a decoy online, on the phone, and in person talking to potential predators, had just joined PJ a week before our first sting operation on Long Island, New York, af-ter hearing about the organization from a friend.

The reason why we chose to work with PJ in the beginning instead of with law enforcement is because it allowed us to do real reporting on the subject of computer predators. If we had simply watched an officer chat with a predator and videotaped him being arrested when he showed up at a park to meet a child, that would only be telling part of the story and would not have given us much insight into the mind of a predator.

Working with PJ and renting our own home for the hidden camera operations enabled us to be in control of the environment. We could get a pretty good sense of who the potential predators were based on the extensive chat logs with decoys. We could watch them checking out our house. We could watch them come in the door, sometimes uneasy, sometimes with great confidence. And I would be able to talk to these men face-to-face. I would hear their excuses and sometimes their confessions. Some would bolt as soon as they saw me. Some would refuse to leave, demanding over and over that they not be put on national television. These confrontations are a critical part of both exposing and understanding the problem.

PJ has been criticized for tactics that some have called overly aggressive. Some police agencies don't think any civilians should be involved in this kind of work, and there are vocal opponents on the Internet of anyone monitoring conversations in chat rooms. PJ was also criticized early on for outing the men caught in its stings before they had a chance to have their day in court. Once a man had an explicit chat with a decoy and made a date for sex, PJ would post the man's name, picture, and other personal information on its Web site, exposing the man to potential harassment and those close to him to humiliation.

As PJ has evolved, it has gone from vigilante group to computer watchdog group. Once shunned by law enforcement, it is now in demand from police and sheriff's departments around the country. Now its mission has more to do with helping law enforcement prosecute cases in court than merely posting the names of predators on its Web site.

The reality is that PJ has the expertise we needed to investigate this crime and it has never let us down. Internet predation was a relatively new crime when we started investigating it and we had to be innovative in our methods. Some have questioned our extensive use of hidden cameras, saying that using them smacks of "gotcha" journalism. Often hidden cameras are the only way to capture a crime. It's really no different than when we used them in Cambodia to expose the child sex tourism industry and the men from Europe and the United States traveling to sexually exploit young children, or in India to uncover child slave labor in the silk trade. We just turned these techniques toward the crime of child exploitation on the Web.

Point of View and Epidemic

Often at cocktail parties or on airplanes, people will ask me about the "To Catch a Predator" investigations. Am I ever frightened? Has any one of these guys tried to attack me? And eventually, once people get comfortable after chatting for a while, many will lean over and in a hushed tone ask: "Have you ever just wanted to reach over the kitchen counter, grab one of these guys by the collar and throttle him?" Of course, but doing so would be inappropriate on many levels, and the truth is I try not to be overly confrontational because I really want the guy to talk to me. I really want to understand what led him to show up at our house to meet a kid for sex. But I'd be lying if I didn't admit that when I watch a man skulk into one of our investigations and appear almost giddy about an encounter with a minor, I feel outrage on almost every level.

As a parent I find it gut-wrenching to come face-to-face with so many men who would groom an innocent child for sex. As a journalist I have to try not only to understand why they do it but also hold them accountable for their actions. I also see things that could never be shown on television. In the infamous rabbi case (that I'll talk about in detail later) I witnessed a man of God send obscene material over the Internet to someone who said he was a thirteen-year-old boy. And not just run-of-the-mill porn, I'm talking about pictures of the rabbi naked and in one case gleefully performing oral sex on another man. It's none of my business what consenting adults do together on the Internet or in private, gay, straight, or bisexual encounters, but when it involves chil-

dren it is not only illegal, it is outrageous. Especially t
rabbi so confidently, almost with a bounce in his step, wal
hidden camera house to meet the boy.

Showing a sense of outrage also helps me to get the truth o
some of these guys and lets them understand that I know more that
perhaps they think I do. In Ohio, for instance, when alonzo403 paid us
a visit in the middle of the night looking for a fifteen-year-old girl home
alone, I was fairly aggressive in my questioning. He admitted to me that
he left his own teenage daughter at home so he could come to our
house to "party" with our girl. He even brought beer and wine coolers.
He was sheepish at first, saying he was just coming over to hang out.
But when I pressed him about his intentions, asking whether he would
have had sex with the girl, saying: "What is it, yes, no, maybe so?" he
ultimately admitted he very well might have committed statutory rape
that night.

It's important to be fair in these interviews and to try not to go
overboard, and while there are some sad cases that come knocking on
our door, these guys are manipulative and would, in most cases, walk all
over me if I didn't take control of the conversation. The tone is sometimes admittedly prosecutorial, but it more often than not elicits the
truth and gives us all a better understanding of the mind of a predator
and the danger posed to kids online.

There have been critics who question whether our investigations
constitute entrapment. You have to understand that when PJ decoys go
into chat rooms, they never make the first contact. The decoys merely
sit there using a profile that includes a picture that is unmistakably of
someone underage. The potential predator must make the first contact.
Usually once that happens, the man initiates a sexual discussion and ultimately agrees to meet a young teen in person. There is a strict proto-
col that is reviewed by senior PJ members. Unless a man is okayed, he
is not given the address to our undercover house.

However, clearly the decoy must create the opportunity for a meet-

it do in a real-life situation. The decoys will
rs that they will be home alone. They are ulti-
of a sexual encounter with an adult. Some even
it sex.

volved, so have our "To Catch a Predator" investiga-
ntil our third hidden camera operation that a law en-
ncy ran a parallel investigation and actually arrested the
men as they left our house. It was a challenging arrangement. As journalists, we didn't want to be viewed as an arm of law enforcement and
law enforcement didn't want to be seen as a tool of a national TV show.
Ultimately we were able to balance this by having PJ act as the wall between the police and the press, if you will. During one of our operations, PJ supplies us with chat logs and everything else we need to
confront our visitors. It also provides the evidence police need to make
an arrest once the man leaves our house. Many law enforcement agencies do not have the resources or experience to run such a sting operation, and wouldn't be able to conduct such an investigation without PJ
and the national attention brought by a *Dateline* investigation, which
often shows that a town is serious about combating this crime.

As journalists and writers we tend to want to quantify things. How
many children have been solicited for sex online? How many predators
are online trolling for victims at any given time? How many children
have been willing to meet someone in person whom they first met on
the Internet?

The reality is reliable statistics are very difficult to come by. It is true
that the vast majority of children who are sexually assaulted in this country are victimized by somebody they already know, perhaps even a relative. Still, there are statistics cited by respected child advocacy groups that
suggest one fifth of children online have been solicited for sex. Watching
the parade of potential predators coming into one of our *Dateline* houses,
you could get the impression that there's an epidemic. Yet there are also
studies that claim child sexual abuse is down across the board.

An Epidemic?

Who are these guys? Based on my experience there is not one-size-fits-all characterization. About a third of them, I think, are sick, evil, or wired to want to have sex with young teens. Technically, most are not pedophiles; that term refers to someone who seeks sex with prepubescent children. These are the guys who would probably be trying to meet kids for sex whether or not the Internet existed.

Another third, I think, tend to be the younger men who surface in our investigations, the twenty- or twenty-one-year-olds whom I refer to as the opportunists. Some are socially awkward and sexually inexperienced. This group figures that young teens might be having sex anyway and since the girl or boy is really only six or seven years younger, why not go for it?

As for the other third, I believe they would not likely be involved in this behavior without the Internet. For many men the computer provides twenty-four-hour-a-day, seven-day-a-week access to the Internet. And it is anonymous. You can be anyone you want to be online. And it's as addictive as a drug for many men. This mix ends up being a very strong cocktail. The men in this group often start by viewing pornographic Web sites, then come the chat rooms. Their addictions and compulsions develop to the point where the men no longer see the line between fantasy and reality. The only thing that will satisfy them is a face-to-face meeting with the target of their desire.

We don't know exactly how many computer predators are on the Internet at any given time and we don't know how many of our children have been solicited for sex in a chat room or how many of those then act on it. The evidence I have seen indicates that these incidents are underreported. Kids, in some cases, don't share this information with parents. Sometimes it's because they're embarrassed, sometimes because they fear they will lose their Internet access.

I'll tell you one thing, though. I've looked into the eyes of hundreds of men who have traveled in some cases hours to meet a young teen for sex. I have talked to them and have read the chat logs that sometimes reveal their darkest desires. Make no mistake, whether there are 5,000 or 500,000 on the Internet at any given time, they are out there and they pose a threat to your child.

These men typically don't stand out in a crowd. They are cunning and patient. They often have respectable jobs. In our investigations we have caught doctors, a rabbi, teachers, a lawyer, musicians, an actor, and all sorts of businessmen. In a recent investigation near Dallas, Texas, a fifty-six-year-old man had set up three different identities on the Web so that he could have sexually explicit chats with teenage boys. One of those boys was actually a decoy from PJ. In one evening the fifty-six-year-old posed as a nineteen-year-old man, a twenty-one-year-old man, and also had a MySpace profile saying he was thirty-six.

He talked graphically online about all the various sex acts he wanted to perform with the "thirteen-year-old" decoy noonezero93, as well as e-mailing him multiple pictures of penises.

louis conradt: i want to feel your cock
noonezero93: its right here
louis conradt: do you shoot alot?
noonezero93: not telling!!
louis conradt: you're so cute
noonezero93: well I just wish u had said ud come over then not call
noonezero93: or nothing
louis conradt: i know, i'm sorry
louis conradt: i'll have to make it up somehow
noonezero93: you should
noonezero93: and you know how
louis conradt: maybe you can fuck me several times
louis conradt: he he
noonezero93: i'll forgive you the moment I see u

noonezero93: i promis

noonezero93:

noonezero93: in person

louis conradt: has anyone sucked you

He even had a similar conversation with the decoy on the phone. The man never showed up, but in Texas just the conversation was enough for him to be charged with a felony. The next day Murphy, Texas, police obtained an arrest warrant for the man. What did he do for a living? It turned out that the man behind the chat was a career criminal prosecutor for twenty three years. Louis William Conradt Jr. had been the elected district attorney in Kaufman County, where he lived. A few years ago he stepped down to run for judge. When he lost that election he got a job as chief criminal prosecutor in neighboring Rockwall County.

But, in November of 2006, he was on the other side of the law. When police went to Conradt's home to arrest him, he refused to answer the door. Police called him on the phone, but he wouldn't pick up. They suspected he was home because a Murphy police sergeant saw that a laptop computer was on inside the house in a room where it appeared someone had just left in a hurry. A tactical team was brought in to enter and make the arrest. Investigators were concerned Conradt might be destroying incriminating evidence on his computer. After about forty-five minutes, the tactical team arrived and broke in through the back door. According to police, the prosecutor was standing down the hall with a small-caliber pistol in his hand. He said something to the effect of "Don't worry, guys, I won't hurt you." He then pointed the gun to his head and pulled the trigger. The man who oversaw the prosecution of hundreds of criminals chose to die rather than face the same process himself. This may be an extreme case, but it is an example of who is involved in this activity on the Web.

In this book I talk to some of the people who are at the forefront of this issue. The people in the schools hear things from your children that your children won't tell you. I'll show you what can happen to even the best, most careful kids when predators set their sights on them. I'll also take you inside the mind of a predator, and you'll hear from those who have studied sexual predators, to find out if these men can be treated or if their being locked up is the only solution.

Perhaps most important, I'm going to give you specific advice on keeping kids safe online. In the old days our parents taught us not to talk to strangers at the playground or at the movie theater. They warned us not to take rides from strangers. That advice is still good today; however the term "stranger" when applied to the Internet takes on a new dynamic.

Parents need to understand that a potential predator might groom a child for weeks. It's a slow and seductive process that can make a child feel flattered, mature, and attractive. In fact, after several online chats a child may no longer even consider the man a stranger. They may have exchanged so much information that the traditional "watch out for strangers" warning is no longer effective.

That's why parents need to know how a predator works and what the warning signs are when a predator is trying to get involved with your child. I'll give a list of twenty things you should look out for and discuss with your children. I'll also provide specific talking points and ways you can initiate a discussion with your teens. There are also software solutions that can protect your children online and warn you if there is suspicious activity.

For this book my team has interviewed computer safety experts, psychiatrists, law enforcement officers, and groups devoted to children's safety. In my reporting and in this book, I've tried to distill an accurate picture of the crime, the criminals, and the most practical information available that parents can use to protect their children.

Chapter 1

Long Island and Virginia Investigations

If you had told me before our first "To Catch a Predator" investigation that a) so many men would be willing to risk their careers, lives, and families to meet a young person for sex; b) that so many people have apparently uncontrollable addictions and compulsions involving Internet chat rooms and porn sites; and c) that these investigations, when broadcast, would resonate with our viewers as they have, I would have seriously doubted you. But that is exactly what is happening every day in chat rooms and social networking sites throughout the country. And when you consider that many of these cyber meeting places are populated with curious, boundary-pushing teens, it should surprise no one that the potential for a child to be approached by a predator is high.

What would become one of the most successful series ever aired on *Dateline NBC* had an inauspicious beginning in February 2004: I was stuck in traffic on the Throgs Neck Bridge, en route to a sting operation in a suburban home on Long Island where potential sexual predators were about to arrive. My producer, Lynn Keller, was frantic. If the predators got there before I did, it could sabotage the whole operation.

Our first shoot was relatively simple. We had six hidden cameras rigged in an average middle-class house. My biggest fear was that no one would show up. I've had enough experience in television news never to take anything for granted. We'd prepared well, done our homework, and teamed up with Perverted Justice, a nonprofit group committed to combating online sexual predators.

The story was my idea. I was intrigued when I heard about Perverted Justice from Kevin Dietz, a reporter friend of mine in Detroit who'd worked with them on a local TV story and vouched for their credibility. Before we worked with PJ we spoke with some of its critics and investigated some of the allegations of entrapment. None of them proved to be true. In fact, after our first investigation aired, PJ's chief critic called to say we had done a good job. I realized that a prime-time network news program had a huge advantage in this kind of reporting because we could afford to use high-tech hidden cameras—technology that allows us to put cameras in everything from microwave ovens to palm trees. With sophisticated production techniques, the creative input from producer Lynn Keller, and guidance from senior producer Allan Maraynes, the potential was there to come up with something powerful and potentially groundbreaking.

Since *Dateline NBC* is a news broadcast and under the auspices of the news division of NBC, in many cases we are legally able to film people and use their names on TV without first obtaining their consent. In many cases, when they arrive at our hidden camera house they have already committed a crime, because it is illegal to talk online about sex to an underage teen in almost every state in the country.

I was passionate about this assignment. It hit me on every level; as the father of two adolescent boys, I was disturbed that thousands of adults are eager to prey on kids like my own. As a journalist, I felt the issue of online sexual predators was one we're not adequately addressing at a national level. Not at all. It's on the public radar and awareness is growing, but not enough has been done to counter the threat that still exists. Despite organizations like the National Center for Missing and

Exploited Children, i-SAFE, and so many others that have made online safety a mission, kids in many cases still aren't aware of the risks they're facing, and most parents are not sufficiently informed about predators eager to snare vulnerable, trusting, or careless kids whom they meet online and ultimately want to meet in person.

I kept reassuring Lynn that I'd get there, and I did—but with only about forty-five minutes to spare before the first potential predator showed up. Once they started coming, they never stopped. Over the course of the next two and a half days, seventeen men arrived to meet with one of our decoys—who'd posed as underage girls and boys.

As would prove true throughout our investigations, we netted people from every social stratum. There were men who seemed creepy and others who held positions of trust in their communities.

I have done a lot of spontaneous interviews in my career in which I approach someone in a public place who is usually the focus of an investigative report and start asking questions. These people have ranged from gypsies involved in sweetheart swindles to a doctor caught in a hidden camera investigation into sex tourism in Cambodia. Even though I have the element of surprise on my side, I also have my heart in my throat. And this story took the art of interviewing to a level I'd never experienced before.

The men who came to our house were extremely eager. They had all chatted online with a Perverted Justice decoy posing as a young teen home alone and open to the idea of a sexual encounter. For many of these men, a liaison like this was the fulfillment of a fantasy born in chat rooms and porn sites over the course of many months or even years. The excitement and nervousness any one of these guys was feeling was about to collide with the energy and anxiety we were all feeling inside the house.

Imagine this as a work environment: Mitchell Wagenberg and his crew of camera and sound experts are jammed into a back room hunched over monitors in a makeshift control room. Upstairs in a hallway Del and Frag from Perverted Justice are working the chat rooms, lining up the visits and then providing us with the chat logs that I will use in the confrontations. There are two more camera crews who stay in the shadows until I tell our visitors who I am. Producer Lynn Keller is trying to coordinate all this with the help of associate producer D. J. Johnson, and Ron Knight, who does security for NBC, is trying to protect us all.

Among the first men in the door is a guy who calls himself dark-hero73 online. He'd been chatting online with a decoy posing as a thirteen-year-old girl named Beth. The conversation is sexually graphic.

darkhero73:   I want to be your master so badly.
beth: I've only been with one guy.
darkhero73:   That's OK, I'll tell you exactly what to do, you'll be fine. Are you going to pose nude for me, sweetheart?
beth: Maybe if you're really good.

When he walks into our kitchen, darkhero73 talks briefly with Del, who is posing as the girl. darkhero73 is around the kitchen for a few minutes until I walk out and surprise him. At this point he doesn't know whether I'm a cop or a mad father who showed up unexpectedly and he certainly doesn't know at that point that he is going to end up on national television. When I confront darkhero73 with the transcript of what he said online, he says: "I am just a lonely guy looking for a date." I ask him what his plan was and he says: "I'm ashamed. I'm sorry. I didn't mean anybody any harm." Then he reveals something else about his background: "I'm a schizophrenic man. I'm supposed to see my doctor today."

Once the cameras had come out into view darkhero73 figured out what he walked into: "I'm just getting my life in order. You're going to ruin my life." I suggested that he was the one who made the decision to come to the house and asked what he would have done had there really been a thirteen-year-old girl home alone. At that point darkhero73 was really getting agitated. "I probably would have just said hello and how you doing and maybe we could have taken a ride in my car and that's it," he said.

"You were going to take her for a ride in your car?" I asked.

He became defensive, like so many of the men I would meet in this situation: "I just got out of a mental institution a few months ago. I'm just a guy looking for a girlfriend, that's it. You're going to take a guy looking for a girlfriend and put him on TV and say, oh, here's a pedophile. That's what you're gonna do, right, because I came to meet a thirteen-year-old even though I didn't do anything. I think that's ridiculous. I think your story is a piece of shit."

After about thirty minutes of darkhero73 berating my crew and me, we finally suggested that it was time for him to leave, a suggestion he only accepted after Ron Knight stepped in and nudged him toward the door. After our confrontation we ran a background check on the man. Not only did it turn out that he had a long history of mental illness, he also had a history with law enforcement. His former girlfriend had been granted an order of protection against him. He violated that order and pleaded guilty to second-degree harassment and contempt.

Everyone in the house was blown away by the intensity of what had just happened, but there was little time to talk about it. More men were on their way and transcripts of their online chats had to be read.

Before long there was another knock on the door. It was ed_in_nyc, a married freelance television producer in his early thirties. As much as darkhero73 was frightening because of his graphic chat and his admitted mental instability, ed_in_nyc was threatening because of his cunning good looks, and slick approach. He was here to meet a fourteen-year-old girl named Rachel. When he arrived, Del, posing as the girl, invited him into the kitchen. What happened next was a tense standoff between ed_in_nyc and Del for which we weren't prepared. After a lengthy online chat in which "Rachel" made it clear to ed_in_nyc she was fourteen, suddenly ed_in_nyc wanted her to say she was nineteen. We figured out pretty quickly what he was up to: plausible deniability.

Remember, this was the first time we'd done anything like this and as far as the relationship between *Dateline* and Perverted Justice was concerned, we were really just getting to know each other. So there I was tucked in around the corner and down the hall from where ed_in_nyc was. Del was next to me talking to ed_in_nyc. "Rachel, can you read between the lines, tell me you're nineteen," he said. Del was looking at me for some advice and I sort of twirled my hand around as if to say, "Keep him engaged, keep him talking." That's exactly what she did. It seemed more like an hour, but these negations between decoy and potential predator continued for about fifteen minutes before I stepped in and asked ed_in_nyc to take a seat in our kitchen. Right away ed_in_nyc said, "I knew it."

I said, "You knew what?"

"What was going on here," he said. This was the first really creative excuse that I had heard in our investigation. ed_in_nyc's story was basically that he knew this was a sting operation targeting adults trying to solicit kids online for sex and he was just here doing a "research project." Now, remember this was the first investigation so no one was clued in to the "To Catch a Predator" series yet. I asked ed_in_nyc what he did for a living and he told me he was a television producer. I said, "That's interesting because I work in television as well."

It was then ed_in_nyc showed a flicker of concern. He seemed to finally recognize me from my earlier *Dateline* reports. Slowly, he started to sense that he was going to break through from producer to an on-camera role, and not in a way that was going to earn him an Emmy. Still, ed_in_nyc was hanging in there. The man who, online, told a decoy posing as a fourteen-year-old girl, "Picture this, you lying back as I straddle your chest," was now trying to convince me that he was on my side. He even showed his support for our investigation, saying, "I'm very interested in your story. I think it's a great thing that you are doing. I think it's something that you should really do more and more of and bag these people left and right." He shook my hand, offered to help in the future production of our show, and he was on his way.

The Long Island sting also uncovered someone in a position of authority and trust, someone you'd never expect to be soliciting a young teen online. At twenty-four, ryan4686 was supposed to be one of New York's bravest, a firefighter stationed in Brooklyn. But when he wasn't fighting fires, one of the ways he apparently spent his free time was going into chat rooms and trying to hook up with girls. Some of these chats even took place from a computer at the firehouse. ryan4686 chatted with the decoy on and off for a few days, sometimes using sexually graphic language and then other times showing a conscience, referring to the girl's age and how inappropriate it would be for him to meet her.

Ultimately, though, ryan4686 did drive over to our undercover house. But just as he did, a police car pulled into the parking lot of a real estate office next to our house. ryan4686 saw the squad car and was spooked. He took off, and at that point he was pretty much off the hook. Even though we suspected his change of heart had more to do with the cop car than any sudden moral awakening, because he changed his mind, Perverted Justice at that point wasn't even going to post him on their Web site as a predator. But then ryan4686 did something that would alter his life for the near future. He drove home, turned on his computer, and started chatting with the decoy again.

He at first accused the decoy of being part of a police sting operation, but then he got comfortable, and once again the chat turned sexual. ryan4686 then turned on his Web cam, exposed himself, and began to masturbate for someone he thought was a fourteen-year-old girl. All the while he was wearing his New York City firefighter sweatshirt. ryan4686 talked about coming back over to our house, but claimed to have had a fender bender on the way and never showed up. That's when I went looking for him.

Early one morning in Brooklyn, New York, I confronted ryan4686 as he finished his shift at the firehouse. I read him some of his online chat and showed him a picture of his online performance. While he claimed that he did not intend for a fourteen-year-old girl to see him masturbate, saying that show was for someone else, he admitted that his behavior was inappropriate. He even offered this advice to other men who might try to do the same thing: "I think, ah, people ought to use their heads, people should know, um, I made a mistake."

Several months after our first investigation aired, ryan4686 was arrested and charged by the U.S. Attorney's Office in Brooklyn with crimes related to his online activities. ryan4686 was looking at up to fifteen years in prison if he was convicted on all of the charges. Ultimately, his lawyer reached a plea deal with federal prosecutors and ryan4686 pleaded guilty to transmitting obscene material to a minor. He was convicted on June 8, 2006, and sentenced to five years' probation and continued counseling. He's also had to register as a sex offender and must submit to random polygraph tests. As part of the agreement, he must also allow his computer activity to be monitored.

The first investigation ran as an entire hour on *Dateline*. Included in the program were two powerful segments: one with a group of parents who were absolutely blown away that this could even be happening, and the other with a group of kids, virtually all of whom told me that they had been approached online by someone who made them feel uncomfortable.

I asked the kids whether they had shared this information with their parents. Not only were no hands raised, but no one could even look me in the eye. None had told either Mom or Dad. Why? They said they were afraid that their parents would take away the computer. (Parents, take note.)

The first hour was a huge success and created a buzz. I watched the broadcast at home with about ten neighbors, who were speechless afterward. After the show aired, Stone Phillips, the anchor, called me at home to say that he, his wife, and teenage son all watched and were riveted. He asked me if I would speak at his son's school. Stone and I are pretty good pals, but the fact that he didn't wait to tell me on Monday or shoot me a quick e-mail made me really think we'd made an impact. I knew then that we'd be doing this again.

Almost immediately, Lynn and I started talking about our next investigation. We'd learned a lot from the first one. Both of us were impressed with Perverted Justice and wanted to continue that relationship. We also had ideas about production, preparation, and using more hidden cameras in better ways. We thought our next broadcast would be even more compelling.

I'm certainly not averse to taking risks; they often lead to great television. But on the night of August 25, 2005, I was heading outside my comfort zone. We were twelve hours away from filming the second in what would ultimately become the long-running "To Catch a Predator" series. Perverted Justice had spent more time working the chat rooms before the shoot so we expected more men than in the previous investigation. I worried about handling the additional volume. Increasing the number of potential predators increased the potential for violence.

There were plenty of other things that could go wrong. I had spoken with the FBI about our investigations. What if word got out around town and the entire operation was compromised? What if local police got suspicious and showed up? At this point, we didn't have law enforcement running a parallel investigation. That would come later.

Our sting operation took place in a comfortable suburban home in Fairfax, Virginia. If all went as planned, men would begin arriving the next morning, seeking out young teens they'd solicited online for sex whom they'd been led to believe would be home alone.

This time the house had been rigged with nine hidden cameras, both inside and out. It was a more lavish operation than our first one and had taken a week to prepare. (As our subsequent shoots grew more ambitious, NBC would be spending tens of thousands of dollars just to equip the house with hidden cameras, microphones, and other technical gear.)

Dateline NBC averages about eight million viewers a broadcast. Some weak stories can often be padded out with other elements and additional interviews to make them succeed. But once again, this was make or break time. If sexual predators didn't show up, I had no story. *Dateline NBC* would have sunk tens of thousands of dollars into a boondoggle with my name on it.

Law enforcement officials and child advocacy groups who work on this issue estimate that the number of predators online at any one time could be in the tens of thousands. An exact number is obviously hard to gauge, but given that millions of children are online and that, statistically, one in five is solicited for sex, the dimensions of this problem are serious and huge, according to the National Center for Missing and Exploited Children, which closely monitors this issue. Based on its research, fewer than 10 percent of the preteens and teenagers approached for sex ever tell authorities about it. Even when scared, children usually feel too embarrassed or too ashamed to talk about what has happened.

Predators are cunning and duplicitous. Before they sink their hooks into children they groom them first by gaining their trust, praising them, and treating them like adults. This appeal is particularly successful with children who have low self-esteem. Suddenly they feel empowered and cool. Predators are savvy in kid-speak and able to feign interest in the TV and music that kids like.

Once they've won a kid's trust, some predators in the most extreme cases use threats and intimidation for manipulation: "I know where you live. If you don't do x, y, or z, I'll find you and hurt you. . . ."

We had teamed up again in Virginia with Perverted Justice to lure predators to our hidden camera house. In its early days, Perverted Justice did not work with law enforcement. There was concern among police departments and the FBI that the group's techniques bordered on entrapment. That image has changed.

PJ volunteers pose as underage minors by posting dummy pictures. The starting point is usually regional chat rooms on Yahoo! or AOL. They then move on to popular social networking Web sites for kids like MySpace.com.

What usually happens is this: a man sees a profile set up by a PJ decoy that includes a picture of a boy or girl who is unmistakably underage. The potential predator then sends an instant message. Most men are seeking kids between ten and fifteen years old. Once the man initiates a conversation about sex, the Perverted Justice decoy responds. In most states, charges of entrapment are avoided as long as it's the predator who makes the first sexual overture. PJ volunteers keep chat logs and turn over complete transcripts of a conversation to the authorities, which often lead to arrests. When we first began working with the group, it was averaging about two convictions a month.

PJ members are a mixed bag of characters. Some, like Frag, a middle-aged guy who worked with us in Fairfax and beyond, have successful businesses and the spare time to take on this crusade. Others, like Del, have worked with or known victims of predators and have seen the ravages of sexual exploitation and want to do something to stop it. Other PJ contributors have themselves been the victims of sexual abuse. Frag and Del have now made their work for PJ a full-time job.

Perverted Justice volunteers across the country had been working in chat rooms for several weeks on the Fairfax assignment. When I got to Virginia the day before the sting, Del and Frag were confident that men would be showing up and gave me a pile of transcripts of some very lurid online chats. Some men had included photographs of their genitals. I had to read each word of every transcript and know as much as I could about the potential predator to do a good interview. The content was so vile that reading the material was emotionally exhausting.

Del had set up a big bulletin board that had pictures of the men tacked up with the times they were supposed to arrive. She was confident that men would be coming in droves. I was more wary. It's easy to be bold online. In Virginia, the potential predators had already committed a crime by soliciting kids online for sex.

We had our own security person—Ron Knight—who'd been with us since the beginning. He's a retired NYPD lieutenant who spent twenty-three years with the force. He was meticulous in his preparations. We'd rehearsed how we'd operate. All knives were removed from the kitchen, and Ron told me to keep the kitchen island between the predator and me. He would be watching on a television monitor—ready to respond if our subject made a sudden move. Ron told me to ask the men to keep their hands out of their pockets and, if they were willing, to sit on a kitchen stool.

Even with careful strategies, we had no way of knowing if any of these guys would be armed or high on drugs. My gut feeling was that these guys were more likely to want to run away than turn violent.

I did a run-through with my producer and Del, who turned out to be an invaluable asset. She was twenty-two at the time and had an uncanny ability to make her voice sound like either a boy or girl. She did telephone verifications with our potential predators to make sure they were still planning to come. With a smile in her voice she'd be coy, shy, and flirtatious. But in baggy shorts with a baseball cap on backward and a lower modulation of her voice, Del easily passed for a fairly hip dude.

What viewers never saw on TV were the dynamics of what happened behind the scenes among the rest of us. There were twenty of us in all, and our success depended on working together smoothly as a team. But our personalities were different and we were cooped up in the same house for several days. A day could last for seventeen hours, and we all got tired and stressed. Ultimately, we were always able to work out whatever issues surfaced, but there were some highly charged moments that made me feel like I was on an MTV reality show.

Sometimes there were moments of almost comic relief. During our first investigation, one of the cameramen had a birthday. We got him a cake and as a joke had what we felt was a clever plan to surprise him. One of the other crew members went out to get the cake from the van. He was then going to pretend to be a potential predator and walk into the house carrying the box. When the cameraman having a birthday walked into the kitchen filming, he'd be presented with the cake and we'd all sing "Happy Birthday."

Only problem was, in the middle of all this, a real potential predator arrived at the house. We managed to scramble and reposition ourselves. After the confrontation with the potential predator, we were finally able to go through with the birthday surprise.

The night before the Virginia sting I called home and talked to my wife and boys before I went to bed. Hearing about the preparation for the upcoming school year and the antics of our dog helped center me in a more normal world than the one I was about to enter. I had a hard time getting to sleep that night. Everything was ready. Now all we could do was wait.

. . .

My fears were unfounded. We were besieged. The first man through the door was a rabbi. Within a few hours, it became clear that men were not only coming, they were coming slightly ahead of schedule, which created traffic problems for us. We didn't want to blow our cover by having guys running into each other as they were arriving and departing. We were inundated so quickly that I knew our first investigation was no fluke. I understood—in a way I had not before—that there is indeed an epidemic of online sexual predation. I was seeing the faces that went with the statistics.

In three days, nineteen men arrived at our house. What was chilling was that, for the most part, they all looked benign and rather nondescript. Men who had used disgusting language and e-mailed pornographic pictures of themselves to our decoys showed up in sandals or in sweatpants and running shoes. Forget the tattoos, cigarettes, and un-kempt hair; these guys could have driven up next to you in the parking lot of Ikea and you would not have looked twice.

Our operation worked like this: when a man entered the house, Del would call down from upstairs saying she'd be there in a minute and tell him to wait in the kitchen. When a man walked into the kitchen, I did, too.

"So what brings you here?"

With those words, we got started. Several men turned and made a fast exit, running away down the block. Most thought I was the child's father or someone from law enforcement and sat down when I said, "Have a seat." No one realized he was being secretly filmed in a house with hidden cameras or that I had read the entire transcripts of his per-verted online chats. Each hedged, dodged, and lied about why he'd come. That didn't surprise me. But when confronted with the tran-scripts of what they'd actually said, most insisted that this was the first time they'd ever done anything like this.

Aladdin was fairly typical. His online name was the_sphinx59. He had set up his rendezvous at the house thinking he was meeting a twelve-year-old girl who gave oral sex to her boyfriends. Aladdin was an Egyp-tian waiter at a Holiday Inn. At first he tried to lie his way out by saying he'd heard the house was for sale and he was there to check it out.

The transcripts told another story. When I pointed out to Aladdin what he had said online, he confessed and then, feeling faint, lay down on the kitchen floor. He seemed hapless and pathetic, the kind of sketchy guy I had expected to meet. Aladdin didn't threaten any of my preconceived notions about who these men were—fairly innocuous and powerless guys taking on larger personas online and seeking power over a truly powerless kid on whom they would act out their sexual fantasies.

What blasted away all my preconceptions were the men I met who held positions of trust in the community: a special education teacher, a rabbi, and an emergency room physician. I once went an entire year without using the word "shocking" in a *Dateline* script because I thought the word was overused, but there was no better word for what we were seeing in our house. I was shocked, and I don't shock easily. There was nothing pathetic about these men. They were conniving, determined, and deeply embedded within mainstream society.

The special ed teacher turned out to be fifty-four. He had been talking to a Perverted Justice decoy who was posing as a thirteen-year-old boy about oral and anal sex. The decoy asked him to bring condoms. When I asked the teacher if he brought them he said he had, but added that he always carried condoms with him.

At first he lied to me and said he thought the boy he was coming to meet, named Brandon, was an adult: "He said he was twenty-three, what's the problem?" When I pointed out the spot in the transcripts where the decoy gave his age as thirteen, he was shaken. "I thought I'd come see him." "See him for what?" I asked. "I wanted to meet him." Ultimately he said he "made a big mistake." A mistake that led to a guilty plea and a five-year prison term.

The ER doctor was cagy. He bounced into the kitchen in running shoes and sweats, and when Del, posing as a fourteen-year-old boy, called from upstairs, the doctor headed in that direction and threatened to blow our cover. I confronted him immediately.

Gbabbnsp was a fifty-year-old divorced dad with two adult children. He cast himself as the Good Samaritan, insisting he hadn't come for sex, but to comfort a teenage boy who seemed distressed at being left home alone. Gbabbnsp wanted to take him out to lunch. His online chat had been careful—"I don't think I even want to have sex until you're old enough for us both not to get in trouble over it." But Gbabbnsp did go on to say he wanted to cover him with "hugs and kisses," and "cuddle you and make you feel safe and loved and cared about."

Gbabbnsp acknowledged that he was in a situation that made him look bad, but he conceded nothing more than that and tried to maintain a deliberate composure before my grilling. But while his hand shook as he ate chips from a bowl on the table, he insisted he would not have ever done anything illegal.

The rabbi was something else entirely. Of the nineteen men who walked into our kitchen during our three-day sting, he was one of the most disturbing to me. While the ER doc remained evasive about his intent, the rabbi was not. He hid nothing. "I'm prowling for young men," he said at four A.M. when he was online using the screen name of REDBD.

Rabbi David Kaye worked as a staff member of a Jewish organization that developed educational programs for high school students. When the Perverted Justice decoy told Kaye he was only thirteen, the rabbi said, "That's rape." But moments later he added, "I've never been with a young man like you. But I would like to."

Kaye also sent photos of himself engaging in oral sex with another man. The photos were too pornographic to be shown on television. We had to edit out most of the picture and ended up showing part of Kaye's face with its strange smile. What was so striking about Kaye was how confidently and comfortably he strode into our house. It was the middle of the day in a lovely upper-middle-class neighborhood in Fairfax County, Virginia, about thirty minutes from Washington, D.C. With his hands in his pockets and a smile on his face, the rabbi walked right into our kitchen. Del, posing as the boy, said: "I just spilled some Diet Coke; I have to go change my shirt." When Kaye said "okay," it almost came out as a giggle.

During his earlier online chat with the decoy, Kaye said he could come over at lunchtime and visit, but he had a dinner date that evening with his girlfriend. He left open the possibility of another visit after he left his girlfriend. That's why Del asked him, "You gonna still be up for tonight after your date?" to which Kaye responded coyly: "We'll see." He chuckled for about three seconds before I walked into the room and his facial expression changed dramatically. The rabbi, who was paunchy with reddish hair, realized he was in trouble immediately. Right away he wanted to know who I was. I said: "I'll get to that in a minute." First I had some questions for him. Kaye said: "Look, you know I'm in trouble and I know I'm in trouble, I'm not looking to get into any more trouble, why don't you just tell me who you are?" I already knew from the computer background check we'd done on him what he did for a living, but I wanted to hear it from him.

"A rabbi," he said in a low voice.

"Presumably, in your position as a rabbi you've counseled parents and children?"

"Yes," he said.

I asked him what he was thinking as "a man of God" sending obscene material to a teenage boy and showing up at a house where he was supposed to be alone.

"Not something good," was his response. "Could you please tell me who you are?" he asked again.

"I'm Chris Hansen from *Dateline NBC*." What happened next played out in slow motion in my mind. Kaye came at me after grabbing the transcripts and the copies of the sexually explicit pictures he'd sent. By now the camera crews had emerged from the next room and there was no doubt in Kaye's mind that he was being videotaped. Our security man, Ron Knight, stepped in between us and after a brief scuffle Kaye left.

Between the time of our confrontation and when the Virginia investigation aired three months later, Kaye called my producer, Lynn Keller, several times. He berated her for planning to include him in our program, as if we were the cause of all his trouble. We offered him an opportunity to sit down for an interview and tell his side of the story. He would only do this if we promised to obscure his face, make no mention of the fact that he was a rabbi, and not use the video of me confronting him. These were obviously conditions we couldn't comply with.

In the week leading up to the Friday broadcast of the Virginia "To Catch a Predator," Kaye called us again and this time agreed to an interview without the conditions he demanded previously. On Wednesday morning of that week, Ron Knight and I flew to Washington, D.C., where our camera crews had set up for the interview in a Georgetown hotel. I wanted Ron there just in case things somehow spun out of control. Ron and I were standing in the hotel lobby when I spotted David Kaye walking briskly into the hotel clutching a briefcase.

He ordered me to sit down on the couch in the lobby and proceeded to tell me his conditions for the interview. As best I can remember he said: "My face will be blurred, there will be no mention of what I do for a living, and you will not use any of the video from the house in Virginia."

I said, "Rabbi, we've been through this. You know we can't agree to those terms." With that, he stood up and stormed off.

One of the men I met on that first sting was a military intelligence officer from a nearby army base. How could a guy in his position ask someone online who he thinks is a twelve-year-old girl to have sex with a dog before having sex with him? He said he wanted to know how that would feel. He later told me he had a serious Internet addiction, one of many I would hear about.

"To Catch a Predator Virginia" aired as the entire *Dateline NBC* hour on November 4, 2005. Ratings for the broadcast were exceptional; an estimated eleven million viewers watched the program. Because of the tremendous response we did a follow-up broadcast a month later updating our audience on the problem and the fate of several potential predators we profiled.

I was not prepared for the reaction to the Virginia investigation. On Saturday, the day after the original story aired, I took my sons and some of their friends to play paintball out in the country. It was a beautiful fall day and I wanted to join the kids tromping around in the woods playing war games. That was not to be. The cell phone would not stop ringing and my BlackBerry would not stop buzzing. People from work, child advocacy groups, Internet safety organizations, and law enforcement agencies all were weighing in with reactions.

The next day I took off for China to work on an investigation into counterfeit prescription medicine. There was no way to predict what would happen while I was traveling. The subject of computer predators was all over our cable network, MSNBC. Virtually every show devoted time to the story and used excerpts from our Virginia investigation.

Some of the hosts of the MSNBC shows and some of the guests expressed outrage that the men exposed in our investigation were not immediately arrested and charged with crimes. The Fairfax, Virginia, police department was taking a lot of heat. Lieutenant Jake Jacoby of the department had been interviewed for the story so he knew how many men had surfaced in our investigation and what some of them did for a living. He even commented on what crimes they may have committed.

That, of course, was all after the fact. It wasn't until after our story aired that Jacoby and his officers received copies of the online chats between the Perverted Justice decoys and the men who showed up at our hidden camera house. The police had to do their own investigation and develop prosecutable cases with the district attorney's office. I understood this. Some of the people who watched "To Catch a Predator" did not. When I returned from China a week after the show aired, there was still a lot of buzz about it, and when I appeared on various cable news programs, I made a point of explaining why the Fairfax police couldn't immediately make arrests based solely on a TV newsmagazine report. It was then that I realized that if we ever conducted another investigation we'd have to deal with the thorny issue of how to involve law enforcement.

Ultimately, some of the men in the Virginia investigation faced justice. The rabbi resigned his position shortly before the *Dateline NBC* broadcast aired. Nearly a year later, he was indicted by a federal grand jury on charges of enticement and coercion of a minor for sex and traveling with the intent to have sex with a minor. After reading the transcripts of the rabbi's online chat, the judge refused to let him out of jail on bond, believing he was a danger to the community.

Kaye waived his right to a jury trial and took his chances with a bench trial, where testimony is given and evidence is presented before a judge, and the judge alone decides whether the accused is guilty or not guilty. Prosecutors presented excerpts from the *Dateline* story showing Kaye coming into the house and being confronted by me.

While Kaye admitted in court that he had struggled with sexual identity issues over the years and had had a number of homosexual relationships with adults, he said he thought the person he was chatting with online was actually a young adult in a role-playing situation. Still, U.S. district court judge James Cacheris said the evidence against Kaye was overwhelming, and in September of 2006 found him guilty of both of the charges against him. On December 1, 2006, he was sentenced to six and a half years in prison followed by ten years of supervised release.

The ER doctor was fired by his hospital the day our program aired, and his medical privileges were suspended. He moved to California and tried to renew a license to practice medicine there. In March 2006 state licensing officials, however, were aware that he had surfaced in our investigation and suspended his license. The special education teacher was also fired. He was later charged with soliciting a minor for sex and pleaded guilty.

And we weren't the only ones conducting investigations for potential online predators. The Fairfax County police department mounted a series of sting operations nearly identical to ours that year, and they nabbed thirty men.

Chapter 2

Kacie Rene Woody

Rick Woody pauses before he speaks. The memories come easily, but sometimes the words do not. "It's things you can't put into words. It's like someone reached in there and grabbed part of your heart, there's a part of you, gone."

He is quiet for a moment, then another.

"You have to get to the state that this is not something that is temporary, she is gone forever."

The weight of his sadness fills the silence that follows.

"If I could do anything in the world right now," Rick Woody says, trying to contain his tears, "it would be just to hug Kacie."

It's a while before he can speak again. Words seem too small to carry the burden he is bearing.

"She had so much love in her. It's something that you get used to, something that you enjoy, seeing how much someone can brighten up your life. And then, all of a sudden—it's gone."

He speaks slowly, as if putting himself together again from all the broken bits inside. "It's the deepest hurt and pain that I have ever felt. I can't imagine anything being worse than looking at your little girl laying there in a casket."

Kacie Rene Woody was abducted from her home on December 3, 2002, and murdered by a forty-seven-year-old San Diego man she met in a Christian chat room who had pretended to be a teenager. Kacie had been raped and shot in the head. She was thirteen years old and found chained to the floor in the back of a van.

Rick Woody was working late that night as a police officer in Greenbriar, Arkansas, a town north of Little Rock with a population of just over three thousand. Kacie was home alone that December night. Her brother, Tim, a college student, was studying at the library and due back around ten. His friend, Eric Betts, who was taking an electrician's class and staying with the Woodys, was due home around the same time. Kacie's aunt lived just a few houses away.

Kacie checked in with her dad on his cell phone early that evening. The family had lived quietly for eighteen years at the end of Griggers Lane, a dead-end gravel road in rural Holland, Arkansas. The sign on the way into town says it has a population of 597.

"I talked to her on the telephone about seven o'clock and as far as I can remember, there wasn't anything that was out of the ordinary," Rick says. "I always asked, 'Have you got your homework done? Have you practiced the saxophone?' She'd done some laundry that night. Just a pretty normal conversation."

Kacie was an honor roll student and a dependable child. She was caring, sensitive, and wise beyond her years, having already been tested by tragedy. When she was seven, her mother was killed in a freak automobile accident. Two horses bolted into the path of the car her father was driving. One landed on the passenger side of the car, crushing Kacie's mother, Kristie, to death. Kacie, who was in the backseat, was not injured, and saw everything.

Woody devoted himself to his three children after his wife's death. Kacie's two older brothers, Austin and Tim, had graduated from high school and gone on to college by the time Kacie turned thirteen, but Tim was still living at home. Her dad adored her. They sang along to his Elvis CDs together in the car, and on Friday and Saturday nights, he said, they sat home together and watched the Disney channel. "We watched a whole lot of *Lizzie McGuire*.

"My biggest fear was that I was worried about the future. Here I was a single dad with a teenage girl. When she turned thirteen, all of a sudden there was a little bit of an uneasy feeling there, but still, I wasn't panicking yet like I knew I would when she turned sixteen. I'm telling her, 'You're going on your first date, I'm going with you.' I was very protective of her. She was my little girl and I know guys."

But Rick didn't know about the dangers of Internet chat rooms.

"I didn't understand that they were using these chat rooms to prey on these kids. I didn't understand how many predators were out there. I'm still old school and I was worried about the guy in the trench coat in the corner of the playground. I'm not thinking about them on the computer screen."

Kacie's computer was in the living room, facing a window and just a few feet from the kitchen. Rick knew Kacie chatted with her friends online, which actually saved money since they lived so far from town that talking to them by phone meant long-distance charges.

Her dad had rules about the computer. Kacie couldn't get online until she had finished her homework, done her chores, and practiced the saxophone she played in the junior high band. Rick felt her Internet use was harmless. Kacie was home and in the living room—what could happen? His fears were what might happen outside the house, not in it. Kacie's online chats seemed like an extension of Kacie's outgoing personality.

"She loved people, she loved talking to people, and she was a good communicator. I think it was just a way for her to express her giving personality, to get online and chat and make new friends.

"I knew she was going into chat rooms and talking to people. I would look at the conversations; the computer was right there by my

recliner. It was right there where anybody walking by could walk up behind her and see. I looked at several conversations and they were all innocent conversations."

Rick had told his daughter not to put her personal information online. "The problem is I didn't really know how to keep Kacie safe online
because I didn't understand about the predators out there. I didn't
know anything about chat rooms at all because I didn't have any interest in them."

He didn't know that a forty-seven-year-old San Diego man would
pretend to be a hip southern California teen to meet someone like Kacie and manipulate her goodness and trust for his own vile ends.

By seventh grade, Kacie and her two best friends, Samantha Mann
and Jessica Tanner, were all boy crazy. Rick smiles, remembering how
serious and how silly it could be. "It would be this boy this week and
another that week. Fortunately for me, she was still a daddy's girl."

Rick knew Kacie was chatting with Scott, a fourteen-year-old boy
in Georgia. But it seemed like nothing more than a cyber version of
puppy love. He was a few hundred miles away and he and Kacie never
talked about actually meeting. "They considered themselves boyfriend
and girlfriend. They were in love forever. It could have very well been
the boy at school," her dad recalls. "It just happened to be on the Internet."

There were other times when Rick would ask his daughter who she
was chatting with and where she had met them as her fingers flew over
the keyboard. "Her answer always was, 'In a Christian chat room.' I'd
be like, 'Great, talking with Christian guys.' Little did I know that was
where the predators would go to find innocent girls."

It was in a Yahoo! chat room for Christian teens that Dave Fuller
from San Diego "met" Kacie Woody.

Kacie posted a picture with her profile. Her screen name was
modelbehavior63, an amalgam of a favorite Disney movie and her
brother Austin's football jersey number. She said her name was Kacie

and that she was from Arkansas. In the More About Me section, Kacie wrote about her hobbies. "I write love poems, play alto sax, am in the school band and recently tried out for soccer. I'm thirteen now."

Under occupation, Kacie described herself as a "Messenger of God."

Kacie was spending the night with her best friend, Samantha Mann, when she met the man posing as Dave on the computer whose screen name was jazzman_df.

Samantha said, "When we met Dave in the chat room it was at the end of our sixth-grade year. She was over at my house, it was New Year's. Mom had brought up some grape juice in a wine bottle thing so we thought we were having a big New Year's party. We were on the computer and we met him and started talking to him all the time."

Samantha and Kacie had been friends since first grade but didn't become *best* friends until sixth. Sam remembers Kacie as goofy and out-going, but said what made her different from her other friends was that Kacie really cared. "She listened. Most people would be like, 'Huh?' 'Yeah,' 'Okay,' 'Anyway' and keep talking but she would listen and say, 'Yeah, I know, I understand,' until you had nothing to say. You'd be okay and then she'd be like, 'Okay, are you going to tell me anything else?' and you'd say, 'Nope.'"

But that New Year's Eve wasn't a time for heart-to-heart talks. It was a time to chat and have fun. Samantha remembers that the first con-versation with Dave started like any other. "He's like 'I think you're pretty, ASL?'" ASL is online shorthand for "age, sex, location." "She told him twelve, female, Arkansas, and we just started talking. Age, sex, location, that's pretty much what all the conversations start out with."

Something clicked with the guy in California who said he was sev-enteen. "We stayed with him on the computer and talked for a really long time. We didn't even get to see the ball drop because we were on the computer." Samantha said there was nothing memorable about the conversation—they talked to Dave about their interests, the weather in San Diego, things at school.

The girls looked at the picture of Dave that was part of his profile. They thought he looked like a young Fabio: strong, muscular, and with long hair. "I don't remember exactly what his face looked like," Samantha said. "I just remember his long hair. I remember thinking he'd be cute if he cut his hair off and Kacie was like, 'He's cute with his long hair.' And I was like, 'Okay, whatever.'"

Kacie and Samantha each counted Jessica Tanner as their best friend, too. Jessica remembers Kacie's excitement about her new friend, Dave, whom she remembers hearing about from Kacie for the first time in spring. "I was over at her house and she said, 'I met this really cool guy in a chat room, his name is Dave, here's his Yahoo! ID, add him into yours,' so I added him to mine."

After adding him to her Yahoo! buddy group, Jessica chatted with him online. "We introduced ourselves, he was like, 'My name's Dave.' 'My name's Jessica, I live in Greenbriar.' He was in California and we talked about how the day went and how my life was and how his was."

Jessica remembers how special Dave made the girls feel. "We were all curious at twelve and thirteen. Being able to tell someone 'I have an older friend, he's seventeen, he's really cool and he lives in California'; we'd always have something interesting to talk about to our other friends."

But Dave also made Kacie feel like a confidant—the one person who could really understand what he was going through. As he explained to Kacie, he had an aunt in Arkansas who was in a coma and probably going to die.

Samantha remembers how much Dave talked about his aunt. "He kept saying it's getting worse and worse. She's in Arkansas and he doesn't know how long she's going to live."

"He used that a lot," Jessica remembers. "Kacie was like, 'Your aunt and my mom will be best friends in heaven.'"

Jessica and Kacie tried to help Dave cope with the sorrow about his aunt. Jessica's father had died when she was three months old. "When his aunt would come up in conversation we'd be like, 'We understand, we've lost somebody that we've loved, we cared about them a whole lot. It will take a while to get over them, but sooner or later, you'll feel a lot better. Your heart will heal.'"

Rick Woody said that what made his daughter vulnerable was her sensitivity and desire to reach out to others in pain. "These predators look for the kids that are at risk, the kids who need someone to talk to in their lives. Kacie didn't fit the profile of a lot of these kids. She was vulnerable in the area that she was bighearted, she was full of love and understanding, and she loved to help other people."

There were times when Dave would call Kacie on her cell phone and she would conference in one of the other girls. Jessica thought Dave had a really deep voice, much deeper than their friends. But that seemed normal to Jessica for someone a few years older who'd been through puberty.

There was something about him that seemed odd to Samantha when they talked on the phone. "He used really outdated words like 'groovy' and stuff. But I just figured that was because he was from California and Californians are weird. They're not like all of us from Arkansas. I figured people from California talk like that. But his voice didn't sound like he was forty-seven. He sounded seventeen or eighteen, however old he was at the time. He changed ages so much."

That was something else Samantha noticed. When she and Kacie first talked to Dave he said he was seventeen. That summer he turned eighteen, but then "in September or October he said he turned nineteen. He didn't play that one out very well." But by then, Dave was such a nice guy and such a cool friend to have Sam didn't think much about it. She does remember once asking Kacie if she had any intention of going to San Diego to meet Dave. Sam said Kacie replied, 'No, I'm not stupid.' I was like 'What if he comes here?' She said, 'I've read a book about it. I'm not going to go and do that. Do you not remember the book? It's called *Katie.com*." The book, written by Katie Tarbox, and now retitled *A Girl's Life Online*, described how she was sexually molested by a man she met online when she was thirteen.

Jessica considered Dave a close friend, too. What touched her about him was that he was so unfailingly kind. "One night I was sick and I was staying with Kacie and I was like on her couch. My stomach hurt so bad. He got on the phone and he was like, 'I'll pray for you, I'm doing all I can, I'm praying that you'll get better and it's just like a twenty-four-hour bug.' It just seemed like I felt better, knowing that someone was praying for me."

Chatting helped relieve the frustrations of being in middle school. There is always someone willing to listen to you online. Too young to drive and get jobs, too old to play in the backyard as they did when they were younger, middle school girls are eager for acceptance and connections—eager to shed their self-consciousness and the anxiety around being pretty, popular, cool, and smart.

Dave always knew the right thing to say. Samantha said he helped her figure out a lot of things. "You could talk to him about all your boy problems at school. He was a guy and he like knew everything about it, you know? He'd be like, 'You don't need a boyfriend anyways because boys are stupid.' I'd be like, yeah, you do."

Both girls said there was a time early on when Kacie called Dave her boyfriend, but that was short-lived. Kacie met a guy at school and she told Dave that he was now her boyfriend. But Jessica remembers that Dave wasn't fazed at all. "He was like, 'Oh, fine, as long as we can still be friends, let's still talk.'" According to Jessica and Sam, Dave never made demands, never talked about meeting, and never steered conversations toward sex.

Except for Samantha's flicker of doubt about Dave's age and clumsy use of no longer hip language, there were never any serious concerns about him. "He always had a consistent story," says Jessica. "Every day he'd tell us about school and on weekends he'd go and hang out with his friends and talk about how his parents and him were arguing about how dirty his room is. Just teenage things."

Rick Woody remembers that sometime in October 2002, two months before she was murdered, he asked Kacie who she was chatting with online. She told him that her friend Dave lived in San Diego. Rick asked her how old he was and when Kacie said he was eighteen, her father said, "That's too old." He asked her to stop chatting with him—not out of fear—but because he was five years older than Kacie, which just didn't seem right to her super-protective dad.

Samantha said when Kacie told Dave that she'd have to stop chatting with him he said, "'Well, if you can't talk to me on the computer, you can talk to me on the phone,' and she said, 'Yeah.'"

Kacie had been crowned the Fall Festival Queen shortly before her thirteenth birthday and wore a long black dress—her first formal—to the festival dance. Daddy's little girl looked like a princess that night.

Rick Woody gave in to his daughter's persistent requests and got Kacie a Web cam for her birthday on October 17, 2002. He knew how much she and Jessica liked to make silly pictures with goofy grins. "It goes back to me being naïve again. I didn't realize she could turn around and put those pictures on the Internet. I think Dave was saying 'Send me a picture.'"

That's exactly what Kacie and Jessica often did. "We sent a lot of pictures to him through the Web cam. They were just still pictures. I think maybe four or five times we'd get on the camera and actually wave to him," Jessica recalls. "He always had a compliment like we looked good, we looked pretty. He always kept it pretty mellow." Never did Dave say anything that made Jessica feel uncomfortable. Nor did Kacie ever confide any feelings of unease or fear about Dave. When Dave talked about meeting someone, it was Scott.

Kacie and Scott, the boy in Georgia, had officially become boyfriend and girlfriend two weeks before her birthday. They'd been online friends for about six months. Kacie hung his picture in her locker at school. He was wearing his football uniform and a wide smile. She and Scott chatted incessantly online—his screen name was tazz2999. He was romantic and unabashed about expressing himself. Kacie shared some of his romantic messages with her friends—". . . ur everything and so much more to me ur my moon and my sun u light up my world you're my angel My love for you will never end."

Kacie had even introduced Scott to Dave and they talked twice by phone, mostly about cars.

Jessica remembers one scary incident that November when she was spending the night with Kacie. The girls were getting off the computer and talking to Dave on the phone. "We were walking through the bedroom and at that time, the kitchen floor squeaked really bad and we shut the door." The girls were home alone except for George, Kacie's miniature Yorkshire terrier.

What spooked them was that they both knew the kitchen floor didn't squeak on its own. "In order to make the kitchen floor squeak, you have to weigh more than a dog or an animal, you have to be at least human," says Jessica, the fear of that night still lacing her voice with urgency. The girls told Dave that they thought someone was in the kitchen.

Dave was reassuring. "Nobody is in your kitchen." The girls shoved a dresser up against the door in Kacie's bedroom for protection. The squeaking in the kitchen stopped. Jessica said they feared someone was just outside Kacie's bedroom door. She and Kacie called out for Rick, Tim, and Eric, in case one of them had come home unannounced. There was no answer.

Dave urged them not to hang up. "Don't get off the phone. What if he or she comes in?" Jessica said they bantered back and forth with Dave for about ten minutes. The kitchen floor squeaked again and then the front door shut. The girls called Kacie's brother, Tim, and told him what happened. When he got home he said putting the dresser in front of the door was the safest thing they could have done but said they should have hung up on whomever they were talking to. Jessica remembers how mean that felt. "We thought it was rude."

Investigators are convinced, based on credit card receipts, that Dave Fuller made at least two trips to Arkansas, in October and November, before finally returning a third time in December to murder Kacie. "He was patient, he waited on his time. He was truly a predator," says investigator Karl Byrd. "Predators take advantage of the situation to obtain their prey."

Tuesday, December 3, 2002, was a day like most others at Greenbriar Middle School, except that a fight that had started the day before between Kacie and Samantha was continuing. Now their friends were taking sides. The scrap began over the picture of Scott in Kacie's locker. "She got mad at me at school," Samantha says. "I said her boyfriend was 'hot,' and she thought I said 'fat.'" Kacie had been telling all their mutual friends that Sam had called her boyfriend "fat."

Samantha went to see Diane Kellar, the school counselor to six hundred middle schoolers. Calm, thoughtful, and gracious, Kellar has been steeped in education for at least twenty-five years, migrating from English teacher to guidance counselor. "She and Kacie were having what I call 'little girl fuss fights,'" says Kellar. "Samantha came in and wanted to talk about Kacie. She was concerned." Sam sat in the white wicker chairs that Kellar has arranged to look cozy in her office.

Samantha told Kellar that she thought Kacie was giving out too much information online. She said she'd given out her phone number. But Sam was worried about Scott, not Dave. "I wasn't concerned about Dave because he was my friend. Scott wasn't my friend." Samantha thought Scott might be "some guy who put a picture of his grandson in a football uniform out there."

Kellar called Kacie to her office and left the two girls alone to calm down and sort through their misunderstanding about Scott. Then after fifth period, Kellar spoke to Kacie alone. "Kacie assured me that everything was okay, she was being careful and knew what to do." Kellar talked generally about the potential dangers online. But Kacie reassured her that her dad knew she gave her phone number out to people she met online and approved of who she talked to.

Diane Kellar was not at all alarmed. "I had a false sense of safety. We live in a small rural town, there's not a lot of crime, we know everybody and it just didn't occur to me—those are things that happen in large towns in metropolitan areas—not in Greenbriar, Arkansas."

By the end of the school day, the crisis between Kacie and Sam had dissipated like smoke. They walked with Jessica and their friend Jacqueline to the school buses together. "We were saying, 'Bye, Kacie,' and she said, "'Can I stay the night with you tonight?' I said you don't have a note, you dork." She asked Jessica and Jacqueline about a sleepover and they said the same thing—without a note from her parents that was then signed by the principal, it wasn't going to happen.

Sam said Kacie didn't seem worried. "She was like, no one's going to be home and I don't want to practice my saxophone." But when she realized that there was no chance of a sleepover, she just said good-bye. "She laughed her weird little laugh," remembers Samantha, "and she's just like 'Okay, I love you all,' and gave us all hugs. That was the last time I'd see her."

Samantha's poise and energy suddenly dissipate. The facts are familiar, but the feelings are still so overpowering.

Rick Woody had just been promoted the year before from dispatcher to police officer. But on December 3, he felt lousy from a sinus infection and debated calling in sick. His chief told him to take it easy when he came in at the start of his four P.M. to eleven P.M. shift. But no luck. Before long he was called out on an auto accident. The freezing rain and the wind made it feel like it was spitting sleet. It was a bad night to be on the roads.

As she told her dad when she talked to him that evening, Kacie had done her homework and practiced the saxophone. She was in for the night and after having some ramen noodles for dinner was on the computer. She clicked on her Yahoo! messenger list and sent a group e-mail to her closest friends at school.

"Just a lil message to let everyone know I love y'all."

Those would be her last eleven words to her friends.

Scott sent Kacie an instant message and started chatting, full of news and affections transmitted in staccato bursts of words and abbreviations.

```
tazz2999:          Hey Sweetie
modelbehavior63:   hey
tazz2999:          how are you my angel?
modelbehavior63:   ok u
tazz2999:          better now that ur on sweetie
```

Kacie told Scott about the day's big news; she was one of twenty-three kids picked out of one hundred thirty to sing in front of the school board. She also filled him in that evening on her spat with Samantha and the trip to see Mrs. Kellar.

```
modelbehavior63:   So guest what I got . . . a lecture
tazz2999:          awww im sorry baby
modelbehavior63:   on how you could be a 80 year-old rapest . . . lol
tazz2999:          lol
modelbehavior63:   hehe . . . and that the picture was ur grandson
tazz2999:          how many times have u gotten that 1 hehe
modelbehavior63:   um . . . I lost count . . . well . . . then . . . she is
                   like "do ur parents know u talk to ppl u dont
                   know?" i was like "yeah" and she was like . . .
                   well be careful . . . and don't agree to meet
                   them less ur mom or dad is with you i was
                   like . . . okay . . . and she was like remember
                   this lil talk . . . I was like . . . ok
```

While Kacie was instant messaging with Scott that evening she was also carrying on a conversation with Dave. He called to tell her his aunt was dying that night and Kacie described to Scott how she was trying to console him.

modelbehavior63:	tonight . . . Dave's aunt is going to meet my mommy
tazz2999:	Im soso sorry baby . . . at least we know that she will be happy there with your mommy . . . I am sure she will look out for her . . .
modelbehavior63:	yeah . . . i think they will be best friend . . . hehe
tazz2999:	I hope Dave is alright
modelbehavior63:	he is . . . I am on the phone . . . he has been laughing at me . . . bc he know it is the best . . .
tazz2999:	at least he is laughing

Dave Fuller was on the phone because he could not be on the computer; he was driving toward her house in a rented silver minivan.

Kacie wanted Scott to know how bad the weather was that night. She clicked on a weather Web site and sent it his way.

modelbehavior63:	look at what it feels like outside!
tazz2999:	awww *holds her tight and rubs her arms to keep her warm*

When Kacie was home alone she turned on all the lights inside.

tazz2999:	hehe ill always be with u my angel because ur all I want to be with

Kacie didn't respond right away so Scott kept on.

tazz2999:	hehe I put my screen saver as the picture I have in my locker.

tazz2999	ur the most beautiful angel in the world Kacie

Kacie fell silent.

tazz2999:	r u ok sweetie?
modelbehavior63:	yeah

It was 9:41 P.M. Kacie Rene Woody was never heard from again. Dave Fuller had slipped in through her unlocked front door and pressed a cloth saturated with chloroform over her face. There were signs of a brief struggle. Kacie's glasses were found in the recliner. Fuller then dragged or carried the thirteen-year-old into the minivan. She was wearing what she always wore to bed: a gray sweatshirt and a pair of blue sweats that had "Baby Girl" written on them.

Meanwhile in Alpharetta, Georgia, Scott felt something was amiss. This wasn't like Kacie, not at all.

tazz2999:	u there baby?
tazz2999:	sweetie ru okay . . .
tazz2999:	please talk to me baby
tazz2999:	when u r ready to talk ill be here
tazz2999:	are you mad at me baby?
tazz2999:	please talk to me baby

Scott tried for half an hour to get a response from Kacie. His messages became increasingly desperate.

tazz2999:	Please GOD let her be okay
tazz2999:	Kacie please talk to me
tazz2999:	please . . . please
tazz2999:	Kacie I'm so so scared I dont know what to do.

Thirty-six minutes after his last communication with Kacie, Scott called her house at 10:15 P.M. There was no answer.

tazz2999: why isnt anyone answering the PHONE!
tazz2999: UGH
tazz2999: Please
tazz2999: PLEASE PICK UP KACIE
tazz2999: PLEASE
tazz2999: GOD PLEASE LET HER PICK UP

Scott sent an e-mail to Jessica, asking her if something was wrong with Kacie, but Jessica had already gone to bed and didn't see the e-mail until the next morning.

Scott tried once more to reach anyone at the Woody home.

"Eric, Tim, Daddy, Danny—anyone—please be there to help her, please. I know something isn't right. Please please please."

Two minutes after Scott left his frantic phone message, Eric came home from his electrician's class. The house was quiet. He assumed Kacie was asleep. The computer was on but he didn't bother to glance at it. Nor did he check the messages on the Woody phone. He turned on the TV and threw in some laundry.

At eleven thirty, when he went back to the utility room, he noticed that the light was on in Kacie's bedroom, but she wasn't there. When her brother Tim came home minutes later, Eric mentioned that to him.

Tim called his dad, who said he was sure Kacie was at home. Rick said he'd come right home and sent Tim to check and see if Kacie had gone over to her aunt Teresa's house nearby on Griggers Lane.

Something didn't feel right about this. Kacie was supposed to be at home. Rick called the sheriff's office and raced back home.

At first glance, nothing seemed out of the ordinary when he walked in the door. But when he went into the kitchen, he saw that both of Kacie's coats were hanging there. Her shoes were by the computer desk. "I didn't feel good about that at all," Rick says.

Tim had canvassed the neighbors but no one had seen her. The state police arrived and asked Rick if she might be a runaway. He assured them she was not.

He went to sit in his recliner, moving the towels Kacie had left there after doing the laundry. "I found Kacie's bent glasses and one of the lenses was popped out, lying in the chair. Then I noticed that the chair was pushed all the way against the wall instead of being pulled out like it normally would have been," Rick says.

George, Kacie's dog, was limping.

"Your whole insides are in knots and you know things aren't looking good but you are constantly trying to find something logical to make this be all right." But Rick knew the facts pointed only one way. "I knew that someone had come in and got her and that she didn't leave voluntarily."

One of the boys, either Eric or Tim, noticed Scott's frantic messages. Both stayed at the computer trying to contact him, but he'd gone to bed. No one realized that his number was on their caller ID.

The FBI was called during the night when it became clear from Scott's messages that this might be Internet related. By dawn agents were processing the house, and one turned up a crumpled piece of paper in Kacie's trash that had the name "David Fagen, San Diego," written on it. The name was something to pursue.

• • •

Samantha had been awakened during the night by a phone call. "I remember the exact time because you can't forget things like that. It was 1:11 A.M. I picked up the phone and Rick's like, 'Hi, Sam, this is Kacie's dad. Is she at your house?' I was like 'No-oh.' I thought they were playing a joke because she had asked to stay with me earlier. He goes, 'Well, she's missing, do you know anybody whose house she could be at?'" Sam mentioned the names of a few people who rode Kacie's bus.

Sam tried to sleep again but couldn't. She went down and woke up her mother and asked her to pray for Kacie because she was missing.

On the school bus the next morning a boy hollered out to Sam. "Did you hear about that Kacie girl getting kidnapped?" Sam tried to hold it together.

But when she walked into the first-period science class with Miss Moreland that she and Kacie shared, it hit her. Kacie's desk was empty. It was right next to Sam's.

The two empty desks made Sam start to cry. Miss Moreland sent her to Diane Kellar's office.

Jessica hadn't been able to check her e-mail before coming to school so she'd not seen Scott's message. She didn't find out until she walked into her first-period consumer science class and a girl said that Kacie had been kidnapped. Jessica was dismissive. "I think I would have known. I watched the news last night." The girl told her it happened after the news and Jessica burst into tears.

When Sam and Jessica saw each other they collapsed into each other's arms and sobbed. Diane Kellar put them in a room by themselves. They cried and talked, talked and cried. Both concluded that "it had to be Scott."

FBI agents interviewed both girls at school and told them Scott had been eliminated as a suspect. He was who he said he was and in Georgia.

After they answered the agents' questions, Samantha and Jessica sat in Diane Kellar's office going over everything they knew about Kacie, trying to think if they'd left anything out. "What's something different?" Jessica asked. "Dave was going to come to Arkansas to see his aunt because she was in a coma," said Sam.

"Oh, my God, it's Dave," shrieked Jessica. "Do you not get it? He came to Arkansas when?"

"A couple of days ago," said Sam.

"It's Dave, it's Dave," said Jessica.

Sam didn't want to believe it. She liked and trusted Dave too much to think of him as capable of harming her friend.

The girls told Mrs. Kellar that they needed to talk to the FBI agents again. They did. The investigators thanked them for what they felt was a good clue.

• • •

Following up on the name pulled from Kacie's wastebasket, detectives in nearby Conway were asked to canvass local motels and see if there was a David Fagen or any other David registered from California. The second call gave investigators their big break. It was about one thirty P.M. on Wednesday when a clerk at the Motel 6 said there was a guest registered by the name of David Fuller. He had checked in two days before and planned to stay for a week. The clerk recalled that he was irritated when the Internet connections weren't working in the room. Fuller's check-in information gave authorities his cell phone number. A quick check linked it to calls made from the Woody home.

Investigators entered the room and found Fuller's laptop. There was little doubt now about Fuller being their guy. By tracking other transactions on the credit card Fuller had used at the motel, police established that he'd rented a silver Dodge minivan.

Arkansas's version of an Amber alert—a Morgan Nick alert—was broadcast with Dave Fuller's name and the vehicle he was believed to be driving.

Rick Woody felt a stirring of hope. The investigation had come together so quickly that what he worried about most was whether the information about Fuller had been given to police in Oklahoma and New Mexico. "I got it in my mind that he was loaded up and taking her to California."

Investigators got another break that afternoon when a further check on Fuller's credit card showed that he'd rented storage space in Conway a month before.

Two FBI agents and a detective arrived at the Guardsmart Storage area shortly after five P.M. They went to the unit Fuller had rented and found the door unlocked. Detective Jim Barrett saw that there was a silver minivan inside, its engine running. Gun drawn, he started to move toward it.

A shot rang out.

Dave Fuller had fired a bullet through his brain.

• • •

After the gunshot, SWAT teams were called in and everyone pulled back. Rick was home monitoring police radios and TV. The hope that had brimmed up inside when he heard there was a suspect and a vehicle diminished when he heard on TV that a shot had been fired.

"I didn't feel very good about the shot being fired, but as time went on, as more time elapsed, the worse I felt because I knew if she were in there, if she were alive, this would be getting over quicker. Then I would try to make that irrational thinking—they are just being careful because she's alive and they don't want her to get hurt. You can imagine all the emotions that were pinging around."

Kacie's closest friends had gone over to Samantha's house. They were on the back porch swing when Sam remembered a conversation she had with Kacie a few weeks before.

"She was talking about how she wanted it to snow so bad and how she was going to be really pissed off if it was another year that we didn't have snow because it hadn't snowed for forever."

Samantha becomes quieter.

"Kacie was like, 'If I get one more thing before I'm a hundred years old and die, I want it to snow. I want to see it snow in Arkansas again.'"

When it started to snow that night, Sam burst into tears. She knew Kacie was gone.

• • •

There had been no sounds or movement at the storage area. After three hours, police moved in. Dave Fuller was slumped in the rear of the unit, a 9mm Luger still in his grasp. He was facing the back of the minivan from which the two backseats had been removed.

Kacie Woody was naked and chained to the floor of the van. She had been raped and shot in the head. A bottle of chloroform was nearby.

• • •

The police radio fell silent. A news conference was called for ten P.M. Rick Woody called an officer he knew with the rescue unit who was on the scene. The officer said he didn't know anything. "I knew that was a lie," Rick recalls. Good news travels by phone. "I knew in my heart that there was a bad outcome and all I was doing was sitting there waiting for someone to come tell me."

Karl Byrd, the lead investigator for the state police and now sheriff of Faulkner County, and detective Jim Wooley arrived to tell Rick Woody that his only daughter was dead.

"Tim and I went into the bedroom with just them. We just cried and held each other."

Rick Woody is a man who's been bombarded by loss. But nothing as cruel as this.

"I lost my mother at nineteen—to me that was the end of the world. We were extremely close. Then I lost my dad and then I lost my wife and thought, 'It can't get worse than this.' Then you turn around and lose your little girl."

There didn't seem to be a great reason to go on. "When I lost my wife, my attention turned immediately to my kids. Not only do I have to keep them protected, but I have to be okay for them. I'm all they have left. I got to work a little harder at being okay myself. But when you lost your little girl," Rick says quietly, "it's hard to keep focused on being okay for anybody then."

• • •

Rick Woody eventually found a focus. It didn't come quickly, didn't come easily for a man who describes himself as intensely shy and "not a get up and do it kind of a guy."

Rick has become an advocate against Internet predators. But he's made it more than one dad's personal crusade. He created an Internet Predator Awareness Team that began going into schools, churches, and anywhere that parents or children might listen and educating them about the dangers of online sexual predators. He created the Kacie Woody Foundation to help create awareness of this issue.

It took time for Rick to feel ready to do anything. Then it took more time to figure out what to do and how to do it. In part because of his shyness, and in part because he knows kids listen to their peers more than adults, Rick enlisted the help of Kacie's friends, like Samantha and Jessica, as well as other teens from the community. He educated himself on the issue—getting the facts and background he needed to match the anguish of his personal experience. He became certified as a classroom instructor on the issue of Internet safety by i-Safe and NetSmartz, two of the important advocacy groups focused on this issue.

Rick bought a laptop and put together a multimedia PowerPoint presentation that is fine-tuned for different age groups. He knew he had to find a way to engage kids, and that just another set of rules and do's and don'ts wouldn't cut it.

The IPA did its first presentation on April 3, 2005. Since then, Rick has done more than 250 presentations. On a trip to Alabama, he did fourteen in a day and a half.

"How do I do it? How do I *not* do it," he says. "If you had told me five years ago I'd be doing this I would have said you were some kind of a nut."

Now he's become a quiet but persistent crusader. He works as a school resource officer in the Greenbriar High School—a job he describes as 70 percent counselor, 20 percent law enforcement, and 10 percent instructor on issues ranging from traffic law to online sexual predators. He's working in the high school now where Kacie should be in her junior year and looking forward to graduating in 2008.

At the funeral home, Rick pulled Samantha and Jessica to the side. Kacie's closest friends brought yellow roses for her with notes attached, which they placed beside her in the casket. Choked with emotion, he hugged them and said, "You girls don't stop coming around. I might have lost my girl, but you are still my girls so don't quit coming around."

It helps to remain connected to Kacie's friends, just as it helps to try and wrest some meaning from Kacie's violent death. "If I didn't do anything, what happened to Kacie doesn't have any value. Kacie liked to help other people, and to me, this was just a way to let Kacie keep helping other people, by sharing her story."

He's struck by how ignorant most parents still are. "What our Internet Predator Awareness Team is running into is that parents don't really know how to keep their kids safe online and they *don't know* they don't know how to keep them safe online."

In the Greenbriar school district, the IPA presentations begin in the fifth grade. Teachers assured Rick kids were already in chat rooms at that age—ten. They are eager and engaged listeners. But Rick knows that kids are still only half the battle, and one of his frustrations is the low turnout when he does presentations for parents. "We can train the kids to death, but if we don't get the parent trained, it's not going to do any good. You can't always rely on twelve- and thirteen-year-olds to make the right decisions."

At a presentation for new students at Greenbriar Middle School, nearly every hand shoots up when Rick asks a group of twenty-three sixth and seventh graders how many of them are online. They tell him they play games and talk to guys. One student, who uses the computer to play a game, said he'd been asked for personal information online. When asked why kids might try to meet someone online, a perceptive kid says, "Because they might be depressed or not like themselves."

Rick tells them that every day an estimated seventy million kids between the ages of five and seventeen are online and that the number of online predators, according to the FBI, has skyrocketed by 3,000 percent since 2000. He points out to his rapt audience that statistics from NetSmartz suggest that one in four kids will be sexually solicited online. Rick later says he believes that figure soars when kids go into public chat rooms. "There I think it's closer to one hundred percent." During this presentation, Rick tells the kids they will be taken into the "Danger Zone," and to underscore that point, a song by the same name blares out as images flash across the screen.

The kids are shown a chilling video produced by i-Safe America in which a young boy is nabbed by a predator. A boy expecting to meet a girl he's chatted with online waits for her at a designated meeting place. When a man shows up in a red Mazda pickup truck saying he's the girl's father, the boy jumps in. What follows is harrowing. The boy manages to jump out of the truck, but the predator pursues him in a Hollywood-worthy chase sequence. The boy manages to finally and safely elude him, but just barely.

Jessica and Samantha introduce themselves. They're wearing bright blue and yellow IPA tee shirts that say KACIE WOODY INTERNET PREDATOR AWARENESS TEAM on the front and ANGELS WATCHING OVER ME on the back. They present a heartbreaking montage of photographs of Kacie's life; the adorable baby becomes an engaging toddler who turns into a sweet child and then a cute teen with a winsome smile.

Forceful and passionate, Jessica tells the kids that "bad things can happen to us in Arkansas. Kacie used the Internet just like y'all do." As Kacie's horrifying story unfolds, the girls tell the students how they, too, had become friends with Dave and shared Web cam pictures and personal information with him and talked to him by phone.

The work is enormously important to both Sam and Jessica. "It helps part of her still be alive in me," says Jessica, who feels it also helps her redeem Kacie's loss. "I'm saving other people's lives by telling Kacie's story, so that her death won't be in vain."

At first, the kids seem intimidated by the man they know as "Officer Woody." But they gradually become more open and direct in asking him questions. "To a predator," Rick says, "you are a puzzle." He explains that the predator's aim is to put the pieces of the puzzle together and that the goal "is always you." Ideally, he explains, the predator wants you to be willing to meet—and he usually has the patience to take the time to "groom" a victim by a painstaking accumulation of details. Rick maps out the steps in the grooming process to his audience: a predator will say he loves and understands you, treat you better than your own family might, buy things for you like cell phones and phone cards, iPods and Web cams.

Kids are warned about the perils of putting too much information on social networking sites like MySpace, Facebook, and Xanga. "You love these Web sites, but the predator loves them, too," cautions Rick Woody.

He tells the students about three main types of sexual predators. "You have the nonpreferential, who will take whatever is available. Then you have the pedophiles who like prepubescent kids, and then you have the preferential that likes a particular age group. According to the FBI the preferential sex offenders like twelve- to fourteen-year-old girls and most of their profiles are the same as a serial killer."

• • •

"He *would* have been a serial killer. There's no doubt." Karl Byrd was the chief investigator for the state police who led the search for Kacie Woody. He lived the case minute-to-minute, and it's clear, nearly four years later, that it lives inside him.

Byrd has been in law enforcement for thirty years. He has seen plenty and then some and has a reputation for being a meticulous investigator. But nothing tore through him like seeing Kacie Woody with her wrists and ankles chained to the floor of Fuller's minivan. It was gruesome. Byrd felt evidence he saw suggested to him that for Fuller, "the act of killing her was part of his enjoyment."

That's what drives Byrd's conviction that Dave Fuller was on the verge of becoming a serial killer. It was the brazenness of the crime, the meticulous nature of his planning, and the fact that he had information about other girls in his computer. "It would have been unbelievable to me that had he gotten away with this, and with the excitement that he had been through, that he wouldn't have done it again. Death or incarceration was the only thing that would have stopped him."

The FBI ran Fuller's DNA through a national data bank to see if he could be linked to any other unsolved murders. He could not. What they did learn was that he'd been communicating with teens in chat rooms for about two years and, at the time he murdered Kacie, he was regularly talking with three girls in Michigan, Texas, and Pennsylvania.

The Michigan teen, according to a fine piece of investigative reporting by Cathy Frye in the Arkansas *Democrat-Gazette*, had been talking to Dave Fuller every day for nearly two years from a computer in the public library. She never told him her real name, never agreed to talk with him on the phone when he said he wanted to hear her voice, and refused his offer to fly her to California. But in two years of chats, she said he always acted like a gentleman, and never pushed the chats beyond the confines of friends, family, and school.

The facts of Fuller's life don't jibe with the monstrosity of his act. Raised in a devout Mormon family, the forty-seven-year-old man was described as slight and nondescript, a divorced father of two who worked regularly in car dealerships. Like most of the potential predators that show up in our *Dateline* stings, Fuller maintained a veneer of respectability. The cracks in that veneer, as reported in the Arkansas *Democrat-Gazette*, were a volatile temper and an arrest for exposing himself to two young girls and an alleged interest in child pornography Web sites.

The possibility of understanding more about Fuller and his motivations ended the moment that 9mm bullet split open his brain. But what is clear is that he was exceedingly patient in grooming his potential victims.

Investigators found that he had made two trips to Arkansas—in October and November—before finally driving cross-country to kidnap and murder Kacie. Part of what made him so dangerous was how methodical he was in planning. "He was a typical predator," says investigator Byrd. "Distance meant nothing to him. He had the resources to come here. He meets a young woman on the Internet that he can manipulate. She's not wise to the ways of the world. He manipulates her to where she has all the confidence in the world in him and gives him all the information he needs to abduct her."

Byrd is adamant that Fuller's goal all along was murder. "He spent a lot of time putting together this plan. Part of the thrill was actually stalking her, like he was hunting an animal, waiting for the kill."

Rick Woody and Karl Byrd have long been friends. But they never talked about Kacie's murder until a late August afternoon nearly four years after her death.

The question that has burned in Rick is: "What was his long-term intention? Had he planned on taking her and taking her back to California? Or was it his intention on killing her from the beginning?"

Byrd asks Rick if he has seen the crime scene photos. He has not. Byrd is convinced that what he saw inside the storage area and what happened inside the van was about murder and murder only. "His intentions all along were to murder her," Byrd says. "There was not anything else going through his mind. I think that killing was part of his excitement."

At six feet four inches Karl Byrd is a towering presence. At nearly 280 pounds, he seems indomitable. When he dissolves in sadness, it feels like a redwood crashing down on the forest floor. Thinking back to what he saw inside the storage unit on December 4 makes it almost impossible for Byrd to keep his tears at bay. No words come—it is unspeakable sorrow. After a few minutes that feel like weeks, Byrd pulls himself together to share what he knows with the person to whom it matters most. "The way she was bound, her wrists and ankles aren't torn up. There were no signs of struggle."

"The chloroform explained it all," Byrd says. What didn't add up for him when he first got to Woody's home that night was the absence of any significant signs of struggle. When he saw the rag inside the van and a half-empty bottle of chloroform nearby, he knew that Kacie was unconscious shortly after 9:41 that night. "The only peace in that is she might not have known; and there were other things at the scene that told me she wasn't conscious a lot."

The chloroform made it impossible for the medical examiner to establish the exact time of Kacie's death. He estimated that it probably occurred in the afternoon. But based on autopsy results that described the contents of her stomach, Byrd thinks she was dead by the dawn that followed her abduction. "He probably killed her early on."

Whatever happened to Kacie began at 9:41 on the evening of December 3, 2002, when her instant messaging with Scott came to a sudden halt. Byrd points out that Dave Fuller accessed his storage unit that night at 10:15 P.M. It had taken just thirty-four minutes to kidnap Kacie Woody. She was hidden before anyone even realized she was gone.

Byrd, like Rick Woody, has tried to piece together a scenario that would have, could have, saved her. The investigation was, by all accounts, fast and flawless. But a thirteen-year-old girl still ended up bound, raped, and dead.

No one who knew her will ever be the same. For nearly three years, Kacie's Yorkshire terrier, George, sat by the front door from two thirty until three o'clock every afternoon, waiting for her to come home from school.

• • •

"That person not only killed Kacie, he destroyed something we will never get back." Diane Kellar was the school counselor who warned

Kacie about giving out too much information online on the day Kacie was later abducted.

"We lost not only a wonderful person, we lost our small town, the rural country safe haven that we thought we had." She pauses as the sadness sweeps in. "I lost a great deal of my trust and the children did, too. They didn't feel safe at home anymore. I got calls from parents—children were afraid to sleep in their bedrooms, both boys and girls."

"My mom had to sleep with me for almost a year after Kacie died because I was so scared," Jessica says. "What if he had an accomplice? What if he were going to come get me?" Her cheerfulness ebbs. "Still to this day, if I have friends over, I can sleep with my door closed and all the lights in the house off. But if nobody is in the room with me, I have to sleep with the door open and the bathroom light on. It still scares me."

Beneath her fear is a reservoir of tears. "If I start to cry, no matter what I'm crying about, if it's boy troubles that will be one stage and the last stage is always 'Why did you have to leave, Kacie? I could call you right now and I could be telling you everything and you could be helping me.'"

Samantha still feels the aftershocks of her best friend's murder. "I have a problem trusting people now, like men in general. I would much rather talk to women because I feel like I was deceived." Sam keeps imagining how her friend would have changed. "To me, everyone thinks of her like a young girl, but I still think of her as my age. What car would she drive? Who would she date? Who would she hang out with? You just wonder." The happiness Sam feels often seems incomplete because Kacie isn't there to share it with her. "You just think how it could be better and how it's not. It's really like a death in the family . . . your friends are your chosen family."

Judy Harkrider was Kacie's saxophone teacher and is the band director at Greenbriar Middle School. "She was in my sixth grade saxophone class. She was the only girl in a class of all boys. She was my bud in that one class. We sat together and put down the boys a lot. The boys adored her. They still do." Kacie's murder devastated the band. "She was literally there one day and gone the next," Harkrider recalls. "It was totally beyond them that anybody would hurt her. She was just a sweet girl, she liked everybody. I never heard her say an ugly or derogatory thing about anybody else."

At the Christmas concert two weeks after her death, the band tied a big yellow bow on Kacie's chair, which remained empty for the rest of the year in her honor. "They had a really hard time going on. I don't think I've ever been prouder of a group for holding it together. They got a standing ovation. There were tears at the end of it because they loved her very much. She was just a sweet girl."

After several decades of police work, Karl Byrd is no stranger to the viciousness humans can inflict on each other. But this case shook him to the core. "Think about it, just think about it," he says with an intensity that is palpable. "That something this ghastly can happen in your own living room. That somebody can drive all the way across the country, from San Diego, California, to Holland, Arkansas, and abduct somebody that he has never met in person." Byrd continues, "When you start considering those facts, it hits you: girls get abducted from the side of the road, from a movie theater, but when it starts happening from the security of their own home, when their father is a police officer and there are all these other people that live in the house, it hits home pretty hard. We all like to have that false sense of security that when we walk into our homes, we're safe. This lets you know that is not always true."

Rick Woody and his sons have not been able to put up a Christmas tree since Kacie died. It's been excruciating to even go through the motions of the holiday that comes just twenty-one days after the anniversary of Kacie's murder. "Kacie was so full of joy at Christmastime, it's hard not to think of her and her smiles and the excitement she had."

His faith has deepened and matured since Kacie's death. "A whole lot of my happiness and joy comes through the Christian life I'm trying to live. Obviously, when you are trying to do that, it makes you feel better. When you have been through as much as I have, you've got to look elsewhere rather than on this earth to try and bring joy to yourself."

But he's found a measure of joy here on earth, too. Rick is engaged to a fellow police officer, Anne Blanton, and plans to be married sometime in 2007. She and her two daughters have widened the circle of love around his life. He says, "There's joy in a lot of places there, but obviously, an emptiness where Kacie is. But there's a thankfulness about the happy times I had with her. When you are three years into it, you can think about those happy times and the smiles on her face and not be totally devastated.

"You never have the same type of happiness that you can have when you're a father looking at your little girl." Rick pauses. "You can't ever be healed from it. But I'm trying to get on with my life the best way I can. Because of the way I loved Kacie, I want to strive to educate everyone I can, to make sure it doesn't happen to anybody else. So it will never be over. When I stand up to do a presentation, it brings it back. I'm at a point where I don't dwell on it. I'm trying to go on with my life, but I think that until the day I die, Kacie will be a big part of my everyday life."

Chapter 3

A Tale of Two Advocates

Detective Bob Shilling had been on the Seattle police force for a decade when he was tapped by the chief of police to work in the sex crimes unit. He balked big time. "I was, quite frankly, afraid I would end up killing somebody. I didn't want to deal with that kind of crime," says Shilling. "I asked to go somewhere like robbery or homicide."

But the chief was adamant. "He insisted that I was going to sex crimes because he said my personality was such that I could get along with all different kinds of people, both victims and suspects. I pleaded with him as politely as I could not to go there. But he decided I was going. The reason I didn't want to go there—and he had no way of knowing this—was because I had been a victim of sexual abuse as a child."

Fast forward sixteen years: Bob Shilling, one of the world's good guys, took on an assignment he was sure he would hate and found his life's calling protecting children from sex crimes committed not only online, but every other way imaginable. But I'm getting ahead of his story.

When he realized turning down the job was not an option, Bob Shilling decided he needed to have what he calls "the talk with Jesus." He's a thoughtful, mild-mannered man, with dark hair that's graying at the sides. He chooses his words with care and intelligence. "I took a week off work, went up into British Columbia, and did absolutely nothing for a week but thought and got a lot of things resolved in my head. That was when I decided to forgive my grandfather for what he did to me because all that anger was affecting me."

Shilling stayed in an old dive motel in Horseshoe Bay, British Columbia. He spent long quiet hours alone, watching the ferries chug back and forth across the bay. "I didn't talk to anyone if I didn't want to. It was very peaceful."

The peacefulness was productive. "Once I forgave my grandfather, it was like a big boulder was lifted off me," he says. It was a boulder that he had shouldered for nearly thirty years.

"My dad left my mom when I was eleven. My sisters were younger by two, three, and six years. My mom was stuck with four kids and had a job at a department store that wasn't paying a whole lot of money," Shilling recalls. The family moved back in with his grandparents, who slept separately. Bob was told to share his grandfather's bed.

"This was an absolutely terrible time in my life from when I was twelve to sixteen years old. We shared the same room, the same bed. It happened whenever he wanted it. I was beside myself. It was a very difficult time. I had actually considered suicide. One night, when he was sexually abusing me, my mother walked into my room and I thought, 'Oh, thank God, it is over.' She walked in, turned around, pulled the door shut, and she left."

Decades have come and gone since that moment, but the pain is still raw and still real for Bob Shilling. "That was the most helpless I had ever felt. I thought, 'Oh, my God, if my own mother can't protect me, how am I supposed to protect me?' I finally decided something had to be done. I finally got enough courage to tell him, 'If you put your hands on me again, I will kill you.' I ended up moving out to my sister's dollhouse that my grandfather and I had built in the backyard. It was probably four feet by six feet, and I lived there until I graduated from high school."

Bob Shilling returned from British Columbia with a deep sense of resolve. "I came back determined that if I was going to be a sex crimes detective, then I would be the best detective I could be." Shilling read and studied, took all the classes he could find, went to all the conferences he could manage to attend. "It was not only therapeutic for me, it also taught me a whole lot of things I didn't know about sex offenders and protecting the public."

In sixteen years, the job he tried to avoid now feels like something he was destined to do. He's the only municipal police officer in the United States to be appointed to Interpol, the International Criminal Police Organization. Shilling serves on the specialist group on crimes against children. "How do you go from the kid who is contemplating suicide because you are in your darkest hour, to someone who is at the apex of their career? It's been quite the journey," he says. I might add that it's a journey he's successfully completed. When we first met, I was impressed with the deep peace that seems to radiate from the core of his being.

Some of the work he has done with Interpol has been in the areas of Internet child pornography—a business of exploitation that is rampant worldwide. The investigations often involve multiple countries and painstaking detective work. Shilling described the successful investigation of a recent case that was called "Kindergarten." No one knew where these children were being photographed. Where do you start when you have the whole world to comb?

"Norway stepped up to the plate and said they would take the lead for the investigation. They worked closely with a lot of other countries and ended up hiring a biologist to tell them where some of the flora and fauna that was found in the pictures could have come from," Shilling says. The biologist was able to determine that the vegetation in the child pornography was indigenous to Canada and the Scandinavian countries. That left only a few hundred million people, right? "They hired a geologist because there was a picture of a little girl on a rock.

The geologist narrowed that rock down to a Scandinavian country. The bottom line is that it turned out to be in Sweden, the guy was busted, and all the children were saved from this man. That was directly a result of Interpol. That's the kind of stuff we do."

The man who was arrested had access to children through his kindergarten-age daughter. He took the kindergarten class photograph at her school. "He victimized almost every little girl who was in that class photo and put very graphic, abusive pictures of them all over the Internet." Shilling continues, "They were friends of his daughter. As in so many sexual abuse cases, the perpetrator is someone known to the child."

It's a reality Shilling has lived. Shortly after he started investigating crimes against children, one of his sisters said she was living vicariously through him. "That sent chills down my spine," Shilling remembers. "She told me what my grandfather had done to her. I thought, 'Oh, my God.' Then she told me that one of my other sisters had recently told her about what he had done to her and pretty soon, we found out that all of us had been victimized and none of us knew. We were all living under the same roof, and none of us knew."

Despite his concerns and involvement with Internet predators, Shilling hammers home the message in community meetings that "children have more of a chance of being sexually abused by someone you know, perhaps someone living in your own home, than they do by a stranger out on the street. When we talk to them about stranger-danger, we are doing them a disservice because when it does turn out to be someone they know they think 'Wait a minute, this isn't a stranger. Did I do something to cause this?'"

The passion he feels for this work energizes his words. "You would be amazed, it would actually make you sick—I could retire if I had a dollar for every time a victim told me, 'I told Mommy or I told Daddy and they didn't believe me.' You think, 'Oh, my God,' you just want to grab the parents by the ears and shake them and say, 'What was going through your head?'"

Parents tell Shilling that they worry about media attention and notoriety that will fall on the family if they press charges. Community notification about sex offenders brings attention to the entire family and some people want to avoid that. They will say to Shilling, "What if the child isn't telling the truth?"

"I explain to them, not believing your child has done more damage to them because they were looking to you for support and help and what you have told them is that keeping Daddy or keeping Uncle Joe from going to jail is more important than you are. What damage does that do to a child growing up?"

He pauses. "I know the effect it had on me when my mom walked into my grandfather's bedroom and then turned around and walked out. She had her reasons, but I remember the betrayal I felt."

Victim, advocate, law enforcement officer, Bob Shilling has a unique perspective on how to tackle the problems related to child sex offenders and Internet predators. His credibility is unassailable and he's paid a stiff price for his insights into these complicated issues.

When we sat down and talked recently over a few glasses of wine, he told me that he feels part of the strength of the *Dateline* broadcasts is that "it shows people that these aren't people with three eyes who wear trench coats and jump out of bushes. This is a rabbi, a doctor, a firefighter, these are normal-looking people."

They are, in fact, guys like his grandfather—an outwardly decent man who took his grandson to see the Los Angeles Dodgers play baseball, or to ghost towns where they'd look for rocks to collect. "We did all sorts of fun stuff that as a kid you think is so cool. But then there is that other side of him that was just a monster," Shilling said. "You start having feelings, 'What did I do wrong? If I tell somebody is anybody going to believe me?'"

Shilling makes an important point that is exceedingly relevant to the question of mandatory sentencing for first-time sex offenders. His own background as an incest survivor made him strongly oppose a measure in Washington State—which was defeated—which would have sent first-time violent sex offenders to prison for life without the possibility of parole. Why was he opposed?

"If I knew my grandfather was going to go to prison for the rest of his life for this offense, I definitely would not have told anybody. I wanted it to stop and I wanted him to get help so he didn't victimize me or anyone else. I have publicly argued *against* some of these initiatives that have come up to make it one strike and you're out for sex offenders. Wait a minute! You are going to have a chilling effect on people being willing to come forward and testify. But if it happens a second time, then all bets are off."

Beyond that, he says there aren't enough prisons to hold the population that legislation like this would generate nor money to build new ones. "That money has to come from somewhere. Unfortunately, what ends up happening is other programs that are very good suffer because the money has dried up. Sometimes those end up being victims' programs so it is counterproductive."

Shilling feels we get more bang for our buck by investing in treatment for sex offenders—whether they are predators who prey online or whether they abuse kids in other circumstances. "I absolutely believe in treatment. I think that's one area where we really need to put more resources. I know there are a lot of studies that say treatment works and I know there are some studies that say it has no effect. I can tell you from somebody who deals with sex offenders on a daily basis that there is a huge difference between sex offenders who come out of a treatment program and sex offenders who have spent their time in Walla Walla— the penitentiary—and are now coming back into the community."

The difference Shilling sees in the sex offenders who have been through treatment is that they are able to talk in an open way about their issues. "They can tell you about what some of their triggers are, they can tell you about their high-risk behaviors and their offense cycles. They know what they can do to intervene in that offense cycle . . .

they learn interventions to keep them from re-offending." He's too experienced a cop to think that treatment is a magic bullet. Shilling knows that there will always be a danger of some men re-offending. "The trick is determining who those offenders are who are going to be less likely to reintegrate successfully into the community and focus our efforts on intensive treatment and supervision for them."

Contrast that with men who have not been in treatment—the ones Shilling meets coming out of prison. "There is no victim empathy. They are still blaming the victim. They talk like they were the victim. Trying to talk to them about anything to do with their sex offense, other than that they were the victim, is like pulling teeth. It is completely opposite with sex offenders who have gone through a treatment program."

The treatment program Shilling has been involved with has a recidivism rate of about 4.5 percent over fifteen years. "Is it as good as we would like it? No. But it's a heck of a lot better than what most people think." When Shilling talks at community meetings he asks people what they think the rate of recidivism is for sex offenders. "The answer I get most often is somewhere between ninety and one hundred percent. They are shocked when they find out it is as low as it is."

The other myth Bob Shilling wants to slay is about residence restrictions for sex offenders. He thinks they are counterproductive. "A lot of states have jumped on the bandwagon and decided sex offenders can't live within two thousand feet of a school or can't live within two thousand feet of a playground. If someone really wants to harm a child, two thousand feet isn't going to make a difference. We know from research that sex offenders are like everybody else—they need pro-social support, they need to have a job and a roof over their head, they need all the types of things we need. Most of these crimes are of power and control."

Imagine then, he says, that a guy comes out of prison and wants to do the right thing. "But because of the fact that we won't let them live in a spot where they have a roof over their head, or we don't allow them to have a job because the employer has no place to contact them or fears getting picketed for hiring a sex offender—now they can't pay their legal and financial obligations, they can't pay the crime victims' compensation fund, they can't do everything we have asked them to do. They start losing control over their lives, they start going into what they call 'the whirlwind' and they just start spinning. What does a sex offender do whose crimes are of power and control when they don't have any power or control over their life?" You and I know the answer to that. The danger is they end up taking power and control over someone else's life and re-offending.

This is what has Shilling on fire. "We end up creating the very situation we are trying to avoid! When you put it to citizens like this, it's like the lightbulb goes on."

His analysis is backed up by hard data from Iowa. Tough residence restriction laws bar sex offenders from living within two thousand feet of a school or child care center. Some cities added libraries, swimming pools, parks, and bike trails to the off-limit areas. The law, which has been in effect for over a year, has backfired. What's happening is that when someone can't find a place where they're allowed to live, they go underground.

"It has pushed some of them off the map," says Bill Vaughn, who is the chief deputy of the Polk County Sheriff's Department in Des Moines. "We have individuals who have been pushed out to where they are sleeping under bridges, rest areas, at parks on trails, and of the roughly one hundred thirty we are responsible for tracking, there are between twenty and twenty-five of them that we had no idea of their whereabouts."

The Iowa Coalition Against Sexual Assault, which represents victims, says that citizens are less safe since the law was enacted than before. "Probation and parole supervisors cannot effectively monitor . . . offenders who are living under bridges, in parking lots, in tents at parks or at interstate truck stops," said Elizabeth Barnhill, the Coalition's executive director, in an interview in the *Los Angeles Times*.

The state prosecutors' association also now opposes the legislation. "Those laws were passed for the safety of politicians, not children," says John Sarcoma, the attorney for Polk County, which includes Des Moines. Sarcoma is an experienced prosecutor and former head of the State Prosecutors' Association. "The result, if you look at it, in our county, is that probably ninety-six percent of the single-family dwelling places are off limits and ninety-eight percent of the multiple-family dwellings are off limits. What sense does that make?"

With no place to live, offenders get pushed out into rural areas where it's even harder to monitor them. The other aspect Sarcoma points out is that only about 3 to 4 percent of the offenders they are tracking committed crimes against strangers. "I think that it does give people a false sense of security. It doesn't make them any safer. I also think that it destabilizes some of these offenders. When that happens, you are probably going to end up with more of these things occurring. We just don't think it was well thought out."

But it is undeniably political red meat. Iowa's legislature has so far refused to modify it. In a moment of rare candor, Republican senator Larry McKibben told the *Los Angeles Times*, "We live in a nasty political environment, and I certainly wouldn't have wanted to take a vote that somebody could turn into a direct-mail piece saying I was going soft on sex offenders." McKibben was in charge of the task force that assessed the impact the law was having in Iowa.

So now police, prosecutors, and victims' advocates agree a law on the books is making Iowans less safe. It should be a legislative slam-dunk, right? But for now, at least, in Iowa, politics is getting in the way.

This is why Shilling feels that communities have to be smarter in approaching this issue. Most sex offenders will get out of prison or jail. The risk is always that if they fail to reintegrate, there will be more victims. "I'm not telling people that you need to roll out the welcome wagon or invite them to dinner. But leave them alone. Let them get on with their lives, keep an eye on them, know what they've done, but let them be taxpaying members of society."

He can't help but be surprised when he hears himself speak at community meetings these days. "I can tell you that never in a million years would I have believed when I was sixteen years old that I would be standing up in front of people telling them, look, we don't make society safer by chasing these people from place to place," Shilling says. "If we think as citizens we are safer because we have chased them out of the community then we have another thing coming. They are still there. But we the police don't know where they are anymore and we can't tell citizens where they are. It guts the sex offender registration laws, it guts the community notification laws, and it really does make society a lot less safe because we have created this situation where they are unstable. We put them in that situation of the 'whirlwind.'"

While Bob Shilling opposes one strike and you're out laws for violent first-time sexual offenders, he takes the opposite view for second offenses. He teaches two classes at the sex offenders' treatment program at the Twin Rivers Corrections Center in Monroe, Washington. He says a mandatory sentence for a second offense is a powerful deterrent. "There is not an inmate in there who does not know about two strikes and you're out. They all realize that if they do this again, they are going away for the rest of their lives."

His approach to the issue of sex offenders is based on gritty reality—Shilling has been a police officer or a detective for twenty-six years—and his belief in our shared humanity. "These people aren't just bugs that you can squish and walk away from and be done with. They are products of our society. We have a responsibility to deal with these problems."

As Bob Shilling educated himself and learned about every aspect of sexual offenders and childhood sexual abuse, he felt he knew the answer to why his mother closed the bedroom door and walked away after she saw him being abused by his grandfather. But having a theory in his head was not the same as knowing it in his heart. He knew he needed to ask her directly so he would really know—even though it had been decades since the incest occurred.

"Bless her heart, she died two years ago, and prior to her dying I said, 'Mom, I just have to ask you something. I know the answer. I just have to hear it. Why was it that day you walked in and turned around without doing anything?' She started crying. She said, 'I am so sorry. This has haunted me ever since that happened.' She said, 'Your grandfather sexually abused me and I didn't know how to stop it for me. I certainly didn't know how to stop it for you.' She just held my hand and said she was so glad to get it off her chest."

He is quiet for a moment. Life has come around for him full circle. He has ransomed the terrible pain of his past in a way that he knows is making a difference. "I have been doing this work for sixteen years. Some of my colleagues say, 'Oh, my God, how can you do this work that long?' I do it because it's a passion and if I can help educate people as to who sex offenders are and how they are able to do what they do and help remove that veil of secrecy, then we are better able to keep these things from happening."

Shilling has seen the worst that humans can possibly do to each other. But he remains resolutely optimistic. He feels that our *Dateline* broadcasts have helped illuminate an important problem and I'm proud that our broadcasts are one of the reasons why he is optimistic about the future. "I am very hopeful or I wouldn't have been doing this work for sixteen years. The brighter the light we can shine on the problem, and the more we can get out and educate the community and have them partner with us on sex offender management, the safer the community will be."

At the opposite side of the country is a woman who is Bob Shilling's counterpart in dedication, compassion, and optimism. How Parry Aftab became involved in these issues and where they have led her is compelling.

Aftab had no intention of becoming an advocate for Internet safety issues. She was living a life that she enjoyed and others envied. Aftab, a smart, vivacious woman, shot to the top in the legal profession while still in her forties. She did hostile takeovers on Wall Street and started her own law firm in 1990 with offices in New York and Moscow. Aftab had money, status, and prestige—and an elegant suburban home in New Jersey for herself, two children, and a golden retriever. She had great clothes, took terrific vacations, and enjoyed the perks that come with being able to bill at $450 an hour.

She was not discontent nor midlife crisis material. Just the opposite. Aftab worked hard to get where she was in life and wasn't about to change. Her interest in children's issues was in the less-than-zero range. On children's issues she said her attitude was, "I don't do kids, that's for soccer moms, not for me. Thank you very much, go away." She had every intention of making law her career. That was then.

This is now: Aftab is talking to five thousand kids a month about keeping themselves safe online. She started and runs a nonprofit organization called WiredSafety.org and has written several books, including *The Parent's Guide to Protecting Your Children in Cyberspace*. Aftab is now one of the foremost authorities on Internet safety issues. She has an army of volunteers who are part of her organization. At last count there were 11,200, spread out in at least seventy-six countries.

But this is something she never intended do. The voracious commitment she makes now began casually in 1997. Aftab was invited to be on a local cable TV show to talk about the Internet and related issues like pornography. It was a call-in show and one of the callers was Donna Rice Hughes. Hughes gained notoriety before her marriage when she was photographed in 1987 with then-Senator Gary Hart on his boat called *Monkey Business*. The photo sabotaged Hart's presidential bid. Hughes has gone on to become an Internet safety advocate in her own right.

Aftab was shocked when Hughes said that her stepson had come to live with them because his mother allowed him to use the Internet. "I went nuts," Aftab says. "I was so busy trying to protect the Internet in those days from people who wanted to shut it down or say it was evil for children. I was not nice."

A big Supreme Court case in 1997 on the Communications Decency Act kept Aftab in the media spotlight as an Internet expert on CNN and other networks. She was a volunteer on AOL and Court TV's legal helpline. She got tired of people asking her for advice on children and the Internet. She asked her sister, a pediatrician, to find her a book to recommend. Her sister dug around and said there wasn't one. Aftab ended up writing and self-publishing a small book called *A Parent's Guide to the Internet*. Much to her surprise, the ten thousand copies that had been printed started to sell. She was increasingly in demand as someone who knew about protecting kids in cyberspace. Except that it wasn't what she wanted to do. "It was awful. Clients complained. Here you are supposed to be this tough, ruthless lawyer they've hired and you're on television doing all these other things."

Aftab dialed back a bit. She still felt committed to protecting the Internet and her eyes were being opened to the benefits it had for kids. While researching her initial book, she contacted a man who'd made a Web site for his daughter with cerebral palsy. Aftab asked him why he'd done it. "'Because online, no one knows you are in a wheelchair. Online she is just a pretty little girl. Everybody else, when they are online, has to sit down, too. No one points.' I sat back, tears in my eyes, and realized, that's why I have to fight for this, because online all children can walk, talk, and see."

The Internet was also color-blind. Aftab realized that online, children could be judged, in the words of Dr. Martin Luther King Jr., "by the content of their character and not the color of their skin." There was no denying the Internet's benefits for kids. But her passion was law, not advocacy. In doing her book, she felt she'd done her part.

In 1998, the turning point came. She volunteered to pitch in when a friend needed help with his Web site for a few weeks. A woman from

South America sent in a link to a child pornography site and said, "Shut down this site and put these people in jail." Legally, Aftab knew a lot about child pornography. She'd just never looked at it. All of that was about to change.

"I saw a three-and-a-half-year-old being raped on the Internet in 1998." Her words are hard to hear. But seeing was obviously so much worse. That one picture eventually worked a sea change on Aftab.

"When you see child pornography, it is like having a branding iron to your brain. You are just never the same. This little girl had her eyes closed and she was facing the camera sitting astride this animal. He was lying on his back. You never see their face. You just see everything else. Full penetration. She had her eyes closed because somebody was making her pose for the camera. It changes you," Aftab says quietly. "You are not the same. It's like September eleventh—there is a before and after.

"I saw this and I was devastated, just devastated. I cried. I vomited. I was one of the first Internet lawyers in the world. I turned to my partner and said, 'We have to do something.' Her partner agreed. Aftab started doing pro bono work that gradually took over a large part of her firm's resources. She also began trying to find the little girl she'd seen in the picture. "Because of the work I had done, I knew everybody in law enforcement on the international level, and we had offices in Moscow where a lot of child porn was coming from. I was able to do a lot of things that a lot of people couldn't do because I had a credibility most people didn't have."

Her work as an Internet lawyer set the stage for her activism and advocacy. She could pick up the phone and call top people at Yahoo! or AOL. Her initial passion was based on trying to stem the mounting tide of child pornography which has, in just over a decade, been transformed, according to Aftab. "In 1991, law enforcement says there were maybe one thousand images of child pornography that existed in most places. The Web was launched in 1993. In 1996, the first numbers were being measured by law enforcement in Manchester, England, where they have a great cyber crime unit. They measured about twelve hundred images at that time on the Internet, total. When we were full blown—by '99 until 2001, we were running—by that I mean finding and reporting—about six hundred child pornography sites a week and each site had an average of a hundred fifty images." Now she says the pedophile groups that trade in child porn trafficking sites require people to have collections of a hundred thousand images to join.

She searched relentlessly for the little girl she saw being raped in the photo. "I looked for her forever," she says quietly. "I looked for her forever. I used all kinds of technology and brought in clients who could do all sorts of cool things, but we never found her." The picture affected her in almost every way. "From the moment I saw the child porn picture, I stopped dating. I was seeing someone at the time, another lawyer. He went to kiss me and I had a flashback to the little girl. I just couldn't and I stopped dating."

Life as she knew it was coming to an end. She sold her law firm in 1999 and put her big house on the market. Her son, Michael, was in college; her daughter, Taylor, about to start. "I sat them down and said, 'Our lives are going to change because I need to do more of this, not less.' They thought I was nuts. They still think I'm nuts. But they turned to me and were like, 'You've got to do what you've got to do.'"

It was no small sacrifice for her children. Her son had to transfer from a private college to a state school and work as a night security guy in the parking lot of a health club. They had to find a new home for the family dog when they moved into an apartment. Like her brother, Aftab's daughter also had to settle for a state school when she'd hoped to go to a private university.

It doesn't take much time to figure out that when Aftab is obsessed she is nothing short of formidable. She dropped out of college to put the childhood sweetheart she married through medical school. When it was her turn to pursue her education, she tried to talk her way into New York University's law school—one of the nation's most prestigious—

without having an undergraduate degree. When that didn't work she raced through Hunter College in two years and was valedictorian. Then she went to law school at NYU.

By 1999, Aftab had created Wired Safety.org and had recruited the first five teenagers that grew into her "Teen Angels" program. These are high school kids—who now number 450—who are trained in Internet safety issues and work in their schools and communities.

A feature story in *Reader's Digest* in March 2000 brought a tidal wave of volunteers. There were 1,400 when the article came out in March; by September, there were ten thousand.

"I was running all the time, online an average of nineteen hours a day. Sometimes more. You didn't stop." Aftab said it was not unusual for her to answer 1,200 e-mails a day. She ate a lot and not well. Her diabetes spun out of control. But she couldn't stop. "I had no life. I couldn't look back, the moment I stopped I would have flashbacks.

"I racked up tons of credit card debt to do this. I had given up on the 'me' part. I didn't exist anymore. I joined a health club for a year and when they called to say, 'It's up,' I said I hadn't even gone there yet."

Her success fueled her drive to do more. "We infiltrated a sex trafficking ring and in a three-month period alone, sixty people went to jail because of our bust." The intensity was killing her. But she couldn't stop. "I'd eat old pizza and sit on the computer all the time. My daughter was furious and my son was furious. They would say, 'You can't keep doing this.' I would say that I had to. They'd say there were many others who could do it. I said not with my credentials who would work for free.

"In some ways, I feel like I'm on the other side of Oz. I don't have the money I used to have," Aftab says. For years she had no health insurance, although she does now. "Even now, chief privacy officers, friends of mine who are big partners at big firms, are saying, when are you going to stop this and get back to being a lawyer? Judges I run into sometimes still say, 'Oh, you were a good lawyer, it's nice, you did some things for mankind, but enough already.'"

But you could never convince her of that. She's found her destiny and, compared to most people, lives in overdrive. She feels that our *Dateline* specials have helped parents wake up to the dangers online. "So for the first time, I'm speaking to packed houses. I get more media in this area than anyone has over the years. Now it is standing room only because parents are really freaked. What I do more than anything is talk about MySpace, Xanga, Bibo, Facebook, and all the social networks."

She has a straightforward message for parents. "The essence is that they need to be involved and they need to talk to kids about using these social networks intelligently. The days are long gone when you can tell the kids not to have a profile. They need it for their social lives and there are valid reasons for it. Parents need to take off the brown paper bags they have over their heads. Their kids, all kids, are doing this stuff. We need to recognize that, not panic, and get involved."

She said that our *Dateline* broadcasts have had a similar impact on young people. "Kids are scared now. That we can attribute to the *Dateline* specials. For the first time ever, in all the years I have been doing this, kids are afraid. So that can be very helpful. They are more careful and they are thinking about it and they are talking about it and they are looking out for each other a little bit more."

Aftab is about to launch a new and innovative program she's calling Wired Moms. "If we get the moms involved, I can protect a lot of kids. There are mothers against drunk driving, this is mothers against Internet sexual exploitation of their children." The more excited she gets, the faster she talks. "We are getting them up and running and giving them a package that includes PowerPoint presentations and tools they can use to teach each other about this stuff."

Aftab also feels strongly about something else. "We need to do and know a lot more about how sexual predators operate in cyberspace and the ploys predators use, all of the different things so that when we are educating kids we can say, 'Forget this don't-talk-to-a-stranger, you need to talk to strangers, but if somebody says this to you they are probably a slime bag.'"

Destiny seems to be keeping Aftab on its radar screen. After three marriages, Aftab was just as sure that she'd never marry again as she was that she'd always be a lawyer. "The man I'm marrying booked me for a speaking engagement a year and a half ago in Canada," she says. She flew up a few days early for a bit of a breather and he took her lobster fishing. The hotshot attorney turned advocate almost froze to death. In May. "I had yoga pants and a fleece without anything underneath but a sports bra. I was freezing. There was still ice in the ocean."

But a friendship formed. Allan McCullough runs a nonprofit organization in New Brunswick, Canada, that he founded, the Child Safety Research and Innovation Center. Their two nonprofits started doing projects together. He hadn't dated for six years—he was too engaged with his work. Aftab had given up all aspects of her social life. Both understood how and why the other was consumed by their work. McCullough appreciated how demolished she was by seeing the picture of the little girl. She grasped how the rape and murder of a fifteen-year-old girl in Maine had launched him into the work that led him to create his nonprofit. "He's devoted twenty-three years to child sexual predator issues and he's only forty-four. He's created a computer game that measures a child's vulnerability to sexual predators in real life."

Aftab said that for her, seeing the computer game he developed was like "being handed the keys to the kingdom." Nothing like this has ever existed before, she says. The game, which is called Sydney Safe-Seeker and the Incredible Journey Home, is scheduled to be out in spring of 2007. "There are nine ploys sexual predators use, and only in Canada have they done the research on this stuff. I was amazed. In the U.S. we are still anecdotal. Parents can measure a kid's vulnerability. The kids think they are just playing a fun game but you can measure different types of vulnerability to different types of ploys—'Help me find my puppy,' 'Do you want to be a model,' 'I've got a job for you,' whatever. I wouldn't have met him and we wouldn't have clicked in the way we did if we hadn't had this. All the pieces come together."

After their engagement, Aftab asked him what he would change if he could change something about her. "He said, 'I'd like you to be less angry.' I have become very angry over the years. You still see it. But he's done a great deal to help me get there. When he walks into the room, I breathe differently."

Gastric bypass surgery helped Aftab bring her weight and health back under control. Her two children are settled into their adult lives. "I'm proud of my kids. They turned into really great kids. But they still think I'm crazy."

Aftab is also enormously proud of the other kids in her life: her 450 Teen Angels who are out in their schools and communities educating parents and peers. "I am so proud of the Teen Angels. They are just amazing, amazing kids. Everyone talks about kids, and how kids don't care. I got the kids who care and there are a whole bunch of them out there."

The work she does has taken her to some of the darkest places imaginable. But she feels it has also shown her just how fine people can be. The thousands of volunteers who work with WiredSafety.org have lit up her heart. "All of my volunteers do this just for the kids. They do this to help others. They don't get to be on television. This has given me an incredible, incredible faith in the good of mankind. It has given me a firm belief that there is a plan—that things do come together."

Life is coming back together now for Aftab in a more balanced way. She beams as she shows off an exquisite engagement ring but quickly points out that it's a fake. "Every dime we have goes into our work. Allan knows I'd kill him if he bought me a real one."

Missing pieces of herself are returning. "I used to be known for my laughter. Then I wasn't anymore. It used to be that you could always tell

I was around because I always laughed. I stopped doing that. But I'm starting to laugh again, which is interesting."

There is much more joy now in her life beside the sadness, the sadness of the little girl Aftab still sees every night before she falls asleep, the little girl with her eyes squeezed shut tight as she's being raped.

Chapter 4

California Investigation

The phenomenal response to our initial hidden camera operations gave an undeniable momentum to this issue. A recent article in *The New York Times* credited *Dateline NBC* as being the "tipping point" on the online predator issue. The enormous success of our first two investigations led us to create a third. *Dateline NBC* was getting great ratings, and we were proud to bring important national attention to this issue.

This time we went to the opposite side of the country: Riverside, California. We partnered again with Perverted Justice, but set it up differently. After seeing our earlier "To Catch a Predator" broadcasts, Perverted Justice was contacted by the Riverside County Sheriff's Department about conducting a joint investigation into online sexual predators. Perverted Justice jumped at the opportunity.

Many viewers had objected that we permitted the men from the earlier investigations in New York and Virginia to just walk away—and potentially harm real children. Fair question, but working with law enforcement was going to present many challenges.

As journalists we didn't want to be an arm of the police. We wanted to conduct our investigation independently, which included me being able to confront and interview the men coming to our hidden camera house before the police were able to arrest and interview them. Some law enforcement agencies would not be willing to cooperate in such an endeavor or give up that much control over a sting operation. The Riverside County Sheriff's Department was willing to take the risk. Lieutenant Chad Bianco and Deputy District Attorney Michelle Paradise were determined to make it work.

Perverted Justice acted as the wall separating *Dateline* and the sheriff's department. After PJ contributors finished their chats with potential predators and made a date for them to come over to our house, a copy of the chat log was given to me and another one to the deputies. Frag and Del were in radio contact with the sheriff's department at all times.

For this operation we were set up in a five-bedroom home in a relatively new subdivision. Once again PJ had set up its computer operation in an upstairs bedroom and Mitch Wagenberg and his team had taken over the master bedroom and turned it into a television control room.

Lieutenant Bianco and his team were set up in a motor home parked in the driveway next door. Bianco had fifteen men assigned to the operation and they didn't get much rest over this three-day weekend in late January 2006. Our past two investigations had averaged eighteen men. An overwhelming fifty-one men would show up in Riverside.

The plan was to have the men show up, I'd confront and attempt to interview them, and then when they left the house the sheriff's deputies would arrest them and take them away for interrogation and booking. As it turned out this would take a fair bit of flexibility and we were always ready to scramble.

In southern California, fourteen men showed up on the first day alone. This investigation revealed the most diverse group we had ever seen. The men who visited our home ranged from nineteen to sixty-eight years old. We met an actor, a teacher, a Homeland Security agent, and something we had not seen before: men with violent criminal histories.

Among the first men in the door was the actor. His screen name was Cbeachdude and he rolled up to the house in his Mercedes convertible. The thirty-four-year-old was here to meet a thirteen-year-old boy with whom he'd been chatting online. Del, posing as the boy, invited him into our kitchen. Cbeachdude had chatted in graphic detail about what he wanted to do with the boy, which basically involved lots of sex in the shower.

Imagine the adrenaline rush this guy was feeling. He drove all the way to Riverside from Hollywood, parked his sports car, and then walked around to the back of a strange house and came in through the sliding glass door at the patio. He was anxious.

"Just hang out at the counter for a second, okay?" Del called from the next room.

Then as only she can do, she playfully asked: "So I know I showered once; do you still want to shower again?" Cbeachdude giggled nervously: "Well I'm kind of stinky." The mood was clearly ruined when I walked into the kitchen from the next room and confronted him. "What's up?" I asked. He wasn't sure what was happening, but he clearly knew it was not good.

At first he tried to lie his way out of his predicament by saying he thought the young man he was coming to visit was eighteen. Of course that excuse didn't fly because I had the transcripts of his conversation with the decoy. What happened next turned into a tearful performance from an actor who told me he had bit parts in films like *Godzilla*, *Pearl Harbor*, and *Never Been Kissed*. He continued, "I'm ashamed, I wasn't thinking right and I feel terrible and this was seriously the first time. And I knew I was taking a huge risk." He also said that he knew what he was doing was wrong.

Cbeachdude was just the beginning. Each one of these investigations is intense. I have to read every word of every explicit chat log. I discuss it with my producer, Lynn, and we strategize about what tone to take with each guy who comes in. Besides her role as producer, which means she has to be responsible for the overall look and feel of the story, Lynn continually helps me to see the big picture. She is great at not letting me get too focused on one particular element of the shoot, plus she's a good friend and pleasant to work with, which, when you are cooped up in a house for three or four days, makes the whole exhausting experience much more tolerable. Lynn also preps me for our visitors, as in if he says this, what will you say? That kind of coaching is invaluable, especially in preparation for some of the more high-profile men who have come knocking on our door.

Take kinky_man_in_corona. On the surface he was just an average guy dressed in a polo shirt and jeans. He looked like any other forty-three-year-old out and about on a Saturday morning running errands after a stop at Starbucks. But when he walked into our house in Riverside, I already knew more about him than perhaps he was able to admit to himself. I certainly knew more than his wife and kids did—or for that matter the students in the math class he teaches at a high school within miles of our undercover house.

His chat with the PJ decoy named BUBBLEBETH2005 left little doubt about his intent.

kinky_man_in_corona: Yes I do want to come over and I would love to get you naked.
BUBBLEBETH2005: 4 real? I've never done that before?
kinky_man_in_corona: well we'd do more than that
BUBBLEBETH2005: like wut
kinky_man_in_corona: well I would get naked too and we would have sex.

The teacher even schooled our decoy on oral sex, telling her that if he ejaculated in her mouth, it would roughly be the consistency of pancake batter. Now, the high school math teacher, married with kids, was parked in front of our house. Surveillance cameras caught him slipping off his wedding ring and then sliding into the back patio door. He was visibly anxious. Del, acting as the twelve-year-old, invited him in, saying: "I'm just brushing my teeth, I'll be right down, okay?" "Okay," he replied as he roamed around the kitchen checking things out.

That was when I walked in. kinky_man_in_corona immediately asked if he was under arrest; he had no idea our hidden cameras were rolling. I offered him a seat and asked him, "What are you doing here?

"Getting my ass kicked," he said. He must have thought I was with law enforcement because then he told me: "I need you to arrest me and take me to jail and execute me."

Part of the reason so many of these men stay and talk to me during these investigations, I think, is because many feel confessional and I am genuinely curious to find out why these guys would risk everything for a sexual encounter with a young teen after an explicit online chat. And in this case when I posed that question to kinky_man_in_corona I think he was being honest: "I am a sick son of a bitch. I talk about it online all the time." He claimed, though, that he'd never actually met someone in person after an online chat: "I have never done anything with anyone besides my wife. Ever."

He was reluctant to admit to me what he did for a living: "I'm in education."

"You're a teacher?" I asked.

"Um hm" was the response. kinky_man_in_corona was a father himself and admitted that if some guy came into his house to hook up with one of his kids when no adult was at home that he'd be "pissed."

Like the other men who showed up in Riverside, the teacher was arrested and put in jail until he bonded out. But here's the unbelievable part of the story: two days after he came looking for sex with a twelve-year-old girl he was back in his high school classroom teaching math. It wasn't until six days after his arrest that the sheriff's department and the teacher's lawyer contacted the school and he was suspended without pay. While some of his students were surprised at his arrest, other suggested the teacher had a history. A girl named Christina said of her former math teacher: "He has looked at my butt or looked down our shirts." Other students said the same thing, although the school said it never received any formal complaints against the teacher.

While the thought of a teacher doing something like this was shocking, there were other men who showed up in Riverside who had a history of violence and sexual crimes. Some of them were registered sex offenders. Online he called himself Pavlov1234 and claimed he was twenty-eight. But when he walked into our house wearing shorts, tank top, dyed hair, and mustache, I was pretty sure he was much older. It turned out he was sixty-eight. He'd been chatting online with a decoy posing as a thirteen-year-old boy. The chat left little doubt as to what he wanted to do with the boy. The decoy said: "Do we need rubbers? Do they hurt?" Pavlov1234 said: "I don't fuck guys, but if you want to you can do me."

Pavlov1234 claimed it was just rhetoric and that he really just came over to talk. But there was something about this park maintenance worker's background that suggested he was lying to me.

He had been arrested just five months earlier for having sex with a fifteen-year-old boy. We knew this before he arrived because we'd done a computer background check on the man, but we didn't have all the details. I would need to get them from the potential predator himself. I had a printed copy of his registered sex offender record with his picture on it. "So you had intercourse with an underage boy?" I asked.

The man told me, "I didn't even know he was fifteen. He told me he was eighteen." It turned out that Pavlov1234 was still on probation for that offense and as a part of that sentence he was required to see a counselor, whom he had seen just two weeks before this confrontation.

"And what did you talk about with your counselor?" I asked.

"Various things," he said. I asked him if he told his counselor about his sexually charged conversation with a thirteen-year-old boy. He told me he did not and then conceded that it appeared he had not learned his lesson after his last crime.

A few months after we aired the Riverside investigation we learned from law enforcement there that this story was even more sordid. The fifteen-year-old boy Pavlov1234 admitted to having sex with was HIV-positive and prostituting himself. So had there really been a thirteen-year-old boy in our house, he too could have been infected.

Then there were men who had left a trail of victims on their way to our hidden camera house. CasperN909 is a good example. Twenty years before he walked into our house trying to meet a thirteen-year-old boy for sex, he was convicted of molesting three children in one family in Washington State. The children's mother had met CasperN909 through a mentoring program for kids who didn't have fathers. One by one he worked his way into the bedrooms of the three siblings. Finally one of the kids told her mother, who called police.

CasperN909 pleaded guilty in that case and was sentenced to ten years in prison. Not long after he was released, he was caught again, this time in Santa Barbara, California, molesting a teenage boy. Another guilty plea followed and once again CasperN909 went back to prison.

Skip ahead another ten years and he was in a chat room using the screen name CasperN909, chatting with a decoy posing as a boy named Luke struggling with his sexual identity. He flattered the boy: "Cute guys you're supposed to love and cuddle and talk and stuff to." Luke said he liked to wear his sister's clothes and got this response: "Oh well, one day i'll take you shopping, we will buy the stuff, and you come over here and dress up and then we can make love while you are dressed like that, okay."

And then late one night in January 2006, CasperN909 poked his nose through our patio door and asked: "Where are you?" When I walked into the kitchen, he bolted so fast, I barely got a look at his face. He took off down the driveway and was tackled by sheriff's deputies. Later with blood still dripping down his face from the takedown,

CasperN909 refused to tell a detective about his criminal past, even though he knew he'd eventually be found out.

It got so busy in Riverside that we actually had three men show up within minutes of each other. The first guy pulled up in his car and parked across the street from our house. A second walked up and started pacing in front of the house. Then we discovered that yet a third potential predator was parked on a side street.

Finally the man standing in front, who called himself jazzeman04, decided to come up the driveway and into our kitchen.

He's nineteen and here to meet a girl he thinks is twelve. As the other two men continued to wait in their cars, jazzeman04 decided to cut our conversation short and race out the door. Within seconds the deputies sprang into action, first arresting the man in his car across the street, then the man parked on the side street, and finally jazzeman04. Only six minutes had elapsed from the time the first car pulled up. We were stunned to learn that one of the men arrested was a federal agent working for the Department of Homeland Security who came to meet a girl he thought was thirteen. It got so crazed that Lieutenant Chad Bianco ran out of manpower. "I had no one available. All of my investigators were dealing with people we had arrested and you still had people coming to the house," Bianco told me later.

Bianco's team actually had to stash several of the suspects in the sheriff's motor home. The men were handcuffed and told to keep quiet while still more men showed up and were arrested. Finally one large group was taken to the processing center.

Behind the scenes it was difficult to keep up. There was not a spare moment for anyone, not PJ, not the crew, and not me. Fifty-one men showed up after explicit online chats and I had to try to read every word of every one of them. Every night we'd return to the hotel exhausted, grab four or five hours' sleep, and then head back to the house.

The Riverside investigation marked the first time that we had men show up who had seen our previous shows, knew that they could be walking into a sting, and came anyway. People ask me all the time why these guys keep showing up. After interviewing nearly two hundred men in this situation and reading countless lines of explicit chat logs, two things come to mind: first, I think that many of these guys just don't think it can happen to them. They figure *Dateline*, or the police, for that matter, can't be every place and that the chances of getting caught on the Internet are so vast and remote.

The other reason speaks to the addictions and compulsions many of these men develop. They have twenty-four-hour-a-day access to chat rooms and porn sites and they have a sense of anonymity that they feel protects them. Soon the line between fantasy and reality gets blurred. It's not unlike the alcoholic who is fine with a drink or two and then needs three, four, or five. As chats progress, they can become more and more explicit until an actual meeting is arranged. By that time, the predator has been able to convince himself that the kid, in this case a decoy, is a willing, if not eager, participant.

Consider the case of one of the guys who walked into our investigation in Riverside. southbayguy310 drove by our undercover house and he saw deputies arresting a previous visitor. Concerned, he called the PJ decoy posing as the girl he wanted to meet for sex, and asked what was going on. Thinking quickly, Del told the man there had been a drug bust next door, but the coast was now clear.

Sure enough, a few minutes later, he pulled up to the house and walked in. Not only had he seen the deputies, it turned out that he had seen our earlier report on computer predators and, to top it off, we learned that he had been caught by PJ volunteers in the past.

Men arrived at our Riverside house bringing Viagra, condoms, lubricants, sex toys, beer, wine coolers, hard liquor, sandwiches, jewelry, and clothing. By the time we finally wrapped up the shoot late on a Sunday night, we had also nabbed two men who arrived together, apparently to have sex with a boy, and a sixty-five-year-old man who had hundreds of child pornography images on his computer, along with a successful business executive who wrote music in his spare time. (Hard-chuck1, the sixty-five-year-old man, stopped taking his heart and blood pressure medication in jail while awaiting trial and died.)

The Riverside investigation aired as a two-hour *Dateline NBC* special in February 2006. The reaction was overwhelming. We had a special setup in the studio so that I could blog live and answer viewers' questions. There were so many I couldn't keep up. I stayed up until one in the morning. Bleary-eyed, I finally went to sleep knowing two things. We'd be doing another "To Catch a Predator" investigation, and it would have to involve law enforcement.

*As of this writing, Cbeachdude, kinky_man_in_corona, Pavlov1234, CasperN909, jazzeman04, and southbayguy310 have all pleaded not guilty and are awaiting trials.

Chapter 5

The Other Victims

Her e-mail to me was riveting.

"While I appreciate the fact that your program exposes and removes these vile beings from society, clearly saving potential child victims from these predators, I have yet to see any program on this subject recognize 'the other victims' of this horrific crime . . . the unsuspecting spouses, children, family, and friends of these sick individuals.

My ex-husband is now serving time in a federal prison for having been busted through a different Internet sting operation in which he chatted with an undercover FBI agent who posed as a single mother with a seven-year-old daughter. He spoke with this woman on the phone, gave graphic details of the sex acts he wanted to perform on her child . . . and tried to convince the woman to meet him. Yes, he has ruined his own life.

The FBI? They removed a man from society who very well could have gone through with his perversions . . . scarring some innocent child for life . . . I am happy this did not happen . . . so grateful. But what of the lives of this man's grown children, who have to deal with the fact that their father is a sexual predator? Their pain is very real, too. I have seen it firsthand and it kills me to know their faith in those they are supposed to be able to look up to and whose trust has been ruined. To make matters worse, they have to suffer the embarrassment of having people find out . . . they now go through their life wondering . . . who knows? Does he know? Does she know? Who is going to find out next about what my dad did? What about the way *their* lives have been affected?

We are victims as well. We carry an unearned . . . undeserved stigma, which merely adds to the already painful and humiliating aftermath . . . for something *we did not do*. We too are punished, serving a sentence."

Her e-mail is an articulate, passionate, and painful acknowledgment of the fact that repercussions from the behavior of sexual predators run far and deep. Caught in the undertow of their sick acts are those whose lives have often been linked to them by love: their wives, parents, siblings, and children.

People have looked at the "To Catch a Predator" reports and wondered, what's the damage? No children were harmed. It was "just" a sting.

Because she has a young son, the woman who e-mailed me said she would share her story for this book if she could speak anonymously. She has no qualms about being identified, but she would do nothing to risk compromising or complicating her son's future any more than it already has been by her husband's predatory behavior. I agreed.

"Julia" is not her real name nor is "Alan" her husband's. But everything else you will read is painfully true.

• • •

It was a few weeks before Christmas and Julia's husband was off to a conference. Her grandfather had died two days before, but Alan said he was going to the conference as planned and would probably miss the wake.

"I can tell you what he wore: green shirt, khaki slacks. He looked handsome. 'You're going to get a reimbursement for today, right?'

'Yeah, right,' he said. 'Give me a kiss. Call me. I hope you can make it to the wake.'"

At 7:15 A.M. he was off and Julia began her day. Thomas, her three-year-old, had preschool, and she had a lengthy to-do list of things to get ready for the family who would be in town for the wake and funeral. She pulled on her jeans, a purple sweater, and sneakers. By late morning, she was getting her son dressed for preschool.

"My son had one sock on and one sock off," Julia recalls, "when the phone rang. I had a green phone. Thomas was watching *Franklin*, a cartoon on Nickelodeon."

It was 11:56 A.M.

The FBI agent introduced himself and said he had her husband in custody. He reeled off the charges that included words like "sexual solicitation, underage minor . . ."

"I was speechless. What? No. No. He's at a conference. No. No. I couldn't believe it. Then they interrogated me to rule me out, that I wasn't part of it and that I had no knowledge." The FBI agent asked her about her grandfather's funeral, apparently trying to corroborate things Alan had said.

"Alan was facing a hundred sixty years, sixteen counts, and a million dollars bail," Julia says with traces of incredulity still evident as she remembers the moment her world blew into smithereens—shattering everything she thought she knew about herself, her husband, and their fifteen-year relationship.

Alan had been arrested at a Days Inn motel where FBI agents were waiting for him when he arrived thinking he would meet parents who'd brought their two young daughters to have sex with him.

The FBI agent put Alan on the phone. "It was just a fantasy. Nothing happened." His voice was reassuring.

"What am I supposed to do?" she asked.

"Nothing, I'll take care of it, I'll take care of it," he said.

Julia took her son to preschool and called Alan's parents. They came over to her home to help her unravel what was clearly a huge mistake. "We all thought he went on the wrong site and somehow got led around."

Alan called again and reassured his parents that nothing inappropriate had happened. Everything could be explained. It was all a gross misunderstanding. He only went to the Days Inn to make sure the two girls who were supposed to arrive there were not harmed. "He said everything you've ever heard on 'To Catch a Predator.'"

But when it happened to Julia, it was several years before our series first aired. She had never heard of behavior like this. Who would try to meet children for sex? She knew her husband. He had a good job at a local business, worked hard, and was a kind man. The marriage had been under strain for a while and she had just had a miscarriage—her sixth in their nearly ten years of marriage. Their son had been going through the terrible twos and had upended the predictable part of their lives. Alan had seemed to pull away from her after the birth of the baby, but that was common among her friends. Children change everything in a marriage.

Predator? Pedophile? No way. Nothing could cut into her shock and disbelief. A few words and a couple of phone calls could not dent that decade and a half of intimacy she had shared with Alan. "I hoped they were being nice to him. I was very sympathetic, very empathetic. I would not have had a child with this man. I am smarter than that."

It would be years—three, in fact—before Julia understood that she had been up against a master manipulator and that what happened at the Days Inn was not her fault.

• • •

Julia was twenty and Alan twenty-three the night they met at a party when she was a junior in college. "I thought he was attractive, but I didn't like his mustache." But she was excited about meeting his friends, who were very connected to each other and had a lot of fun.

"I remember dancing to Bruce Springsteen's 'Dancing in the Dark' at the bar, wanting Alan to dance with me. He didn't want to, but did, and his one friend said to me, he must really like you, he never dances. I remember thinking, he never dances? That's not what I want."

Julia was seeing someone else at the time and remembers saying to her friend after her second date with Alan that this wasn't a relationship that was ever going anywhere.

Her own family life had been strained. Julia was the middle child who tried to make everything okay. Her mother was an alcoholic. "My parents' communication was very sparse—they were not fighting, but certainly not enjoying each other. I made up the *Brady Bunch* side of life. I really thought that was achievable."

When she met Alan's parents, something clicked. Her parents had separated the year before. Alan's parents were her fantasy come true. They loved and were devoted to each other and their three children. "When I saw the way they parented Alan, it was nice; not only was I interested in him, I was interested in that whole environment. I was just getting sucked into this whole family. They thought I was a great, great thing for Alan."

Julia was energetic and motivated. Alan had flunked out of an engineering program and was having a hard time finding traction in life. But he started in a local business and seemed to be moving gradually up into more responsibility in the office.

"He was never going to set the world on fire," Julia says now. "He didn't have the drive that my father had, but I did, so it would be all right." He was handsome with his blond hair and blue eyes, and kind. People would always remark on his kindness. It was what set him apart— his friends would say that Alan would give you the shirt off his back.

"My ultimate goal was to have a family, to be that fifties mom, where everything is nurturing and calm— a completely unrealistic view about life as it actually is lived," Julia says now with a smile.

Alan was easy to cast in the role of leading man. She dated him for five years. He asked her father for her hand in marriage and got down on his knee to ask her. One hundred seventy-five people came to the wedding. Julia had been raised Catholic but converted to the Lutheran Church when she married her husband.

There were never red flags early on—the big deal breakers that scream, "Turn back now." But in retrospect, Julia feels there were a few pink streamers. His favorite picture of her from their honeymoon in Hawaii was one in which she was sitting in the Jacuzzi and looked very, very young. "I thought it was odd that would be his favorite picture."

On the rare occasions when he would drink and party too much, Alan would become enraged. Julia said it was like a Jekyll–Hyde personality shift. But it only happened twice in their fifteen years together so it never became an issue.

There was the off-again, on-again problem of his sexual inadequacy. "He had insecurities as far as his sexual performance," she says. But Julia had never been with another man and was sure there was a way to figure it out. "I was sure I could fix anything; that pattern had worked for me my entire life."

She worked so hard to please that she learned to ignore his hypercritical nature that subtly worked to sabotage her self-esteem. She remembers the dinner party she worked so hard to pull off. "My friends told me later that they were appalled at his sniping. He was very undermining. Instead of the roast beef being good, it was dry. I should have had apple instead of cherry pie. He was a master manipulator. He would find the weakness and would know what would get to you." It was subtle but relentless.

There are other moments from the early years of their marriage that seemed strange at the time and now seem to point to his secret. Alan became outspoken about the JonBenet Ramsey case. "He was disgusted with all the beauty pageant photos and was fairly vocal about it. He was a big Republican conservative, and totally had this whole other façade."

Starting a family was Julia's top priority. It was an emotional roller coaster ride because Julia had miscarriage after miscarriage—five—before she finally gave birth to Thomas in 1997. Life was finally sliding into place for her in the way she had always hoped. At long last, they were a family. She was optimistic about the future, despite the crash of hormones and a baby that stubbornly subverted every schedule she tried to create. "He blew me out of the water. He would not eat when I wanted him to eat, nor sleep when I wanted him to sleep. He really rocked my world in every way."

But that's what babies do. She knew it and found support in camaraderie with other women with young children. Alan seemed to lose interest in her—but she was nursing and her friends said that had happened to their husbands, too. The good between them always outweighed the bad; they had a lovely three-bedroom home on a quarter acre in a nice neighborhood in the northeast—a foothold in the American dream Julia was determined to realize.

But then the balance in their marriage began to shift in a way Julia couldn't continue to ignore. Alan stopped paying the bills. It was strange. "I had to go and challenge him at work. I was so angry. Money was going out and I didn't know where it was going. Utility companies came knocking. I had no clue."

Alan made excuses. He said work-related expenses had come up. Julia tried to get him to stick to a budget but without much success. The more she tried, the more Alan seemed to pull back. Sex became almost nonexistent between them.

"I was confused. I wanted so much to be happy, but I wasn't . . . but how many moms say that? I would justify it, get with my friends and say, 'Talk me down off the ledge, this sucks.'"

Her determination to make her marriage work still had a way to go. She and Alan tried to get pregnant again. Children were part of the long-range planning Julia kept focusing on. It was hard because Alan wasn't that interested in sex, but she pushed, and was finally pregnant again when Thomas was just past two.

But eleven weeks later, in the spring of 1999, she lost the baby. In the months that followed, Alan withdrew even more. Her own denial fed her inability to see her marriage for what it was: cracked. "We would get into arguments or discussions where I would say, 'I'm not the crazy one here, Alan, what is wrong? Something is up. You need to talk to me.' I knew instinctively, as a woman—I started to connect the dots and think he was getting his emotional fulfillment elsewhere and it was not at home."

What was beyond her capacity to imagine was that he could be getting it online.

She didn't have that much contact with the computer. He would tell her that e-mail was too hard to learn, that there were a lot of different steps. If she needed to look something up he'd do it for her. Her friends would say that was silly. E-mail was easy. But Julia didn't push it. Nor did she really question the strange way Alan set up the computer—although now she realizes it was so no one could walk behind him and read what he was writing. Nothing quite set off alarm bells. "I was coming *so* close. Only in retrospect do you go, Ah, that's why . . . Why is the video camera moved? The tripod?" It was still beyond imagining for Julia that "he was taking a naked picture of himself and putting it online. In my living room."

The more he pulled away, the harder she tried. "We had date nights." She thought maybe they needed to spend more quality time together. He kept urging her to go out with the girls. She thought they needed to have more fun, so she found a sitter so they could go to a Halloween party in 2000. She was going as a woman from the Victorian era. He was—as it turned out—refusing to go. (During their courtship they went to a costume party. He was a flasher in a raincoat and stuffed panty hose in his trousers to make a big penis.)

Fantasies die hard, and Julia still clung to the dream that she and Alan could create a happy family: "I never doubted my love for him. Once again, he was a kind person." But as she turned thirty-five, she began to think she deserved a good life. "I felt I loved him, but I was loving myself more. I was starting to find myself more and to realize that he didn't love me in the way I wanted to be loved.

"I was starting to think that I could do this without him. I was thinking I have fifty more years." But her goal was to find a way to make her marriage work. She broached the subject of counseling with Alan but he said, "We don't need that."

She tried and tried some more until she got fed up. She called Alan at work and said they had to talk. When he came home she mapped out her frustrations. "I am not going to live like this. This is awful. I'm just done."

Alan was unfazed by her distress. When he finally spoke he said, "What I'm going to say you won't like. I'm not attracted to you."

She had been wounded in the center of her soul. "I said, 'Oh, that's a problem. That's a *big* problem.' So at midnight I went out with the dog, walked around the neighborhood, and talked to God. I said, 'There is something in him; there's nothing I can do. I can work out and be the most physically healthy person but there is something wrong.'"

But she still wasn't thinking divorce. "I didn't want out. I was like, 'God, get me out of this *particular* situation. Guide me, I am lost. This is within him.'"

As frustrated as she was by her inability to fix things at home, Julia was not ready to leave the marriage. She had known Alan since she was twenty. After fourteen years together, divorce would be such a waste, such a failure. They limped along together for another year.

It was May 4, 2000, the day before Thomas's third birthday. Julia buckled him up in his car seat and headed out to get party favors. She saw the Coca-Cola truck cross over the dividing line on the highway, but there was nothing she could do. "The van smashed, the air bag went off, my shoulder broke, my ankle was extremely sprained," and there was blood all over the van. She couldn't see Thomas and he made no sounds.

The paramedics came quickly and assured her Thomas was unhurt. Apparently she was so bloodied that they kept him away from her so he wouldn't be frightened. Alan met her at the ER but seemed strangely detached. After a few hours at the hospital she was cleared to go home. Alan insisted on stopping at Burger King even though she was vomiting in the car. He said he was going to work the next day so she had to find child care. He discouraged her from taking her pain medication. "You don't need that," he said, while downplaying the accident to the rest of Julia's family.

Julia's dad and stepmother came to help out for the weekend. Her father was nurturing and caring in a way Alan no longer was. Julia had always felt close to her dad and, up early one morning and out on the deck, she blurted out her fears to him. "'Something is wrong with Alan. There is something seriously wrong.' Dad didn't know what to do. He was like 'recover from this and then heal that.'"

Everyone seemed to think that there was a solution—but it felt just beyond reach. There were so many things that Alan wasn't—an alcoholic or drug addict, physically or sexually abusive, unstable or irresponsible at work—that whatever the problem, it couldn't be that bad. Neither Julia nor anyone close to her could fathom who Alan really was or the other head-on collision that was now just months away.

• • •

Julia and her grandfather had grown closer in the final years of his life. He had moved from assisted living into hospice and was in his final days. The call came on December 2, a Saturday, that Granddad had taken a turn for the worse. She visited that night and again the next day. Her father and the rest of the family started flying in.

She cheered up when she got home because Alan had set up the Christmas tree and straightened up around the house. "I thought that was so strange. It was completely surreal. He had this sort of vibrancy."

He seemed excited about the conference on Tuesday that he was planning to attend. Julia was pleased that he seemed to be taking more initiative at work. Maybe, just maybe . . . She was finishing the long months of physical therapy on her shoulder and now might be the time when she could really focus again on getting her marriage back on track.

Julia spent most of Sunday at the hospice and was at home when the call came shortly after seven o'clock that her grandfather was dead.

Alan was remote and couldn't respond. The only comfort for Julia was in hugging her child. Her husband's strangeness was inexplicable.

When she called him the next day at work to say she'd just learned they'd be inheriting a small sum of money from her grandfather's estate, Alan was nonplussed. "I said, 'This is a great thing. You can get a new car or whatever.' He was not there."

The next morning, Alan left for his conference just after seven A.M. Julia had four hours left to live her life as she knew it.

• • •

In the immediate hours after Alan's arrest, Julia and his parents pulled together to rectify the terrible chain of events that had somehow overtaken their son and led to his arrest by the FBI.

His parents spoke to him and said they, too, were sure it was all a mistake. He was just tying to make sure some young girls were safe and he got caught in the web. Alan's dad started working on pulling together money for bail and Julia's dad started to put together a legal team.

Within hours, a caravan of news vans was parked in front of her house. Cameras were pointed into the windows of her home, which heightened her sense of violation. In order to leave her house to pick up her son at preschool, she donned a long black hooded raincoat, "my shield of armor," she now recalls, and left looking like a Franciscan friar. "It's the piece of clothing I put on because my entire world was gone."

The shock that descended over her was so immense that it is hard for her to remember much of what happened during the first few weeks after Alan's arrest.

She desperately wanted to go to her grandfather's wake and funeral, but found when she got to her father's house that first night all she could do was stare at the sofa. Nothing was sinking in. She couldn't cry. She doesn't remember Christmas that year. She and Thomas stayed with her father and stepmom for several weeks. Going back to the home she shared with Alan was unthinkable. By New Year's she had pneumonia and was hospitalized briefly.

"You lose and mourn and grieve. You almost wish it was a death. You wish it was anything but this deviant life that you had no clue about." Julia pauses before continuing. "Then you beat yourself up because you didn't see it. How did you let this get by? It's really absolutely unbelievable."

A turning point came at the beginning of February 2001. Julia went back to her house for the first time. She wanted to look through the house herself and see if there was anything she could find. An e-mail hit her like a spear. Alan had been communicating with "Heather," a sixteen-year-old in a nearby county. It would turn out they had been together—both online and off—since she was fourteen.

"Even the FBI didn't know about it. I went, 'Oh, my God.' This is not the isolated incident that I so badly wanted to believe. I was somehow wanting to believe that he was set up and just that stupid! I wanted to hold on to my life as I knew it."

Her denial was shattered. The man she married because she loved and wanted to create a family with was attracted to young teens and children. The e-mail had been dated December 6, a few days after his arrest when he was free on bail. Julia was beginning—just beginning—to see her husband for the man he really was.

But his parents weren't. They believed what their son was telling them: "Alan would feed them these lines. 'I tried to be physical with Julia, but she turned me away. I absolutely was there for her, but she just got so distraught over the miscarriage.'"

She was incensed. There was no turning back. She started to make to-do lists, and began considering selling and packing up her house, thinking about where she'd live, starting counseling and finding a lawyer.

The first attorney she spoke to said she'd never get full custody and would have to pay her husband alimony. He wished her luck. She walked out of his office, ripped up his card, and got in her car. "That Gloria Gaynor song, 'I Will Survive,' came on and I drove out of that damn parking lot saying, 'I will make it through this.'"

Her toddler son kept her focused on reality when she so often didn't want to believe the things that were happening to her actually were.

"He was three years old. If Alan was actually what they were saying, a predator, a pedophile, I had to have Thomas examined." His pediatrician said he showed no signs of molestation. Therapists advised her to tell her son basic and age-appropriate information.

"I lived for therapy. Oh, my gosh. Lived for it. I couldn't wait. I had so much to deal with every week." Unsure of what her life would be like financially, she said she found a wonderful therapist through Lutheran Family Services who agreed to see her on a sliding scale for ten dollars a session. A second therapist with experience in the legal system also was instrumental to her survival, she says. She said she could always reach out to them in between sessions when her life felt like what she describes as "1-800-Oh-My-God!"

"I blamed myself. As in anything, it takes two. Do you know how many times you hear that? 'It takes two.' What was my responsibility in this whole thing? You go down that path too much and then you are in a mess. The person you are intimate with, the person who knows your ins and outs has totally led you astray. How could I not have seen this? Then I'd think, Julia, he's a manipulator, he didn't want you to see it. He hid it. That was part of the whole thrill for him."

For the first year, Julia said she existed, did damage control, and went to therapy twice a week. She moved from the house she shared with Alan into a town house nearby so Thomas's life could stay the same. He continued in preschool and had supervised visits with his dad. In the rubble of her new life, everything felt different. Even something as simple as going to her son's preschool recital made her afraid. "I lived in fear," she says. What if someone said something to her? "There are people in my old neighborhood who, to this day, think it wasn't serious. There are people who sided with him, believe it or not. He was nice-looking, he was not that dark predator on the street."

Most unsettling to her as the months wore on was just how deftly she had been manipulated. "All the pink flags alone did not give cause for the major alarm. That was what is truly frightening." All she could suggest to someone who felt the same vague but unsettling feelings about her spouse would be "not to settle for a manipulative answer—to think I better do a little more 'investigating.'"

Julia's world had flipped so completely from one realm to another that September 11, 2001, was almost a comfort to her. Not that she wished anyone any tragedy or death—it was deeper and more symbolic than that. Evil could strike out of the blue. Without warning. What was once powerful could become ash. In an instant. "It was devastating and horrible but it was huge because it really showed me that the world is a bigger place than my little place. It distracted me, and made me appreciate my life. It diminished my immediate horror. Everyone was with me on this one. The newspapers were all about that and not Rocky Creek man arrested in blah, blah, blah."

Julia edged a little further out of her own claustrophobic black box. Life felt precious and worth fighting for again. "Alan's journey and mine began to separate after 9/11." When Christmas came she decided to make a genuine effort to celebrate and make the day magical for Thomas.

After the first year of shock and damage control, she was able to take more action in her life and move beyond mere existence. She found a part-time job—that was easy. Finding a babysitter, letting herself trust someone with her child, was hard. Part of her action strategy was to figure out where she would move with her son. She took a year, visiting cities up and down the East Coast. She would strike out on her own and establish new roots in a new town.

The day she pulled out of her driveway at four A.M. with her sleeping son and dog in the van she burst into tears. Moving . . . and moving forward was always frightening. Healing came slowly and incrementally, but it came through intensive therapy. "I came to the conclusion that there was no way I could have seen it. He wanted to hide it. We're not all-knowing. It was about three years after. Even with extensive counseling it still took three years."

Thomas understands that his father did illegal things with the computer and had to spend time in jail. Alan was sentenced to four years in prison and was released after serving three and a half years. Under the terms of his probation, he can't see his son until Thomas is eighteen nor can he have contact with women under twenty-one. "As the years have passed," Julia says, "I'm seeing that having an ill father, a predator father, a pedophile father is far worse than not having a father at all.

"Someone told me their son shaved for the first time and I thought, 'How is that going to work?' The father-son pumpkin carving at school . . ." Julia's voice trails off at the pile of unanswered questions that she knows will only resolve themselves in time.

Julia chose not to read the weeks of chat logs between her husband and the FBI agents who were posing as decoy parents willing to let their daughters have sex with Alan at the Days Inn. It was more information than she's wanted to know. Her father-in-law did say that he thought Alan's e-mails were "well written," a comment that struck her as bizarre.

She's done part-time work and managed financially because of some money she inherited. The life she is living now does not feel like second-best or an "instead of" life. "I now have a life that I never before saw was reachable. It's there. It takes a lot of effort and a lot of strength and it's scary as heck. I still have a while to go. I have yet to tackle many issues, like parenting a teenager or intimacy with another partner." Dating has been the one precipice for Julia that she hasn't been ready to face.

"My counselor said, 'I promise that when you get through this, life will taste sweet.' For the longest time it wasn't, but now parts are tasting sweet and it's so great. It's so great."

• • •

"Anna" lives several hundred miles away from Julia in a quiet town by a lake. (She, too, asked that her identity be protected to spare her children further pain.) Although she and Julia are separated by miles, they are connected by the emotional journeys they have made. They are women who have been forced to say to themselves, "I had a child with a pedophile." When Anna blurts out that sentence it startles with the terrible force of the reality it conveys.

At forty-four, Anna has a vitality that is contagious. Her brown eyes sparkle and her dark hair shines. She describes herself as someone with "five pairs of running shoes and five hundred books. No, make that five thousand." The picture windows in her living room open out to the sweeping views of a gentle countryside gilded in autumn colors. It's a gorgeous view and a complete contrast to the claustrophobic hell she's endured since April 2005, when she found out that her husband, Mike, a prominent attorney, was under arrest for viewing and receiving child pornography over the Internet. At first the news didn't sound as earth-shattering as it would soon turn out to be. It certainly didn't sound like anything she couldn't take in stride.

"I didn't get the phone call that said, 'Here's what I've done.' I got, 'I'm being investigated for looking at pictures of child pornography, but they are really slick, it is like *Playboy*.' The implication was that they were adults dressed up like kids," Anna recalls. "When you first hear it, you don't process it that quickly. You want it not to be true. When I heard about digital images in the beginning I thought, 'God, they are not even kids. They are digital images!' I tried to put it in the prettiest box I could until I couldn't do it anymore."

Pedophilia? That wasn't a term she had ever given much thought to or really understood. It certainly didn't seem to have any connection to the man with whom she'd had two children and had been involved with for twenty-five years. Mike? Not only was he the smartest man most people knew but he was also one of the most admired. "He's the most loved man in every room he walks into," Anna says with a wry smile. "They call him 'King Mike.' He's just enormously liked, respected; it's unbelievable. It's also often part of the profile of a pedophile, how they are idolized."

Anna first married Mike when she was nineteen. Mike was a few years older, out of law school, with a foothold on a secure and successful future. Both of them grew up mostly in the west and began their newlywed life there. She had always believed in the Cinderella story and Mike fit the part of her prince. "You grew up, got married, and you lived happily ever after."

The fantasy died fast. "We got married and the next day he was Dr. Jekyll. I was just standing there going, 'What the hell happened?' I was so young, I didn't tell anyone. It wasn't his behavior, he was just gone emotionally. Just gone. Didn't exist emotionally."

She was miserable. Mike had interest in sex but there never seemed to be an emotional connection in it for him. "I didn't share with anyone how unhappy I was because on the surface, what did I have to be unhappy about? Mike would come home and not talk to me. He would come home and sit at the end of the bed watching sports—there was an indentation in the mattress."

Anna thought she should try harder. If she were a better wife, maybe Mike would be more responsive to her. Children were something they both wanted, and when they made the decision to try to get pregnant, Anna was thrilled. "The day I found out I was pregnant, I was just like a kid. I find this book called *David, We're Pregnant*." Anna had seen a doctor that day thinking she had the flu. When she found out she was expecting, she came home, gift-wrapped the book, and called Mike at work. "I have this vision of him sweeping me off my feet. Every sit-com show you've seen, like Darrin and Samantha from *Bewitched*—that's my image of telling my husband. I was in bed, he's standing there and I give him the book. He opens it, looks at it, and says, 'This is what you called me home for?' I feel *this* small. That was it. He turned around and went back to work."

She kept hoping he'd change when their baby was born. When she gave birth to a boy, she was ecstatic. Once again, her fantasies soared. "I have this image of what happens when you give your husband a son. He's going to come to the hospital with an armful of roses and shower me with affection." Anna continues as memories from twenty-two years ago spill out. "I am so dumb. I don't know you can ask for pain medicine. I lie in bed in pain. I just had a baby. It was like two A.M. and I called him up. 'I can't sleep,' I said.

"He said, 'Well, I can.' He hangs up on me. Then he doesn't come to the hospital the next day. He'll go to work and be in that afternoon. No flowers, no nothing. I left that hospital knowing my marriage was over. I just didn't know how to go about doing it. Divorce wasn't big then."

But it wasn't easy for Anna to give up on what she calls her *Leave It to Beaver* view of life. She thought she should be able to jump-start her marriage. "There was this one time I decided I have got to try and save my marriage. Again, I have all these ideas in my mind. I spread candles around the room, I get a black negligee, we'll have a wonderful night of passion and I will save this marriage! I lay there and I could have been a cardboard cutout. There was nothing. It was so bizarre."

She became adept at pretending sex wasn't an issue between them. "He'd ask me periodically over the years if sex was a problem in our marriage. I, of course, being a woman, spared his feelings and said no.

It was awful. I told him that, just not in those words. I would say, 'Sex for a woman is an emotional connection. There's nothing there.' The other thing I did was act like I didn't like it. I led him to believe I didn't like sex just to spare his feelings."

But the idea of divorcing him and jettisoning everything she knew was huge. Then one night she had a revelation. "I went to this dinner with some of the other wives in the law firm, and they were older and they had two, three kids and they were all flirting with the busboy and they were drinking. I just see my life flash before my eyes that I'm going to be some drunken woman, who is unhappily married and hitting on busboys because I am trapped in this life I can't afford to get out of."

That was the wake-up call. When she brought up the possibility of living in the east during the summer, which was still a few months away, Mike said, "Why don't you go now?"

She did. She and her son moved nearly two thousand miles away. She and Mike divorced, but traveled back and forth a lot so he could keep and build his connection to his son. This quickly settled into a routine that would last for two decades. Anna lived in the east and Mike out west. But they spent every holiday together; he had a separate bedroom in her house.

Anna got an associate's degree in business administration and then went on to get an undergraduate degree in psychology, which eventually lead to a master's degree in human performance and paved the way for her work in the fitness industry. Mike's career skyrocketed. He was a business attorney for the most powerful law firm in the state.

Anna had always wanted more children. When her son was eight she started to really think about it seriously. She and Mike were divorced. Both had dated but never remarried, were on friendly terms and parenting their son together. Anna pursued adoption, but when a baby became available, she backed out so the child could go to a couple who had no children of their own.

Then she had an idea. Maybe she and Mike should have another child together. It was a strange idea, but not outside the realm of possibility in her mind because they spent so much time together. Mike was going to be the baby's de facto dad regardless of how she got pregnant. Anna brought up the subject with him; they thought about it for a year, finally deciding to take the plunge into parenthood again—via artificial insemination with Mike's sperm. "The family kind of freaked out that I would have a child and we wouldn't be married so we said, 'Fine. If it matters that much, we'll get married.'" For the second time in their lives, they became husband and wife, living separate lives on opposite sides of the country.

Their daughter, Charlotte, was born twelve years ago when Anna's son, Steve, was ten. Their novel arrangement worked. "We spent every holiday together and we had a life together without sex. Frankly, most of the married people I know, after two kids and twenty years, that's what they have, too. My entire adult life has been spent with this man."

There was only one clue that hinted at Mike's secret life. Anna remembers she was still nursing her daughter when Mike called. "Anna, has Steve mentioned anything to you about a book he found?" Distracted by the baby, she said she wasn't paying much attention as Mike continued. "There is this guy in my office who asked me to give him the legal opinion on the constitutionality of it." Anna said she thought it didn't seem like any big deal. Her son had recently been out there with his cousin. "He's like, 'There are pictures of kids.' I said, 'Pictures of kids?' Mike said, 'I'm really sorry. I forgot all about it. I left it at the house and the kids found it.'

"That was a completely plausible story. You know, he brought work home, that was what it amounted to. But I remembered it. Why did I remember it? Subconsciously did I know something? You question everything. But that was it. That was the only thing after all these years."

Why would she suspect anything? Mike seemed detached so much of the time, but she thought so did a lot of supersmart people who seemed to operate in their own worlds. "He just seemed like the most innocuous human being on earth. Never had any real emotion. I even said to him a couple of years ago, 'I have known you for over twenty years and I have no idea how you feel about anything.'"

Child pornography, online predators, belonged to an orbit far from Anna's world. "It was kind of like terrorism used to be. It doesn't happen here. Not in our backyard." And certainly not involving the father of her children. "We really believe if we do certain things, certain things shouldn't happen to us. This is one of them."

She knew in her bones that the Mike she knew would be upset at the idea of children being raped: "If he saw a child being raped in a picture he would do everything he could to find that child and save her." But that was the Mike she thought she knew.

The phone call from her husband in April 2005 was the shout that brought down the avalanche. Within the next forty-eight hours all the computers were seized from Mike's office out west and one from the office she shared with him near her house. (Mike and Anna were co-owners of a small business together.) After his arrest, he went to a treatment center in Texas. Soon she was there with Mike's family for a marathon two-day therapy session.

Mike's family expressed disbelief that the things they were hearing about him were true. The thought that he could have become obsessed with child pornography made them incredulous. With backgrounds in law and psychology, his family members were trained to probe and challenge. "They were arguing about the definition of whether or not he is or isn't a pedophile. That's when Mike said, 'I'm a pedophile, get over it.'"

"Devastating is too small a word," Anna says when she remembers the shock of those first few months. "I feel like he stole my life," Anna says. "If he had walked up to me and said, 'Hey, I'm sexually attracted to children, or sexually stimulated by children, want to have two kids with me?' That's just what makes me crazy that I married this man who pretended to be everything I wanted intentionally, to cover his lifestyle, addiction, interest, disease, and alter ego. I feel like he stole my life."

As his story was gradually revealed, she learned that Mike had been deceiving her ever since they married for the first time. "He said he had had the problem since law school, and I met him after he graduated." In the therapy sessions she went to in Texas with him, more details spilled out. "He claimed he always had a sexual addiction, that throughout our entire lives he went to prostitutes and peep shows and bought pornographic magazines and videos—every aspect of that underground world of sexual deviancy. None of that did I know." When they talked about child pornography, the question of child rape photographs came up. "He said he didn't seek them out, but when he saw them, he didn't move away from them," she recalls.

"He even said he pretended to be a nice person because he liked what it got him. He doesn't know who he is," Anna says. "He said, 'I just can't help it. If I don't look good, I have to change the story.'"

One of the things that made it possible for him to view child pornography was his lack of empathy, according to his ex-wife. "Mike said the person he most identified with as a child was Mr. Spock in *Star Trek*. Mr. Spock had no emotions. That's why when they look at those pictures they don't feel bad for that child. They don't have those feelings, they even think those kids enjoy it." But Anna said Mike always knew his obsession with child pornography was wrong. "He would say, 'I feel bad afterwards and say to myself I'm never going to do it again.'"

Anna hoped there might be some explanation in Mike's childhood for his predisposition toward prepubescent girls. The Association for the Treatment of Sexual Abusers (ATSA) estimates that within the general population, 14 percent of males and 32 percent of females have been sexually abused as children. Where the numbers jump dramatically is in the percentage of the abused who become abusers. "Recent studies from within the past five years suggest that from seventy to seventy-three percent of child sexual abusers report experiencing sexual abuse in childhood," says Dr. Susan Strickland, a forensic social worker in Atlanta who specializes in sexual deviancy. "In my experience, I would say that pedophiles—those who are attracted to and aroused by prepubescent children—have an even higher incidence of childhood sexual abuse than child molesters who are sexually interested in both consenting adult partners and pubescent children."

Anna felt knowing Mike had been molested would help her comprehend what had happened. "You need to explain it so you can understand it because this random thing is the hardest part to deal with. Hearing that they were molested as a child, truth be told, makes us feel better. There's a reason. But he said he wasn't molested. Throughout his therapy he said, 'I don't have a trigger. My only trigger is boredom.' He would describe this drumbeat in his head that pushed him on to do it."

Hundreds of pornographic images of children were found on her husband's computers. As Anna learned the details of the criminal charges against him and spoke with investigators, she realized that Mike had been warned about his behavior several times in the six years prior to his arrest. But because of his prominence and power in the community, no one made very big waves nor did anyone realize at that time the magnitude of the problem.

Anna said she saw a document that suggested his first warning came in 1999. The following year, Mike was netted in an FBI child pornography sting. But there were problems with the case and it fell apart, never making it to court. Nevertheless, Anna said she was told the head of Mike's law firm was tipped off by someone aware of the investigation that "Mike is on the FBI watch list. He almost got caught in this sting; tell him to knock it off."

In 2001 the firm was warned again that Mike was visiting pornographic sites at work. "So they take away his Internet access," Anna says. "Then something happens again, and now he is learning to access it elsewhere." Everyone was willing to cut Mike a lot of slack. "He got all of these warnings, but I think what happens is it is so unbelievable and we are talking about a guy that is considered to be the nicest guy in the world." After his arrest, investigators also told Anna that Mike made a trip to Thailand—a popular destination for sex tourism. Although they found no evidence that he engaged in illicit sex, it was a red flag for his wife.

Subsequent to his arrest, Anna learned Mike was spending up to eight hours a day in cybercafes and had been doing so for nine months. Some cybercafes are the modern version of peep shows. They're legitimate businesses where anyone can get on the Internet to view pornography in a booth by feeding twenty dollars an hour into a machine. Adult pornography is legal, but there is no monitoring in cybercafes, so they're a perfect place to view child porn. Since the drives are erased daily, there is never a trail of evidence left behind. Mike admitted to investigators that he was using cybercafes.

Anna said she had virtually no awareness of the reality of child pornography. Hurtled into it by her husband's arrest, she awakened to its awful reality and the explosion of violent video and pornographic images of children that are readily available online. "I once asked a prosecutor what was the worst thing she ever saw—and she didn't even give me a chance to say don't share it with me—she said, 'The worst thing I ever saw was a five-year-old girl screaming her head off while a man ejaculated into her mouth.'"

That's why when people refer to child pornography as "just pictures," Anna becomes incensed. "I hear it all the time," she says. "'He didn't hurt anybody. It is just a picture.' How do I respond to that? It's not just a picture, it's a picture of somebody's pain. It's a crime scene. Those children are in pain, they are being tortured, and they are not willingly in that picture." Looking at that picture also supports the industry that produces those pictures and ensures that more child pornography will be made.

Equally disturbing to Anna in the aftermath of Mike's arrest were those who said, "Oh, he'd never hurt his own child." Anna is upset by that response. "It's almost like he gets points for not hurting his child. What does that even mean? If you hurt someone else's child it's more okay than if you're hurting your own? If you are hurting a child you are hurting a child. Period." Her own naïveté is unsettling to her now. "Now it's like, 'How the hell was I blind to it?' There are so many kids being hurt; we have to stop *not* talking about it, *not* doing something, because it is so horrific."

Mike pleaded guilty to the federal offense of receiving child pornography and was sentenced to five years in prison in May 2006. "Had there not been a mandatory minimum, he would have gotten off completely," Anna says. "Might have gotten probation, that's about it. Would not have had a felony charge, I can guarantee it. When something like this happens to somebody prominent, it goes against everything we believe in and they do get off." He was also placed under lifetime supervision.

"Mike will be a registered sex offender. I look up who the registered sex offenders in my neighborhood are to steer clear of them. And now that is my children's father! That is absolutely mind-boggling to me," Anna says.

The worst part of navigating her terrible nightmare was grappling with its impact on her children. "He is their father. No matter what. Parents do hideous, horrible things all the time. But—that is still your parent. That's a bond I couldn't break, wouldn't even want to." Her son, Steve, was in college when his father was arrested. "My son's first reaction was to defend his father. There is no way in hell my son would ever defend a man like that, but it's his father."

It was more complicated for Anna's daughter, Charlotte, who was eleven when she found out her father was charged with possession of child pornography—all of it involving young girls. "Our daughter hasn't spoken to him since she found out and I never thought she would. I don't think any eleven-year-old on finding out that her father likes twelve-year-olds would want to talk to him.

"Telling her almost killed me," Anna recalls. "Because it was the end of her childhood. It was heartbreaking." She pauses, taking in the enormity of it all. "I know how I feel having had children with a pedophile. But what about being the *child* of one? To have a parent that you are not proud of? He was a lawyer, he was to uphold the law. Your identity about everything is just shattered."

But her daughter has rebounded and appears to be thriving in every way. "I always try to look at the good things that have come out of this," Anna says. "You want your kids to have this wonderful, idyllic childhood. That's what I had. But it really didn't help me in this situation. Life isn't always wonderful and idyllic. It set me up to be this devastated."

For Anna, the road to recovery has been torturous. She has been sifting through the wreckage of her marriage, juxtaposing the husband she thought she knew with the man he actually was. "We had an office nearby. He printed out pictures, laid them on the floor, and would ejaculate. I think of me, driving past the office, not knowing what was happening in there. That still disturbs me. It is so unimaginable."

It took her months before she was able to tell any of her close friends what she was going through. "I went through this alone," Anna says. "If he had had cancer, I would have been on the phone with my girlfriend the first day. This was such an 'Oh, my God, no, it's so taboo.' I did not tell anyone and when I did, I was practically physically ill.

"Everything I thought would happen, didn't. Absolutely no one thought I had anything to do with it because it is not that kind of crime. This is such a well-kept secret that wives don't know." She is speaking candidly in this book to help break the shrouds of silence around women living lives like hers. "I want that rabbi's wife or ex-wife to find me. I want to talk to other victims, other wives—I do believe it lessens it when you know there is someone else."

For the first fifteen months after Mike's arrest, Anna said the going was rough. She set up online bill paying and stopped opening her mail. "I really did just remove myself from life to deal with life." She couldn't sleep and ate only enough to keep herself going. "Just because I am not bleeding doesn't mean I am not hurt. He did so much more harm than a gunshot would. Manipulation is a horrible thing. It's all for gain, for evil."

Part of Anna's healing and recovery has come through her involvement with Internet safety issues and advocacy. She attended conferences and read voraciously to educate herself on the issues. Sometimes she finds speaking to parents disheartening. "When I do these little presentations on Internet safety, everyone is there because of their fear of pedophiles." She talks about that danger, but reminds parents of another reality: "Your child has about a ninety-three percent chance of being molested by a family member—and only seven percent chance of being molested by a stranger." Anna, like other advocates, stresses this point to parents that except in rare instances, "Your child has an almost zero percent chance of being harmed by anyone on the Internet. Parents don't want to hear about cyber bullying, which is much more widespread. They are just there to find out how to stop pedophiles or how to spy on their kids."

She feels parents have to educate themselves on issues, talk to their kids about Internet safety, and set reasonable rules and boundaries on the computers in their homes. "The Internet is so new—it really caught us off guard. We didn't know the power it was going to have. At first it was all good. But we have to teach our kids about the Internet, just as we did about crossing the street and looking both ways. You have to view it a little bit differently, that's all. It took off faster than our ability to understand it.

"We can't be afraid of it. It's a whole new mind-set," she says. "The Internet to children is a *place*. It's a place kids go just like we would have gone to a football game. They go to the Internet to hang out with friends. So how they view it is not how adults view it."

About the only view in her life that hasn't changed is the expansive one from her picture windows. Her husband's secret life forced her to new truths and painful growth. She has found her voice and is no longer hesitant about speaking up—or out.

"Something was just not quite right. Why did I never, ever say that to anyone? I never said that to anyone because I didn't want to be viewed as the bad guy. Why are we so concerned about not making waves—that bothers me and I want to change it."

Her spirit is fierce and her determination to rebuild her life in new and better ways is unceasing.

"I can't imagine coming through this worse off. I could have stayed in denial. But that's not who I am," Anna says. "I want to learn from it, move past it, but I still want to be me when I get through it. The hardest part was to feel as vulnerable as I felt and just be boldly honest with my friends and family about what I was feeling. It had made everyone feel uncomfortable. My not sharing my feelings got me where I am today and I am not going to stay there. That is my part in all of this. It's not that simple, but that is how people get away with it, how bad people get away with it because good people don't want to see the bad."

That's one of the questions that still plagues Darlene Calvin, a woman I met on *The Oprah Winfrey Show* last September. Her husband, Todd Calvin, was arrested as part of an FBI sting for trying to have sex with young boys. Darlene had no idea she was married to a pedophile who had been a member of NAMBLA, the acronym for the North American Man Boy Love Association, since at least 1986, seven years prior to their wedding in a Catholic church in Dallas with five hundred guests.

"You have to forgive yourself," she says. "This is where I'm in conflict. I should have seen something, shouldn't I? I have to forgive myself for not seeing something, even though the world tells you it wasn't there to see."

What she saw when she fell in love with her husband at twenty-five was a handsome man with strikingly blue eyes. He was six years older than she was and just purchasing a dental practice. "He was very attractive, very personable, he loved volunteering, loved kids, and I thought, wow!" She came from a tight-knit Catholic family and wanted her own version of that family with Todd. "I went from my dad's house to my husband's house," she says. "I had a lot of grand ideas of what marriage should be about."

Darlene's master's degree in psychology was no match for her vision of how life *should be* and didn't help her see what was right before her eyes. Todd was emotionally abusive and made her feel like she always fell short. "I never measured up. What I didn't realize," she says, "is that I didn't measure up because I wasn't a young boy. What I thought was that I wasn't good enough."

Sex petered out after their two children were born. "It was his best excuse not to have relations." His reasoning sabotaged her self-esteem: "'You know, now that you've had babies, I don't like how it feels, it kind of grosses me out.' The whole time I'm thinking I'm damaged goods, I gained so much weight, it was constant."

Despite having years of psychological training and appreciating the value of talking about feelings and reaching out for support, Darlene Calvin kept her confusion to herself. "I didn't want to talk about it to my friends. That's the Pollyanna in me. We were the perfect little couple, the perfect little family, and I had the perfect little idea of how the perfect life was going to be. That's my mistake. I wasn't true to myself. If I have learned anything from all of this, I want to teach my children how to be true to themselves."

Like Julia and Anna, Darlene felt that if she only tried harder, she could make her marriage work. "Trying to save my marriage—that's what good little Catholic girls do. There had never been a divorce in my family and I wasn't going to be the first one."

Todd Calvin's dental practice quickly became successful. He had a terrific voice and became known as "The Singing Dentist." But that was the public persona. It was different in private. "We were living on eggshells," Darlene says. Something seemed off in the marriage; she just didn't know what. "A pedophile has got to keep the person he's closest to, the person he lives with, at a distance. There was a lot of verbal abuse, a lot of criticism, control, and dominance to keep me from figuring things out." Whatever demons he had, he hid them well. The NAMBLA material went to a private post office box. There was a box on top of the closet that had teen magazines with pictures of boys in them and some newspaper clippings about a boy from his hometown in northern Arkansas. But the box had been there forever. "I don't think you would have looked at it and said, 'Oh, my God, you're a pedophile,'" Darlene says.

The signs she did see she took at face value. "His demons lived with us. When he stood in the shower and cried because he was worried his practice wasn't expanding fast enough, was he crying for that or because he had made the biggest mistake in his life because he married a woman he didn't want to? He'd chosen a career he didn't really want because he needed to afford what he wanted to do. He needed to be upstanding and a functional part of society. So he had this business, this wife and the kids—he had the boat and the airplane. But you know what? The demons were still there."

Darlene and Todd Calvin divorced fifteen months before she got word that her husband's house was being raided on February 12, 2005. As she approached his house she saw that it was surrounded by police cars and black SUVs. Her ex-husband was the kind of guy who wouldn't even spit his gum on the sidewalk. It was impossible to fathom what he might have done that was illegal. The agents explained to Darlene that Todd Calvin had been arrested earlier that Saturday morning in San Diego as he was about to board a boat that was going to cruise down to Mexico to meet young boys. Darlene heard the acronym NAMBLA for the first time because the group had arranged the cruise.

When she heard "Man/Boy Love" as part of the explanation of the acronym, she felt her world begin to come apart. As she told Oprah

Winfrey, "That moment is so vivid for me. I still feel that kick in the stomach when it dawned on me what he had done."

Her ex-husband's secret life began to unravel as the federal agents explained that Todd Calvin was charged with conspiracy to travel and traveling in interstate and foreign countries to engage in sexual conduct with young boys. The agents segued into questions about her two children; her son was ten and her daughter eight. It wasn't hard to grasp the subtext behind their questioning. Did she think Calvin had been abusing her son and daughter either during the marriage or during their regular post-divorce visitations? (She did not, and the subsequent investigation never found evidence that he had.)

During the raid on his home, FBI agents found NAMBLA literature and a novel, *Diary of a Pedophile*. More NAMBLA material was discovered in Calvin's dental office along with a book of nude men and boys together. As his case continued to unfold, Darlene said she learned that her ex-husband had had a sexual encounter with a fourteen-year-old boy while still in dental school and then again with the same boy two years later. An investigative report in the Dallas magazine *D* said that Calvin also had paid to have sex with an underage boy while vacationing in Costa Rica.

The sense of unreality Darlene felt when her world came undone on February 12, 2005, still grips her. "I still feel like it's an out-of-body experience when I remember how I felt on February twelfth and when I was curled up in a ball and wanted to die. Even when I watched *The Oprah Winfrey Show* I thought, 'Who is that woman that looks like me and sounds like me and is talking about this man she was married to who was a child predator?'"

Darlene doesn't delude herself—she's too focused and smart for that. What happened to her, as with Julia and Anna, was so far outside the realm of what she thought she knew about her husband that it was impossible to integrate into the rest of her life. While an extramarital affair carries profound betrayal, it is comprehensible in a way that pe-dophilia is not.

Todd Calvin pleaded guilty and was sentenced to twenty-four months in prison. He also faces twelve years of supervision, and is re-quired to register as a sex offender in any state he lives in for the rest of his life. During the period of supervision, he's forbidden to have any contact with his children—the children Darlene told on Valentine's Day 2005 that their father was a pedophile.

"My daughter said she was glad she wasn't a boy. My son . . . didn't say anything." As she said that on *Oprah*, her voice choked and her eyes filled with tears.

Darlene has heard her ex-husband say, "I have a life sentence be-cause even when I leave prison I'm a marked man."

"Wow," she says. "What about his kids? At some point someone will ask my son where his dad is. He is going to have to decide in that moment if he is going to say he is dead, or if he wants to say, 'I don't know. I never knew him.' Or if he wants to say, 'He's in prison because he's a child predator.' A child shouldn't have to decide to say that."

She speaks about her life now because she wants people to appreci-ate what it feels like for families of sexual predators when they become "collateral damage."

"It goes beyond what he has done to those he abused and it goes be-yond what he has done in his own life," Darlene says. "The collateral damage is all the people that in some way—in his forty-something years—were close to him, whether they were patient, friend, associate, or parent or brother, or his wife or his children. He has shaken our trust, and the emotional damage that goes along with that, you can't touch it. Not to say we won't heal, but wow, none of us chose this, not one of us chose this. I still to this day think he doesn't understand the damage he did."

But as life so painfully teaches us, we often don't get to choose what happens to us, but we always choose how we respond. Darlene Calvin, like Anna and Julia, could have easily nurtured her bitterness and refined her victimhood.

That's not who she is. She has opted to feel her feelings and grow through her pain. "I need to forgive myself now for hating myself so much, forgive myself for at one point just wanting him dead. Just wanting him to die. I'll admit to those feelings, God forgive me; it would have been easier for all of us if he were dead. People heal, dying is closure. There are support groups for that!"

She prayed for her children's safety a lot when they visited their dad because he often took them flying in his single-engine plane. "What I didn't know when I thought I was praying for their safety I was actually praying that their father would not molest them." There is no evidence that he did. But there is evidence that he molested other people's children.

"I'd say that my relationship with my children has blossomed because we took out something that caused them agitation and discomfort which was the divorce situation and the visitation," she says. "This was an ugly, ugly thing. My children will have to revisit this with each milestone they meet in life. As I said in my therapy, I can forgive Todd. It's a process, it's a journey. But I can only forgive him for me. I cannot forgive him for my children. And someday, when my children are prepared to deal with it, they are going to have to decide whether to forgive him or not."

It's been said that adversity introduces us to ourselves. It might strike some as paradoxical, but Darlene Calvin wouldn't have her life any other way, wouldn't rewrite her past even if she could because every aspect of her life is better now than it was before. "I would never go back and change anything because it would mean erasing my children from my life. It would also mean losing out on the opportunity to truly know who I am. I will tell you something, I know myself better than I ever have. I am so in touch with who I am; on most days, I'm still at peace with that. There is still a lot of conflict inside of me but time and prayer will handle that. I have the best spiritual relationship with God

I have ever had. It was okay before. It wasn't as rooted, it is not about going to a building called church and saying prayers, it is truly about letting go of things and having conversations with a higher being and knowing somehow that you will be taken care of and that my children were saved."

The profound harm these men have done will have lifetime repercussions for their victims and families. That pain and anguish can never be undone. Alan was sentenced to four years, and after serving three and a half years, he's now free. Mike was sentenced to five years in May 2006 and is presently incarcerated. Todd Calvin was sentenced to two years and served twenty-one months; he's now free. The years of supervision, probation, and counseling ahead for Alan, Mike, and Todd Calvin are aimed at preventing any of them from ever harming anyone else again. All three have lost access to their children until they are at least eighteen.

One of the inspiring things about my job for *Dateline* is the people I get to meet. My favorite are often those like Darlene, Julia, and Anna, who profess that they are really no different from anyone else. Darlene put it this way: "I am every parent, I am every woman, I pack my kids' lunches, I sit on the deck and have a glass of wine with my girlfriends sometimes when I have a spare moment, I drive car pools, volunteer as much as I can, worry about my kids. I'm every parent, that's all I am."

I beg to disagree. Any woman—like Darlene Calvin, Julia, or Anna, who can laugh, love, and live again with real gusto after their worlds were sabotaged by pedophiles and sexual predators is an inspiration to all the rest of us. They are quiet heroines whose courage and grace in the face of personal catastrophe has something to teach us all.

Chapter 6

MySpace

Sometimes you get lucky. Every detective knows that, and Lieutenant Jake Jacoby and Detective Peter Charles of the Fairfax County police department, despite their years of training and experience, never take their luck for granted.

Their wake-up call to the dangers of sexual abuse cases driven by social networking sites like MySpace came when a thirteen-year-old was struck by a bolt of fear and balked at getting into a car with a man she met online. "Marisa" (the detectives asked that we protect her identity) was at a swimming pool in a Virginia suburb of Washington, D.C., on August 24, 2005.

She had agreed to meet a man named Joey Dobbs—whose screen name was buttsecks—just outside the pool. He was waiting for her in his car, but when she saw him, she panicked and handed her cell phone to a lifeguard, saying, "Tell him you're my mom and that he should never call me again."

Police were called to investigate. After a few days the case was turned over to Detective Peter Charles, who was with the PCASO team, an acronym for the Protecting Children Against Sexual Offenders unit at the Fairfax County police department. The unit was not yet up to speed on the dangers of social networking sites like MySpace because it hadn't hit any cases. "If you told me ten years ago that someone could go online and have access to information about thousands of kids, I'd never have believed you," Charles says. Charles has years of experience with sexual abuse cases and crimes against children. He was aware of the trouble kids got into with chat rooms and he knew about the peril of online sexual predators. What he didn't know was that social networking sites were giving them unprecedented access to teens. MySpace, Xanga, Facebook, and Bebo had not really crossed his radar screen yet. Just after Labor Day 2005, that all changed.

Detective Charles interviewed Marisa, who explained the online chats that culminated in the scheduled meeting at the pool with Joey Dobbs, or buttsecks. Marisa told him she thought Joey was the assistant of a woman named Jennifer Ash, whom she'd met on MySpace a few days before the encounter at the swimming pool.

"Jennifer Ash," a voluptuous-looking brunette who claimed she was twenty-one, described herself this way in her MySpace profile: "Born in the DC area, lived in LA for the last ten years, and looking to make some friends. I have a boyfriend so I'm not looking for anything with any guys. SORRY, GUYS!"

She said she wanted to meet nice girls in the Fairfax area. "Anyone that would like to go eat some sushi, go catch a movie . . ." Sounds simple enough, right?

In the Details section of her MySpace profile she described herself as five foot one and slim, bisexual, a Virgo, and a high school graduate who didn't smoke but drank and earned $250,000 a year.

An important status symbol on social networking sites like MySpace is the Friends section. This is where a user puts pictures of her friends—people who chat with her and have access to her profile. Friends leave messages and comments. Jen had pictures of 232 people in her Friend Space section. Among the comments displayed were "Jen's so hot! I just wanna get her out of her clothes and see how naughty she really is." Another said, "If we were having a conversation face to face, I wouldn't be able to look past your tits, they're very nice."

Jennifer hit on Marisa—the thirteen-year-old—for the first time on August 23, 2005. She introduced herself, saying:

> I just saw your profile and thought you might be perfect for project I am working on. It pays very well (starts at 3K a shoot) and only takes a couple of hours. Anyway, if you are interested I would love to talk to you about it.

Marisa replied, "Hey . . . sure i'm interested . . . anything that pays that kind of money . . . lol." (online lingo for "laugh out loud")

Jennifer laid out what she had in mind. She said she'd just moved back to the D.C. area to take care of her mother, who was sick with cancer.

> I used to model for adult Web sites and did some dancing. I have a lot of contacts in the adult site community and decided it would be something I would like to try to start up for myself. I have the general layout of the site and theme and all that done, just need to get enough pictures and video for it. Like I said the pay starts at 3k a shoot depending on what you do in the shoot. It can pay as much as 12k.

Minutes after reading her message, Marisa was back to her online and said she was interested. The two switched from MySpace to instant messaging on AOL. (Instant messaging is real-time online communication, just like talking on the phone.)

Marisa told Jen she was only thirteen. But that didn't matter to Jen, who, according to Detective Charles, told Marisa that an audition was mandatory, adding, "We'll put you in some sexy clothes, you'll have sex, and depending on how that comes out, we'll make a film and I'll give you money."

Jen introduced Marisa to her assistant, Joey Dobbs. His MySpace page described him as someone with no interests—"Teach me something." His photo showed a smiling, collegiate-looking guy—but he said his age was "69"—sexual reference apparently intended. Dobbs described his occupation as a "pornographer." He said he graduated from Texas A&M with a degree in computer science and was online seeking "networking, dating, serious relationships, and friends." There were 220 "friends" in his extended network. One of Joey's "friends" commented that, "You have everyone at work fooled," which would soon turn out to be a gross understatement.

Marisa rapidly agreed to an audition. Jen said Joey Dobbs would meet her at the swimming pool and bring her to Jen's apartment.

Marisa had no way of knowing that Joey and Jen were one and the same.

No matter how it's done, no matter what the pretext, it's illegal in every state in the country to use the Internet to solicit an underage teen for sex. In Virginia, the age of consent is fifteen. (You can't drive until you're fifteen and a half, but legally you can be sexually active.)

Detective Charles had enough information by September 12 to obtain a search warrant for the home of the man whom he still refers to formally as Mr. Dobbs. As it turned out, he didn't have to travel far. Dobbs, twenty-five, lived five miles from the police station and was home when the cops came knocking. Dobbs, according to Charles, was very cooperative and agreed to come down to the police station to be interviewed.

"I had already interviewed the girl and had corroborative evidence on what she was saying. There was no 'feeling,' or 'instinct' about him, because he had contacted the child, showed up to get the child, and I knew he was trying to have sex with the child," Charles said. There was no hint of how much more was to come. Detective Charles didn't realize he was seeing only the tip of the iceberg.

At the police station, Charles recalls, "We put him on computers, he called up his profile and hers and said this was the girl he was trying to meet, and this was the girl [Jennifer Ash] that he made the profile of." Dobbs insisted he had no pornography on his computers and was just, according to Charles, "trying to get laid and set up a situation where he could have sex. He didn't intend on paying any money but he admitted to offering it."

Dobbs said he had a girlfriend, and he had a good job working with computers at a major corporation in the aerospace industry. Nothing set off warning bells in Detective Charles or Jake Jacoby, who was running the Child Protection Unit at the time. "When you see a young guy like Mr. Dobbs, it kind of baffles you," says Jacoby.

But there was nothing baffling about the results that came back from Joey Dobbs's computer. Charles and Jacoby had stumbled into a major sexual predator. He had hundreds of pictures of child pornography and two and a half years of online chats with potential victims. "We identified thirty-seven people that he had extensive conversations with on the Internet—some meetings were scheduled and hotel rooms agreed upon. But that's not illegal. I concentrated on the juveniles."

Most damning in Dobbs's computer were videos he had made of himself having violent sexual encounters with girls who were underage. "There were some very brutal aspects to what he was doing that were very disturbing, to say the least," recalls Jacoby. "It ranks up there with some of the most brutal and disgusting things I've seen people do to people. It's basically watching a rape on video."

"In one of the videos he is very controlling," recalls Detective Charles. "He is commanding this girl to do what he wants. She tries to touch him and he says, 'Don't touch me.' Then something happens where he knocks the camera over and you hear her screaming and he said, 'I told you not to touch me.'"

The girls would be forced to assume contorted sexual positions in which they were graphically photographed. "It was more of a master-slave relationship," says Charles. The videos Dobbs made were a way for him to continue to experience the power and domination he felt in the rape, according to Jacoby. "That's why all these perverts still have things. That's why you find evidence. They use them to relive these moments."

After the forensics came back on Dobbs's computer, Charles began painstakingly building his case against Dobbs by matching faces of the young women he saw brutalized in the videos with online chats and photos from their MySpace profiles.

The first girl in a video he identified was "Susan" (not her real name). She was thirteen. Dobbs didn't use the ruse of hiding behind the identity of Jen. "He shopped for her, met her online, had a conversation," Charles said. "He was going to be her boyfriend, she was going to be his girlfriend. But then when he had sex with her, that was it."

Charles had the unenviable job of having to confront Susan with the secret she had successfully hidden from her parents and everyone else in her life in constructing the charges he would file against Joey Dobbs.

"She was a nice young person, from what I could find out. She never acted out. She was involved in what normal kids are involved in." But when Charles met with her at school, she admitted to having gone to meet Dobbs for sex.

"She was very straightforward—yes, I met him online, yes, I went to his house, I took my dog. She was more upset that he didn't drop her off at her house afterward and made her walk home. It was a ways away."

Then Charles had to meet with Susan's parents, whom he described as good, stable people, and tell them that there was more to their daughter's life than they knew: she had been raped by a sexual predator. "The parents were horrified. They are hardworking, they provide for their children, it's an affluent community, they put their children in what is supposedly one of the top school systems in the nation and unbeknownst to them, they think their kid is on the computer doing whatever and she is approached by people who want to do them harm."

In cases so disturbing, Charles said, people want to point fingers at the parents and say they must have been at fault. But he said that in Susan's case, the parents were not to blame. "You can't point your fingers at the parents—the kid is in their own house, who in their right minds thinks something bad is going to happen in their own house? The doors are locked, the windows shut, the air conditioner is on and the family dog is ready to pounce on the first person who comes through the door."

When Susan and her parents agreed to press charges, Charles was able to round out his case against Dobbs. On September 30, 2005, Joseph M. Dobbs was arrested and charged with carnal knowledge of a minor, ten counts of child pornography, and four other counts related to using the Internet to communicate with underage teens for sex.

Lieutenant Jake Jacoby had been running the child protection unit for five years. He realized Joey Dobbs was a new type of predator. "Here's a young guy, not bad-looking, sociable, has a good job, college-educated, money, everything going for him and he's doing *this*?"

Jacoby is used to the old school predator like the man the unit arrested last year. Carlos Rivera was a two-time registered sex offender who was free from prison. He drove to Virginia to meet a fourteen-year-old boy he'd been chatting with online. The boy had told him he'd be there on a trip with his parents.

Rivera booked a room at the same hotel and the boy came to meet him. "He was going to sodomize the kid anally, but he wanted to make sure he was clean first. He was giving him an enema. That's what he started doing and the kid freaked out," Jacoby said. "The guy went into the bathroom, the kid took off. He wasn't able to tell his parents for several days."

What is remarkable is that the boy *did tell*. Jacoby got a call from an agent investigating the case who was part of the FBI's Internet Crimes Against Children Task Force. Rivera had been grooming the boy online for several months. As is always the case, the predator was carefully building a connection to this kid. "They developed a friendship. It was never to the point of I'm going to do this or that to you," says Jacoby. "They are always looking for that trigger . . . they are always looking at what piques these kids' interests when they say things."

It's about pushing the envelope, slowly and cautiously. It's never, says Jacoby, "'I want to see you naked and sodomize you.' The kid would say, 'That's disgusting, are you crazy?' So it's put humorously. You say, 'Have you ever seen a grown man naked? Do you have any hair down there? Are you maturing?' They are always trying a little something to see how far they can go."

As it turned out, Jacoby said Rivera "had sexually assaulted numerous child victims from Virginia to Massachusetts." He had served time on two prior convictions. Now he's back in prison for his third.

"This is the new playground, right here, the Internet," says Jacoby. The kind of predator parents envision lurking on the edges of the school ground are now lurking behind their computer screens. Social networking sites like MySpace have transformed the cultural landscape in ways that were unimaginable only a few years ago. Many parents don't even understand what social networking sites really are.

Their awakening often comes when a teen gets into trouble and it makes the news.

In Connecticut, a twenty-one-year-old man was arrested and accused of raping a fourteen-year-old girl whom he met on MySpace last year. A few months before, a man on Long Island tracked down the work address of a sixteen-year-old girl he met on one of the social networking sites. He convinced her to meet him in a parking lot and sexually assaulted her. Last October, a thirteen-year-old Georgia girl who pretended to be nineteen in her online profile was sexually abused by a thirty-year-old South Carolina man. Several months prior to that, a fourteen-year-old girl from New Jersey met a man on a social networking site who, at thirty-three, was more than twice her age. He sexually abused her when they met in person.

"All bets are off. The MySpace phenomenon has changed child safety as we know it," says Parry Aftab, who runs WiredSafety.org, a nonprofit group dedicated to protecting kids online. "The number of kids who are getting hurt because of this is going to be something we are not going to be able to contain. I have been doing this stuff longer than anybody else—I've been doing it for more than ten years, and I will tell you, this has me scared."

What's scary about MySpace—and the other major social networking sites like Xanga, Friendster, Cyworld, Bebo, and Facebook—is that, unless the kids restrict their page, they give instant access to pictures and profiles that they post themselves. Think of MySpace as a cyber bulletin board that kids decorate with favorite music that they've downloaded and pictures of themselves. That's for them. For predators, think of it as a shopping mall.

Anyone can strike up a conversation with someone they see in a social networking site. Kids can restrict their profiles to just friends and people they know, but many don't and, too often, they put way too much revealing information about themselves online. Even when a profile is restricted, a kid has the option of letting someone in who contacts them and asks to be included in their network of friends. An appealing picture, a friendly query, a similarity of interests, or someone who just sounds "cool" is often more than enough for kids to make exceptions and let someone into their site that they don't, in fact, know.

MySpace has, as of this writing, 122 million registered members of all ages. Nearly 320,000 new profiles are added *every day*. The minimum age for joining is fourteen. MySpace recently heightened security and does not permit fourteen- to fifteen-year-olds having contact with strangers who are over eighteen.

The new security measures were implemented last year shortly after MySpace was sued in a potentially groundbreaking lawsuit. At the center of the case is a fourteen-year-old girl from Austin who claims she was sexually assaulted by a man she met on MySpace. She and her mother have filed a thirty-million-dollar lawsuit against the social networking site, accusing it of having lax security policies.

Here's the twist: an attorney for the defendant and alleged rapist, a nineteen-year-old community college student, said his client is also suing MySpace because the young woman pretended to be fifteen years old in her MySpace profile, which she established when she was thirteen. In an interview with *Time* magazine, his attorney, Adam Reposa, said with regard to MySpace, "More protection is needed to prevent harm to both parties." His client now faces twenty years in prison if convicted. He said the two had been e-mailing for a month and then exchanged cell phone numbers before meeting. They had a hamburger before going to the movies and then had sex in the backseat of his car. The defendant admits to the sex, but claims it was consensual and that she pretended to be older than she actually was.

Adam Lowey, an attorney for the young woman known as "Susan Doe," said in *Time* magazine that she's suffered "horrific" harm because of the alleged rape. He said she'd been led to believe she was going to meet a high school senior who was on the football team.

How culpable should MySpace be? On one side are those who say MySpace is just providing a way for people to meet, and suing the social networking site is like suing a shopping mall or a nightclub after someone is sexually assaulted after meeting there. On the other side are those who argue that MySpace isn't doing enough to keep kids safe. Connecticut's attorney general, Richard Blumenthal, told *Time* magazine that the minimum age is set too low and there should be age verification: "They fail to raise the age threshold to sixteen and take steps to verify age—as I and other attorneys general have repeatedly urged."

MySpace has not commented publicly on the lawsuit. Hemanshu Nigam, a former prosecutor, is the chief security officer for MySpace. He feels confident that MySpace is doing all that it can to meet its security obligations to children. But what about those kids who lie about their age, or adults who post profiles pretending to be younger? Nigam says MySpace is committed to weeding out age cheaters and catches tens of thousands a week. "Every single week we are catching and deleting thirty thousand profiles of people who are trying to get on the site who are not of the right age," Nigam says. "We built internal search algorithms that run on our site twenty-four hours a day, seven days a week, crawling for inconsistencies in a profile. For example, an individual might say, 'I'm twenty-five years old.' Then in their profile they also let you know they go to a middle school. That will trigger a notification by this tool, and we have a team of people who review all the notifications and then we say, 'Is this person of an age to be on our site or are they under the age of fourteen?'" Nigam wouldn't say how many people MySpace assigns to this area. He also said that MySpace is looking into ways to actually verify the ages of teens. The bottom line today is that there is no foolproof technology nor any databases that verify the existence of somebody under the age of eighteen.

Stephen Kline is the chief security officer at Xanga, a social networking and blogging site. "If there was a magic bullet, I'd be selling it and making a lot of money, but there isn't. The risks on social networking sites are similar to the risks people face in the offline world," Kline says. "The biggest risk is the uninformed user. As with any tool, whether it be a car or a Web site, if someone doesn't know how to use it safely there can be a lot of downside."

There is real status for kids in having many "friends" in their extended network because it feels like proof of popularity. Someone with 150 "friends" has much more social status than someone with forty-five. At an age when it's important to be popular, MySpace or other social networking sites are ways to prove that you belong and fit in. "At this age, when they often feel awkward, and unsure of themselves, even if they don't appear like that—this is a way to say, 'Somebody is paying attention to me, somebody likes me,'" according to Dr. Lisa Machoian, a psychologist and author of *The Disappearing Girl*, who specializes in adolescence. "I have heard over and over from teenagers, 'I have to be this way with this group, and that way with that group, and if I say this I won't be in that group.' It's exhausting for them. Online you can experiment with the more romantic and sexual part of yourself that you may feel inhibited to express otherwise."

But describing the power, allure, and danger of MySpace is not nearly as potent as witnessing it. To make a point about the sheer volume of available profiles, Fairfax County detective Peter Charles sat at the computer and logged onto MySpace. He entered an age range for girls—eighteen to twenty-one. He typed in the zip code for the Fairfax County police department—22031. Within thirty seconds he had more than three thousand hits of young women to scroll through who were within a five-mile range of zip code 22031. While this isn't a perfect example because Charles used legal ages—due to search limits—it does illustrate how many young women's profiles are so easily found. It's also important here to note that many teens lie about their age in their profiles. And he could easily have narrowed his search by typing in the name of a high school.

These sites are ways that kids express themselves and communicate with one another. No one denies their social value. Profiles are a new way of self-expression. You can add pictures of your friends and family. Do you drink or smoke? Sexual preference? Bi, straight, or gay?

Parents who haven't explored these social networking sites think they are as innocuous as their own high school yearbooks. For kids who are scrupulously cautious about their profiles, that may be true. But for adolescents who are seeking sexual experimentation, social networking sites are a stage on which kids can play, and play with their sexuality.

"Parents have always said 'Not my kid,'" says Parry Aftab, who has been trying to alert parents to the need to protect their children online. "Maybe the kid down the street, but *not my kid*. I don't need to worry about it. Now they can go to MySpace and see their kid posing in a bra. They can see the kids they trust and think are wonderful with five bottles of beer in their mouth."

Even good kids. What is shocking to parents—seeing provocative pictures of their kids or friends on social networking sites—is not surprising to psychologists like Dr. Lisa Machoian. Girls in particular, she says, are given mixed messages about their sexuality.

The media is saturated with images of scantily clad and overtly sexualized celebrities like Christina Aguilera and Britney Spears. Teen sexuality is flaunted in the media, but a girl who acts on her sexuality can be labeled by her peers as a slut. But how does a young girl find the boundary between being a slut and a prude? The Internet is one way to mediate that.

A "good girl" can experiment with aspects of herself online that she would *never* exhibit within her peer group or in public. "Sexuality and sexual experimentation is a normal part of adolescence," says Machoian. "If a youngster feels inhibited from exploring those parts of her developing self and that part of her sexual identity within the peer group, then the Internet becomes a place where she can explore that part of herself without fear." It becomes a safe way for a girl to experiment with her sexuality in a hidden way that is not going to impinge on her reputation at school.

Brittany Bacon is now in her first year of law school and has worked on Internet safety issues since she was in high school seven years ago. She's one of the 450 Teen Angels who work with Parry Aftab through her WiredSafety.org program. Brittany has given the issue a lot of thought and has listened to a lot of kids talk about what they do and don't do online. Social networking sites, she says, have unique appeal and power. "It gives kids a way to talk to someone without being judged automatically on how they look, how they dress, or on what they weigh," Brittany says. "I think we see from eating disorders and everything else that teenage girls struggle with, self-image is probably one of the biggest issues. The Internet allows you to be whoever you want to be and look like whatever you want and be judged strictly on what you think and how you connect with someone."

Vivian is fourteen and another Teen Angel who works with Wired Saftey.org. She is enthusiastic about the blog she writes on her Xanga Web site and finds that the social networking site has been a boon to her self-esteem. "I'm not the most popular person, and on these Web sites, you can really express yourself. I may be a little bit shy in school, but when I'm in front of the computer, things change. You don't have to talk to people face-to-face and you don't have to deal with people's reactions. When you are online, you can just be yourself without really worrying about it that much."

Vivian is a freshman in a suburban high school in New Jersey. She talks about things she loves online, like her passion for tap-dancing, and she feels that online she can express parts of herself she might not talk about at school. "I think it has opened up opportunities and it has allowed me to step out of my box a little bit at a time." She also points out that kids can meet online who might be in the same big school but not in the same social circles. Online acquaintances can lead to real friendships that might not have happened otherwise. "You can look at other people's Web sites and become friends without having to meet face-to-face first, and then you bring up a conversation in school because you made a basis online."

• • •

When Detective Peter Charles gets his hooks into a case he has a hard time letting it go. He still continues the painstaking process of trying to find the rest of Joey Dobbs's victims, with the hope of bringing additional charges against him. The work feels a lot like doing a thousand-piece jigsaw puzzle, he quips, "that's all in black."

People don't realize in watching our "Predator" shows that there is a huge amount of work that goes into building a case that will stand up in court. The arrest is just the tip of the iceberg. "We get stuck with the rest of the iceberg. It's very labor intensive. People don't understand that it doesn't happen overnight because they watch an hour television show and everything works out great," says Lieutenant Jacoby. In a cast like the MySpace case with Joey Dobbs, thousands of hours went into building the case that would convict him.

Charles spent nine months reading through two years of online chats and eventually managed to identify four of his six underage victims—none of whom had come forward voluntarily.

All were "good girls," and like Susan and Marisa, from upper-middle-class families who were doing well in school and had shown no signs of acting out. Their parents had good jobs and comfortable incomes and were engaged with their children's lives. Yet each of these girls had willingly gone to meet Dobbs. But even after being sexually brutalized and videotaped, they didn't tell or seek medical help. This is why there are such huge concerns about the underreporting of Internet crimes: kids don't tell, even when they have been horribly victimized.

This is not a surprise to Dr. Machoian, who has worked with many trauma survivors. "It's very rare that kids tell," she says. "Shame is a huge piece of it and fear of what might happen if they do tell. We also know that, initially at least, these girls are going to meet someone willingly—but obviously not consenting to be brutally raped. Yet there is always the fear that if they tell they might be blamed and seen as a bad or stupid girl."

Social consequences are as lethal to teens as parental ones. "Can you imagine going back to high school? Imagine being exiled and sitting alone in the lunchroom and people are calling you all sorts of names," Machoian says. "Would you tell? There is no way you would tell."

Joey Dobbs did not threaten his victims in exchange for their silence, according to Detective Charles. But that kind of intimidation is one of the weapons most commonly used by abusers to exert and maintain control over their victims, says Machoian. "A lot of times kids I work with who have been sexually abused are told, 'If you tell, I'll kill you, kill your family.' Usually they will say they will kill someone important to the child."

Before parents can fully understand what is happening on the social networking sites like MySpace, they need to appreciate the seismic shift that has taken place in sexual attitudes among young teens. Sex is just sex. Oral sex is now common in middle school.

By comparison to the casual sex all around them, social networking sites like MySpace offer teenage girls something that is seemingly more meaningful. "What can be appealing to girls about the Internet is that there is a relationship in their mind going on," says Machoian. "They are communicating with someone and it feels like a relationship. Relationships are so important to adolescent girls and so central in their development. It's another huge hook that these predators have. It's not just hooking up, it's very relational."

Parry Aftab has made it her mission not only to protect kids but to understand who the kids are that get into dangerous situations online. After years of listening and working with kids, she feels there are three distinct profiles among girls who are vulnerable online.

The most vulnerable are generally between eleven and fifteen. In the early years of Internet safety awareness, says Aftab, this was the profile that was stressed to parents of young teens who were loners. "Parents whose kids who weren't loners said, 'Oh, good, we don't have to worry.'" What was missed in this assumption were the kids who *don't* fit that profile and *don't* tell.

The tragic case of a Connecticut teen, Christina Long, drove Aftab to reexamine what she thought she had already figured out.

Christina Long was not a loner. She was pretty and popular and, according to Aftab, she was also "the co-captain of the cheerleading squad, she's a member of the National Honor Society and the first one killed, the first confirmed death by an Internet sexual predator."

Long was a sixth grader at a Catholic school. She was being raised by her aunt because her own parents were too troubled. Chrissy was extremely close to her aunt, Shelley Rilling, who I interviewed in our first investigation. Aftab said that Rilling talked to her frequently about online risks. Aftab said that Rilling kept close tabs on Christina's Web site, urged her to use a less provocative screen name, and when asked to change something, Chrissy willingly complied. Yet despite the devotion of her aunt and her efforts to do everything right, her sixth-grade niece was found murdered and abandoned in a ravine on May 20, 2002, by a man she had met online for sex.

"She had an alter ego," says Aftab. She had a profile that she'd share with her aunt and another profile that she didn't. "So the alter ego was looking for relationships with men—her profile said 'I'm up for anything.'"

Initially, Aftab was sure that Long's aunt was to blame and had been asleep at the helm. But Aftab, author of *The Parent's Guide to Protecting Your Children in Cyberspace*, had a rude awakening when she sat down with Rilling. She was completely Internet savvy. "I found out the aunt could have written my book for me." What the aunt didn't suspect was that her niece had a secret online life in which she was seeking danger and thrills.

Aftab sought out a forensic psychologist to try to understand what happened to Christina Long. He told Aftab that when loners—the shy, quiet teens—run into trouble, they tend to be the ones who tell. But Christina Long symbolizes a different profile type—a kid who was out looking for danger and thrills. Unlike the loners, these kids don't tell. Like the victims of Joey Dobbs, they remain silent. "They feel stupid, they feel responsible for it, all these other things that compound the normal, 'I don't want to talk about the bad things that happen to me.'" Unless a kid is kidnapped or killed, says Aftab, these secret lives can stay submerged.

MySpace and its kin have created a third profile. Aftab describes it as "not a slut, just playing one on MySpace." These are kids who act outrageously on social networking sites to get noticed. "If you are one of a hundred million profiles, it's hard to get someone to pay attention to you so you have to do something outrageous," Aftab says. "You engage in cybersex, or you pose in sexually graphic or suggestive ways." That behavior can spiral into something that's out of control and attract the attention of the wrong kind of people. "Most of the Internet sex predators are looking to date young," Aftab says. "They are looking for young kids who don't have sexually transmitted diseases, who are naïve enough to think they have something special."

While many girls are reluctant to tell what has happened to them when they run into trouble online, boys, says Aftab, never tell. "If a boy is sexually molested or exploited, they don't tell because 99.999 percent of the time the molester is a man. When it's a woman, they don't get any sympathy. We've had several cases where boys were molested by women online and everyone makes jokes. 'Boy, what a lucky kid.'"

The pack mentality of adolescents quickly normalizes behavior—everyone is doing it so that makes it okay. The explosive power of My-Space and the other social networking sites makes change that might have happened gradually in the previous generations erupt exponentially.

It's easy to imagine the empowerment that a teenager feels in an arena where thousands of peers are acting out. "If they see other kids posing in their bras or engaging in conversations with adults they think it is okay. It must be safe so there is the whole community phenomenon that is influencing actual behavior."

This becomes a volatile mix when it dovetails with the invincibility that is common to adolescence—"I'm too smart to get caught."

Aftab runs into that all the time now in the work she does. "My biggest problem these days when I talk to kids is getting the ones considered the 'smart ones' to pay attention because they are the ones at greatest risk. They are the ones who are voluntarily doing idiotic things."

But she says she's figured out a strategy that seems to work—appeal to the smart ones to help educate younger peers and siblings. When she starts working with them on the premise that they know all this stuff, they are easy to engage and willing to teach what they know to younger kids they care about. "I say I know you know all about these things, but how can we make it safe for kids who don't know as much as you do, and then they get involved. Once they get involved, then I got them hooked. Once I got them hooked it's like, 'I didn't realize I was doing this.'"

What Aftab and other advocates seem to be in near unanimous agreement on is that there is a danger to kids from parents who feel the solution is to deny their children Internet access. That can only back-fire. "I can protect kids from everything bad that goes on online, but I can't protect them from parents overreacting and shutting off the Internet," says Aftab. "In nearly every single case, the kids have gone willingly to a meeting with a sexual predator. They might have thought he was cute and fourteen but they have gone willingly. That means this is a hundred percent preventable."

MySpace's Nigam also believes that the best technology is still not going to protect a kid as much as education and good judgment will: "A hand doesn't reach through your computer screen and grab you and take you away. An individual has to leave that front door, has to walk out and get into a car or get a ride and go somewhere."

The social networking site Xanga implemented a new security system last spring. Stephen Kline, Xanga's chief security officer, says, "We have a wonderful rating and flagging system that allows us to use the wisdom of twenty-nine million sets of eyes to help us identify what's going on on Xanga. Users are required to rate the content of their site in a system that's similar to the way movies are rated. A, B, C are sites anyone can access. D is similar to an R rating and EX means that a profile has explicit content. To access that, an individual must be able to verify their age. The flagging system encourages participants to report objectionable or illegal material to Xanga." Says Kline, "There are things that computer filters may not be perfect at picking up but humans know them when they seem them. We give our users opportunity to help us with that. It's successful and getting better. It's a distinguishing feature on Xanga."

Social networking sites are a reality of teenagers' lives. Parents have to accept that. Kids can access computers in so many other places—their friends' homes, libraries, and schools—that it's pointless for parents not to accept this. Parents also need to understand that kids are wired and wireless. Kids can communicate on social networking sites through a Game Boy, Xbox Live, or a cell phone, which is why all bets are off. The barn door isn't just open, it's been torn off. "What we need to do is make sure kids have a filter between their ears so they know what to do," says Aftab.

Her teen advocates wholeheartedly agree that parents have to be careful not to overreact to Internet issues with their kids. "It doesn't have to be you against your child to protect them," says Brittany Bacon, the teen advocate and now law school student who has been part of many presentations for parents. "All the parents—as soon as we'd start the presentation would be like, 'So what is my child *really* doing online, my child can't go online unless I'm standing there right by their shoulder seeing every word they type and I go in and check my child's e-mails and her instant messaging conversations, she has no idea—' We'd be like 'whoa, whoa, whoa . . . let's slow this down.'"

"Parents may not realize that their kids are on so many social networking sites," says Vivian. "Usually kids are on more than one at the same time. If parents do find out about a kid having a social networking site behind their back, they should not overreact about it. It's good to limit your kids, but you shouldn't take it away from them. Parents need to understand how to react to their kids online."

While the danger of the misuse of social networking sites is evident, it's important to stress that the benefits in them for kids can be significant. Dr. David Finkelhor runs the Crimes against Children Research Center at the University of New Hampshire and has been engaged in teaching, researching, and understanding the myriad issues that impact the safety of children for nearly thirty years. He points out that social networking sites can be valuable for gay or pre-homosexual boys who are socially isolated and turn to the Internet to try to make sense of the complicated feelings inside themselves.

While he feels the Internet is a useful way to process and test feelings that might be too scary to articulate in other ways, Finkelhor points out that the vulnerability of these kids puts them in jeopardy.

"There are guys out there who give them lots of help and the punch line is, 'Let me show you how it's done.' One of the reasons why these kids are vulnerable is that they are not getting help from other sources."

It's a point well taken; part of what will make kids turn to the Internet is to compensate for what they feel they can't find anywhere else in their lives: a safe place to express who they are and find validation.

For her book *The Disappearing Girl*, Dr. Lisa Machoian interviewed hundreds of adolescent girls. "Over and over I asked girls, what can adults do and what can schools do to help? It was stunning. Over and over the answer came back, 'Listen.' They just want to be heard."

"Girls equate listening with caring," continues Machoian. "These predators are listening to them. If a guy is listening it means he cares and these guys are listening. If there is anything that stands out for adolescent girls, it's listening, listening, listening. These guys are listening and that's a huge hook for them."

Are parents listening? How often do adults really listen to their children? Listen in a way that is nonjudgmental and nondistracted? Not making eye contact, thumbing a BlackBerry, making a meal, or paying bills falls short in the eyes of many kids as really listening. "'If I don't think someone is paying attention, I'll just stop talking,'" Machoian remembers a young girl telling her. "As a larger culture, do we listen to teenage girls? I don't think we do a very good job of that and they have found people willing to listen online." But these people are often not who they pretend to be and are not genuinely sincere.

It's important to point out here, too, that social networking sites are still such a relatively new phenomenon, the data is just not available to substantiate the dangers that have been brought into sharp focus by anecdotal information and chilling cases like the young women who have been preyed upon by Joey Dobbs.

Finkelhor is appalled by the failure of the government to gather adequate statistics. "Look at it this way," he says. "Think how different this would be if it were a disease. Look at that recent E. coli outbreak. They knew there were one hundred thirty-three people in the country who have had an E. coli infection. You would think someone would know exactly how many people in the country have been arrested for a sex crime against a child involving a computer or the Internet. It's something in the same order of magnitude in the anxiety it creates."

Finkelhor points out, and rightly so, that there has been a substantial drop in crimes of sexual assault against children: "The National Crime Victims' Survey, which is one of the main measures of sexual assaults, shows about a seventy-five percent decline in sexual assaults in youth between 1993 and 2004. The National Child Abuse and Neglect Data System, a collection of state figures on child sexual abuse cases, shows a fifty percent decline between 1994 and 2003." While that data is heartening overall, it doesn't reflect what might be happening on social networking sites, since they are too recent a phenomenon to be included in that data.

Lack of good data drives Aftab up the wall. "I need statistics. I need hard research; it doesn't exist. It is still anecdotal. Here Congress can be really helpful right now: crime reporting forms that every police officer in this country fills out when there's a crime don't have a box to check off if the crime is Internet related. So if a child is kidnapped, killed, or if something bad happens to them, there is no box to check so someone can start tracking these things."

Finkelhor strikes a cautionary tone—pointing out that in at least 80 percent of the reported sexual abuse crimes against kids, the abuser is either a family member or someone known to the child. In the absence of hard data about social networking sites, no one knows in fact how vulnerable children are on the Internet. "I'm not saying that we shouldn't be worried, but we need a bigger perspective on it," he says, adding that until there's data, "I think the jury is still out on this. I'm not convinced yet that the Internet or MySpace and all the changes we are seeing are resulting in an increased risk for kids. Certainly some kids are going to get hurt. There are new dynamics in some of these cases. But we are monitoring the sexual assault data and it's all looking good. Sex crimes are down and very dramatically over the last ten or twelve years now."

The satisfaction in doing sex crime work for officers like Lieutenant Jake Jacoby and Detective Peter Charles is in putting people behind bars before they can hurt others. "You are basically saving all these other victims. These people are not going to stop. It's not their first time, it's not their last time," says Jacoby.

Joey Dobbs pleaded guilty and was sentenced to serve eight years in prison.

Jacoby and Charles—like thousands of other law enforcement officers around the country—keep up their valiant efforts while knowing that when it comes to catching online predators, the odds are stacked against them.

"For all the people we catch and for all the people *Dateline* catches, your chance of having a cop on the other end of the computer are still infinitesimal," says Jacoby. "It's like a reverse lottery. The chances of you winning are a hundred trillion to one while it's a hundred trillion to one that you are going to get caught."

But they aren't the only ones hunting. As momentum builds on this issue, more and more people are joining in the pursuit against online predators. Thousands of dedicated FBI agents and police and other law enforcement officers spend millions of hours annually tracking down men and women who are online with malicious intent. Most of us will never know their names or see their faces but we can learn about what keeps them going from guys like Jacoby and Charles. For them, every arrest, despite the odds, is a victory and a measure of adrenaline to keep up the pursuit.

"Even if you only put people in jail for three or four years that's three or four years that people are going to be safe," says Jacoby. "For all the hassles, the long hours, the frustration in putting together a court case, when all is said and done we're protecting the innocence of children. You want children to grow up and not be scarred or victimized by these people."

Chapter 7

Ohio and Florida Investigations

The ride from the Cincinnati airport seemed to take forever, even in the sleek rental SUV. Greenville, Ohio, is a town of about thirteen thousand folks about forty minutes from Dayton. There is one sports bar, no Starbucks, and one of those little downtown areas that struggles to compete with the big box stores a half hour away.

It's a small town. But for its size, it has one awfully sophisticated law enforcement agency in the form of the Darke County Sheriff's Department. Detective Mike Burns contacted Perverted Justice to conduct a sting operation in the spring of 2006. The house we ended up using was across the road from a farm field and belonged to a bachelor builder. It had a seven-car garage and a finished basement where seventeen potential predators would show up over the next three days to meet a young boy or girl home alone.

On the Ohio investigation, for the first time we agreed to pay Perverted Justice for its work during our investigation. After all, I was getting paid, my producer and crew were getting paid, and PJ wasn't going to work for free forever. It mounts a large operation and we needed its contributors to continue our investigations. This did, however, spark some controversy. After extensive discussions we decided to pay a consulting fee. We knew we would be criticized by some, and indeed we were. The sheriff's department also wanted to deputize Del and Frag. Because of a quirk in local law, authorities said deputizing them would allow prosecutors to charge our visitors with a more serious crime. It's something we weren't crazy about doing and it opened us up to criticism in journalism circles that we were too cozy with law enforcement. At the end of the day, it's something we felt we could live with for the limited purposes of Ohio.

In Ohio we tried something different. Besides Del and Frag and the rest of the PJ contributors, we hired a very young-looking actress who was nineteen to play the part of a teen girl on the Internet. We also used a Web cam for the first time so that potential predators could actually see a face and have an interactive relationship with our decoy. The bait was alluring, but even so, it took a long time for anyone to arrive, and that part of the investigation was draining.

Mitchell Wagenberg and his team had once again wired our house with hidden cameras and microphones. With each investigation these guys outdo themselves. There are always a few extra cameras, some incredibly slick remote control device to operate the cameras, and as always, the product is so good, it is hard to imagine that studio cameras weren't used.

Each one of these investigations takes on its own rhythm. Ohio was no different.

I was concerned as I drove into town that maybe we had picked a place that was too rural. Maybe guys wouldn't travel to such an isolated spot. Maybe this sort of crime just didn't take place in small-town America.

The night before the shoot began my producer, Lynn, my associate producer, D.J., and our specialist, Ron, had dinner at a little saloon across the street from our hotel. These dinners are often the last chance we have to relax and have a glass of wine before the stressful and often sleepless three- to four-day shoot that is about to begin.

We work through the details, talk about the challenges of each location, like things as mundane as the fact that in this house there was only one usable bathroom for nearly twenty people. We also go through the list of potential predators already chatting with PJ decoys. On this night we have the easy job. Del, Frag, and the rest of the PJ contributors work the chat rooms late into the evening. The Wagenberg team will be up late as well making sure the house will be wired for the next day. Eleven hidden cameras were used in this investigation. Neither group has ever let us down.

At dinner there was some concern that some local folks had gotten wind of our investigation. Greenville's a small town and word can travel fast. A former law enforcement officer had seen activity around our house, lots of crates being moved in, and guys he knew were current sheriff's deputies. I don't think he got on the Internet and started warning predators, but I do think that people like to talk and word eventually got out.

That could explain the stop-and-go flow of men into our door. But the first day was busy. Just after noon our first visitor arrived. His screen name was greeneyed121, a twenty-three-year-old who was a student at an evangelical university about an hour away. Earlier he was chatting online with a decoy posing as a thirteen-year-old girl calling herself katiedidsing. He was graphic from the start: "My hands will travel down your smooth body, till we reach your pants. Here we will remove your pants and underwear, revealing your beautiful nude body."

greeneyed121 found katiedidsing on the social networking site My-Space. He told her: "I have an idea but it's a little weird. I did it with another girl, but I don't know if you want to. Call me and let me listen to you as you finger yourself to orgasm."

The PJ decoy declined that offer, but it didn't seem to discourage greeneyed121. He later typed: "I have good news; I can come over Friday and stay the night, too!!!" He did come over, but he would spend the night in jail, not in a thirteen-year-old girl's bed.

He walked in through the back door cautiously. Del, posing as the girl, called him in from around the corner, told him she'd be right down. Seconds later I confronted him. He was compliant, almost mild-mannered. He told me: "I didn't know if I would really be able to go through with it." When I read back to him some of his online chat, he claimed he was talking about "fantasies dreamed up online or in your mind, things you might not be willing to do when it comes down to it."

When I informed him that it is illegal to solicit a minor for sex online in Ohio, he replied, "That, I was unaware of." But he was about to get a lesson in the law from the Darke County Sheriff's Department.

During his interrogation, greeneyed121 said that he had never had sex before. Apparently the thirteen-year-old girl was to be his first. Detectives found a box of condoms in his car.

greeneyed121 was the first of nine men who would show up on March 24, 2006. There was a paramedic with a foot fetish, a forty-three-year-old oil executive who came to meet a fourteen-year-old boy for sex, and for the first time in any of our investigations we saw a religious theme. Not only was greeneyed121 an evangelical college student, another young man screen named goodbody1330 actually told me he had discussed his planned liaison with a thirteen-year-old girl with his pastor, although he admitted that he didn't share the girl's real age. For the record, the pastor counseled against the visit: advice goodbody1330 should have taken since, like the other men who showed up, he was arrested and taken to jail.

The next day we experienced one of the longest droughts in "To Catch a Predator" history. For the first nine hours of the day no one showed up. We paced; Lynn and I discussed the possibility that word had gotten out around town about our investigation, or maybe potential predators were getting wise to our program.

PJ decoys had chatted with at least a dozen men who lived nearby, who had made dates to come over for sex, but never showed. And that's why, as I mentioned earlier, we thought the former law enforcement officer who saw what was going on at the house may have inadvertently spread the word we were operating in town. Our first visitor on that Saturday did not come knocking until 8:20 P.M.

He was another man who told us he was church-going and God-fearing. By day he was a mechanical engineer, but at night he turned into netbuckeye, a thirty-three-year-old who in this case was chatting with a decoy posing as a fourteen-year-old girl screen named CHICKY-GRRRL. He was careful not to be too explicit in his online chat, but he did say that he "wouldn't do anything without a condom." netbuckeye did exactly what I asked him to do and had a seat at the bar.

I continue to be surprised when someone like this guy, who is educated, good-looking, and articulate, meets an underage teen online and then comes over for a visit. I asked him if there was a church group or a bar he could go to in order to meet people. That's when he told me that in fact he does go to church every Sunday. I asked him if this church taught him that it was okay to visit fourteen-year-old girls who are home alone. He said: "They would not recommend that, no."

Then he came up with something we had never seen before. He asked if he could show us a note that he had written that was in his car. Del ran out to get it and netbuckeye read it to us. It read: "At 8 P.M. tonight I'm meeting a person who I met online." He went on to write: "If she really is who she says she is my intention is to befriend her and to mentor her."

Detective Burns wasn't buying any of it, saying that around the sheriff's department, the note was referred to as the "alibi letter." "When you look at a vehicle that pulls up in front and stops, drives by, comes back, does the same thing again, if it's his intent that he's going to go in and counsel this girl, why would you struggle with that issue? I think we saw the battle from within as to whether or not he was going to get caught," Burns later told me. netbuckeye told me he was "just a lonely guy," not a predator, but by the end of the night he was under arrest.

Three more men showed up before the night was over. There was meatrocket8, a thirty-year-old university computer specialist who had a wife and kids. His mother was a prosecutor in a nearby county and his dad was a cop. He chatted online with a girl he thought was a fifteen-year-old virgin. "Would you like me to cum in you?" he asked the girl in an online chat room. "I don't want to get preggers," she responded. He assures her: "I'll keep it wrapped." Then, referring to the fact that she's a virgin, he wrote: "Actually I find it quite attractive . . . I'm honored to be considered the candidate for your first."

After that conversation meatrocket8 got in his car and drove two hours in the middle of the night, across dark country roads, for his rendezvous. As he walked in he called himself a "dumb ass" for having such a hard time finding the place. When I approached meatrocket8 in our undercover house he immediately introduced himself and shook my hand. He had no clue what he had just walked into.

He admitted that he brought condoms, but claimed he was "no pedophile" and that he "just wanted to talk" and "kick back." I asked him how the condoms fit into his conversation plans. Sometimes in these confrontations I'll push it a bit to see how the guy will react; otherwise the interview will turn into a stalemate. I asked if he was going to perform "balloon tricks" with the condoms. At this point he was sweating profusely. He stammered before admitting that the only reason someone carries condoms is usually for sex. After I told him who I was, the cameramen came out and he bolted and was arrested.

The last man in the door arrived at two thirty in the morning. As he walked in, Del, pretending to be a fifteen-year-old girl, said she had to change clothes. The man got a laugh out of this. He was a forty-two-year-old training manager for a global transportation company. He had driven two hours for his date.

Online he asked the decoy sadiethesmarty if his sex talk had gotten her aroused. The decoy responded: "Talk doesn't do anything for me." The man, whose screen name was parknride_469, responded: "Well, my tongue will." He stayed pretty cool as I walked out from around the corner. He said he thought the girl was older. But then I read to him some of his online chat in which he said to the girl: "You're only fifteen, a little young for this aren't ya?" and "but baby fifteen can get me twenty," referring to the prison term he could get for having sex with a fifteen-year-old.

Aside from the fact that parknride_469 seemed more than willing to commit statutory rape, he didn't seem like a violent guy, that is, until our story aired and an ex-wife posted a note about him on a Perverted Justice message board. She said he had been an abusive husband and had been arrested in connection with that abuse. Seeing her ex-husband on our show, she wrote, made for the "nicest night we have ever had since we left."

We often learn a lot about the men who show up at our houses in the weeks after they're arrested. That was the case with a twenty-six-year-old sixth-grade teacher and track coach who showed up at our Ohio house around noon on Sunday. In chat rooms he went by the name iurutherford, and when he was talking to princessdanika, who said she was thirteen, it was only about three minutes into the chat before he told her what he did for a living.

They talked about routine things like pets and music. He said he was married, but the relationship was rocky and headed toward divorce. He turned on his Web cam to show the girl his face. She said he was cute. Then our decoy turned on her Web cam. She was really the young-looking nineteen-year-old actress we'd hired for the investigation. iurutherford typed: "Your cute too . . . definitely have a pretty face . . . for . . . jailbait . . . lol."

The teacher then took off his shirt and said: "I could be your teacher. Would you flirt with me?" She typed back: "Wink at you and stuff? ud like that?" iurutherford said: "I'd be flattered . . . not like that's a bad thing . . . innocent enough." But over a three-day period the chat turned into anything but innocent.

iurutherford asked princessdanika to show him her tummy. She did and he said: "Nice tummy hun. I want to lick that." Then he said: "I owe you something now, don't I." He then pulled the back of his boxers down just a bit. He continued: "I knew you were cute but damn . . . and I'm not there naked with you now. Why?" He seemed to seal his intentions when he declared: "I'm so freaking horny . . . You know if you had me naked I'd want more, right? Hope you like me this much in person . . . long drive for rejection," he typed before saying that he's going to try really hard to come over.

The teacher said he would call our decoy before making the two-hour drive from his home in Cincinnati. In fact he said he'd call even if he decided not to come. We never got the call and all of us in the house kind of figured he was going to be a no-show. This happens a lot. There is a long lull in the action. People relax. Some even close their eyes for a minute or two. Then all of a sudden a shiny red Corvette came rumbling down our drive and parked just five feet from our back door.

We scrambled into position. This time our actress, Emily, was the decoy. "The door is open," she said. "Where are you?" iurutherford asked. The teacher was both anxious and excited at the same time. He was youngish-looking for twenty-six. He had short brown hair and was in good shape. "Come here," he said. Emily said, "No, I promise I'll be right back," as she bolted upstairs. Again he demanded that the thirteen-year-old "come here."

It's always a bit of a wager as to exactly when I decide to show myself in these investigations. If I walk out too soon, the man might get spooked and run before he's committed. If I wait too long, he may hear the crew or start to get suspicious. I stepped out from the stairwell. "Actually I want you to come here," I said.

"That's what I thought," was his response.

iurutherford had a feeling this was a setup, but the chat log left no wiggle room as to intent. Because I've already read the chat log and in some cases have been able to do a background check on our visitors, I often know more about them than they first suspect. I asked iurutherford what he did for a living. "I'd rather not say. Who do you work for?" he asked. When I told him that I would get to that in a minute, he told me: "No, I'd really like to know, I'm sure I'm on TV or something right now."

Finally he admitted that he was a teacher and then he revealed something else about his Internet habits: "I thought about this a lot, for years, maybe getting counseling, maybe I should get help, and I said, well, it's not that big of a deal, I've never taken it to this step. I don't know if this week pushed me over the edge." iurutherford was referring to his wife telling him she was filing for divorce.

I asked him if he had ever watched *Dateline* and he figured out pretty quickly what he had walked into. "Oh damn, I've seen one of those . . . that's one of the reasons I thought, why am I doing this?" he said.

"You've actually seen one of our previous programs on computer predators?" I asked.

"I didn't think I was a predator. I wasn't coming here for anything physical," he said. That's a common excuse. The teacher stayed and talked to me for forty minutes. He denied ever crossing the line with any of his students, but conceded his online behavior had grown out of control. When he got up to leave he told me: "I'm sorry and tell the kid I'm sorry."

After his arrest, the teacher told investigators that he masturbated while talking to young teens online, but there has been no evidence that he actually met any of the girls with whom he chatted. From his jail cell, iurutherford called the private Catholic school where he taught and coached to resign.

About a week after our *Dateline* story aired we got a call from a detective in Carmel, Indiana. The detective had been posing online as a teenager and told us she was able to confirm that iurutherford had been soliciting her for sex as well. He has since been charged in that case in addition to the one in Ohio.

Perhaps the most frightening man to walk into the predator home on the prairie was changeforthebetter2006. When he was chatting with our decoy posing as a thirteen-year-old girl, he said he was twenty-seven and looking for a hook-up. "Feeling frisky?" he asked. He asked the girl, DESTINY, if they could have sex and if he could "spend the night." He said he couldn't come over Saturday night because he had church at nine thirty Sunday morning, but he could make it Sunday night.

changeforthebetter2006 is suspicious, though, asking at one point: "I just need to know you are being straight up with me . . . and not a cop. Nothing personal, but I watch what I do." It turned out the man had good reason to be suspicious. He'd been down this path before. He even admits it online: "I did something stupid less than a year ago. I went to court Friday about it. My attorney and I plea-bargained. This next Thursday I go to jail for it for eleven months. I got busted soliciting."

Everyone inside the house was amazed at the admission and how willing this guy was to come over at eleven o'clock on a Sunday night, four days before he was due to be locked up for doing the very same thing. Yet there he was walking up our driveway. He was short, not even five feet tall. After he came in, he made it clear what he was after. Del, posing as the girl, told him she'd be right down after she finished getting changed. He shouted back: "I'll watch you." He was in for a different show. When I first confronted him he declined my offer to have a seat on the barstool. This created a problem because of his height. Unless he hopped onto the stool he'd have been hidden from camera view behind the bar. Finally after several requests he climbed up to take a seat.

He told me that all the sexually explicit talk online had all been "just B.S. talk." He insisted that he had no plans for sex. After all, he said he didn't even bring condoms. But our cameras caught something curious in his car. When I asked him about the black bag, he said it was his briefcase, which contained his Bible. "You're a religious fellow, are you?" I asked.

"Yes I am," he told me. "I thought, well, I'll just go over there and say hi and be done with it and go home," he insisted.

When I confronted him with the fact that he was due to report to prison in four days for doing what he had done tonight, he offered this excuse: "I'm stupid, I'm weak, it's just that I had no intention of having sex with her." It turned out that changeforthebetter2006 certainly wasn't doing what his screen name suggested and he wasn't twenty-seven as he had said in his chat. He was forty-seven and a budget analyst for the military, a job he wouldn't have much longer.

Unbelievably, there was even more to his criminal past—not just solicitation for sex. He was accused of raping a young female relative. Sergeant David Adkins of the New Lebanon, Ohio, police department described the attack: "It was late at night; there was a thunderstorm. She was scared of the storm so she went to his room because she wanted the comfort of an adult because of the storm. And ultimately he pretty much violated that trust and confidence that he had."

Adkins had been after changeforthebetter2006 for two years. He had admitted to the sexual assault in a counseling session but Adkins had to battle to access the records, all the while suspecting that changeforthebetter2006 could be seeking sex with other children: "I would say chances are slim that he's only done this two times. Obviously there's something he can't control there. I mean he knew for a fact that I was after him for a year and a half."

Four days after his arrest changeforthebetter2006 went before a judge in the prior solicitation case. The judge ordered that he become a registered sex offender and sentenced him to eleven months in prison. He later pleaded guilty to raping the young female relative. Like all of the other men arrested in our Ohio investigation, he was charged with attempted unlawful sexual contact with a minor.

If the flow of visitors in Ohio had been sporadic, it was steady in our next location, Fort Myers, Florida. I'd just finished a week's vacation with my family on Sanibel Island, about an hour away. I was rested and relaxed. That would change literally overnight. All of these shoots go late; that's just part of the deal. But Fort Myers was by far the latest, with one man showing up at four in the morning.

The house in Fort Myers was in one of the nicest neighborhoods in town. It was a classic Florida-style stucco home with a guesthouse on the property where the Fort Myers police set up their parallel investigation. Within minutes of arriving at the site, Lynn, the producer, and I were taken by police chief Hilton Daniels to the home of the city's mayor. We chatted with him and his wife for about twenty minutes, then it was back to our house to read transcripts and prepare for the visitors who might be already on their way over.

This time the Wagenberg team rigged thirteen hidden cameras inside and outside our house. There was even a camera hidden in a palm tree that could pan 360 degrees and could zoom in tight enough to read a license plate on a car down the block. The PJ folks were set up in an upstairs bedroom, the Wagenberg group in a first-floor study, and Ron, Emily, and I were in a sunroom adjacent to the living room, where I would confront the men.

Emily had really gained confidence since the Ohio shoot. Del had spent a lot of time working with her, and Frag was talking her through each encounter via two-way radio and earpiece. If a potential predator came over to meet a boy, Del would still play the part, hair pulled back, wearing a ball cap.

The Ohio and Florida stings would play as a four-hour series in May 2006. Even in the fast-paced world of television, that was a very quick turnaround. That meant we were basically editing the two Ohio hours as we were shooting in Florida.

We were a little anxious in Florida because the laws governing carrying a concealed weapon are looser than in many other states. It was our good fortune, though, to have warm weather on this third weekend in April. That meant our visitors wouldn't be wearing jackets and it would be easier to see if they had weapons on them as they approached our back door. And approach they did. Before it was over, twenty-four men came to our house to meet a young teen home alone. The first arrived just after two thirty in the afternoon.

thomascoffen was a thirty-one-year-old handyman who was very direct online when he thought he was talking to a fourteen-year-old girl. "I am into young girls," he wrote. "I like them better than the older girls." When the decoy asked if he had done this before, he admitted that he had with another girl who was fourteen. The handyman told the girl online several times that he loved her and even sent her a naked picture of himself.

When I came out to confront him, however, he said he came here looking for work. "I do blacktop sealing," he told me. About twenty seconds into our conversation he admitted that was a lie, but then he came up with another excuse. "My computer messed up," he said.

I asked: "Your computer, so it just, what, magically typed itself like a player piano?"

"No . . . it's messed up, I'm saying I have a virus in it and stuff."

"What's messed up," I told him, "is this conversation." He claimed he was just there to talk, but the condom in his shirt pocket told a different story. We had to wrap up the handyman interview pretty quickly because our next guest was due any minute.

Eleven men came that first day. One brought rope after talking online about tying up a fourteen-year-old girl during sex. One guy showed up who was deaf. I obviously couldn't communicate with him. Frag had to call the police on the radio to make sure they knew the man wouldn't hear their commands to get on the ground and be arrested. There was a twenty-two-year-old who came over for sex with a fourteen-year-old girl. He brought a rose and some Bacardi Apple liquor. When I told him what he'd walked into, he was more concerned about his father-in-law's ten brothers finding out what he'd done than he was worried about going to jail.

The shoot that first day went on until 4:04 in the morning and ended with one of the most intense scenes I had witnessed up until that point. During these investigations it's not unusual to see men being hesitant to walk inside the house. We had never seen anything like

moff_1960, a forty-four-year-old maintenance engineer at a Florida re-
sort. Online he told the decoy posing as a fifteen-year-old girl that his
wife had caught him chatting online with a teen a week earlier and
threatened to divorce him.

He asked the PJ decoy if he was freaking her out because of his age.
He then asked: "So would you ever fool around with an old guy like
me?" Later, he made his intensions very clear: "OK, how about after I
come in I'll strip."

"LOL for real," the decoy wrote. moff_1960: "Sure, if you want me
to." But when he finally arrived at our hidden camera house, the forty-
four-year-old wouldn't come in. He tried to get Emily to come to his
car instead.

Emily said: "I thought you were going to do something for me in
the laundry room (the strip tease act)." moff_1960 shook his head no.
Emily asked: "Are you going to back out on me? Cuz that's what I feel
like you're gonna do now." moff_1960 replied: "I am just being cautious." It's clear that he sensed something different about Emily. In fact,
there is something different. Emily is not the girl he talked to on the Internet or on the phone. That was a decoy from PJ.

This happens to us from time to time. PJ has contributors from all
over the country working in the chat rooms. They use different decoy
photos and so every once in a while one of those photos will be very different from Emily or any of the actors we've used since. We just have to
wing it.

moff_1960 said: "You haven't acted this way when we talked before." Emily tried to calm his concerns: "Oh really? Well, talking in person's a little different than talking online." moff_1960: "You don't
sound like the same in person as you did on the phone . . . your picture
looks different, too." The odd conversation went on for more than half
an hour. At one point moff_1960 asked Emily to go get a library card
to prove she was who she said she was. Finally Emily said: "This is
ridiculous, I'm going to bed." moff_1960 left the back doorstep headed

for his car. He never made it. He was intercepted by the Fort Myers police take-down team.

I was exhausted. The crew was bleary-eyed. It was 4:40 by the time I got back to the hotel, and I hadn't even checked in yet. I got about four hours of sleep, got up, went for a run, and headed back to the house. Thank God for Starbucks. I often joke with Lynn that it is vital that all of our predator houses be within ten minutes of a Starbucks.

Saturday was busy and ran late. Ten more potential predators paid us a visit. Ten more are confronted by me and arrested by the police. There was a wireless technician who was in Florida working. He lived in Arkansas. He was chatting from his hotel room. A forty-five-year-old drove his Harley over so he could take a fourteen-year-old girl for a ride before sex. A twenty-three-year-old who owned a dog grooming shop came over at around eleven that night after a sexually explicit conversation with a decoy posing as a fourteen-year-old boy. He had seen some of our previous predator stories. He even complimented me on my work and he was prepared for the police to arrest him when he walked out the back door.

Our last fellow of the evening was perhaps the most memorable. crazytrini85 was a man who knew what he wanted and wasn't shy about asking for it when he was chatting online with someone who he thought was a fourteen-year-old girl. He asked the girl if she'll try anal sex. He said it's better than regular sex. When the girl, named Cindy, tells him she has a hot tub at her house, he says: "Ima fuck you in there lol . . . and on your mom's bed." Cindy asked: "Why not my bed?" crazytrini85 said: "That too . . . ima fuck ya in every room so no matter where u go u will remember me."

This was our fifth investigation in five states and by this time I had pretty much figured I had seen and heard it all. Not even close. crazytrini85 asked Cindy if she had any pets. After she told him she has a cat he writes, "U kno what would b a huge ass turn on for me? Watchin you fuk him lol." Cindy says: "I don't think I wanna fuk the cat." crazytrini85 is persistent: "Would you for me? Ppl do that shit all the time. How about suck his lil kitty dick?"

Later on the phone he asked the girl to get some Cool Whip for the kitty sex party. The decoy said she would think about it if crazytrini85 would do something for her: strip naked once he walks into the house. Although we did have a man walk into our house naked in Virginia, we didn't think we'd see a repeat performance. But crazytrini85 didn't disappoint. Seconds after he walked in the door he stripped and was on the hunt for Emily. She had ducked into the sunroom where I was standing. I could see him coming toward the door moving so quickly that by the time I got my hand on the door to open it and go confront him, he was literally right there.

Fortunately, we had a blanket nearby so that he could cover himself up for the interview. "What are you doing?" I asked.

"Making a mistake," he told me. He claimed he was just messing around with the girl online, then he started laughing. He asked for some water, which I got for him from the kitchen.

I said: "All that running around naked must have gotten you pretty dried out there, huh?"

"Yeah," he said.

I said: "So what's going to be happening if I'm not here? You're naked. There's a fourteen-year-old girl. You're chasing a cat around. You've got Cool Whip and you want this girl to do some sex act with the cat and then you'll have sex with her. Is that accurate?"

"Yes," said a now sheepish crazytrini85. He admitted to me that had there really been a girl in the house he would have had sex with her and that he was making a "big mistake." I told crazytrini85 he could keep the blanket; he went back to the laundry room, got dressed, and was promptly arrested as he left the house.

It was three fifteen A.M. when I got back to the hotel and another short night when it came to sleep. So it was just fine by me that on Sunday we only had three men scheduled to arrive. We had proved our point in Fort Myers. So, as far as these shoots go, this was the calmest day of the three. It was about four o'clock when something happened that would have a profound impact on every person in the house.

In PJ parlance, FOTOFIX was a "fast mover." At 2:24 in the afternoon he started chatting online with a decoy posing as a fourteen-year-old boy. At 3:57 P.M. he was parking in front of our home. We all watched from the remote camera in the palm tree, what became known as the "coconut cam." After he parked his shiny new SUV, he climbed out and walked around to the passenger side rear door. I thought maybe he was grabbing some food, perhaps beer. Instead, he unbuckled the child safety seat of his five-year-old son and led him by the hand out of the vehicle and up our driveway.

I'll never forget Frag yelling over the radio: "He's brought his son, he's brought his son." Now, I had a real dilemma on my hands. This guy clearly deserved to be confronted, but at what cost? There was no way as a parent that I could traumatize a child. FOTOFIX had been coy online talking to the decoy. When the decoy asked what he liked doing with guys, he responded: "Don't like typing about . . . you got a cell?" That's when he talked to Del, posing as the fourteen-year-old boy on the phone. FOTOFIX told her he liked to give and receive oral sex, but he wanted to be discreet. Now, with his boy at his side, he was walking into our house.

After I told him who I was, I said: "We are doing a story on adults who try to meet children on the Internet and since you have your child here, I'm not going to pursue this. But I think you know what you're doing here, don't you?" FOTOFIX said he was just going to "take someone out to lunch." I told him that since he had his child with him, it would be best if he left. He agreed and said: "I'm never going to do this again."

Moments later he was under arrest. Frag had let the police know about the boy. A female officer scooped the child up to take him away so he wouldn't have to watch his father's arrest. "I just want my son back," the man wailed. The boy's mother was at work. Police called her and she picked up the boy. There was no indication that FOTOFIX was going to involve his son in any sex act. It seemed he was going to let him watch videos during the planned liaison with the fourteen-year-old.

Amazingly, according to police, FOTOFIX blamed his wife for his predicament, saying it was because she refused to give him oral sex that he had to go looking for young men online. Six months after his arrest, he was back living with his wife. Because Florida child welfare officials were investigating the father, the boy had to live with another relative. That means, at least initially, the woman chose her predator husband over her child. It's hard to fathom.

*Ohio: greeneye121, goodbody1330, netbuckeye, meatrocket8, parkn-ride_469, and changforthebetter2006 have all pleaded guilty in Ohio. As of this writing, iurutherford has pleaded not guilty to the charges against him and his case is still working its way through the court system.

*Florida: As of this writing, thomascoffen, moff_1960, crazytrini85, and FOTOFIX have all pleaded not guilty and are awaiting trail.

Chapter 8

Bobby Grizzard: Determined Detective

Massillon, Ohio, is a small town with big ambitions and impressive success in catching online sexual predators. The former steel town has a main street lined with beautiful old brick buildings that feel more like the twenties than the twenty-first century. For coffee there's still the Chit Chat Café.

This area is known as "the cradle of high school football." Newborn baby boys are given miniature footballs when they leave the hospital. Massillon is a town with 33,000 people and a football stadium that can hold 20,000 of them. Football is a sacrament here. Pride runs deep as a result of Massillon's status as the second in the nation in high school football victories, surpassed only by Valdosta, Georgia.

But Massillon is important for much more than just football—in this quintessential all-American small town there's a king-size effort underway to fight back against sexual predators. An Internet Crimes Against Children Task Force was formed in August of 2002. (The ICAC program is part of an effort by the Justice Department to support state and local communities in their efforts to combat offenders who use the Internet and other communications technology to sexually exploit children.) In just over four years, nearly a hundred online sexual predators have been arrested—including one female sexual predator—and sent to prison for terms ranging from eighteen months to forty-four years.

"We could triple that if we were doing it full time," says Detective Bobby Grizzard, who was hailed in an editorial in a local newspaper for being a "crusader" against online sexual predators. He's gunning for guys like the fifty-four-year-old disk jockey who drove from South Carolina thinking he was about to meet a twelve-year-old girl. In his car, police found a noose, duct tape, rope, a pulley system, handcuffs, dildos, butt plugs, nipple clamps, and an enema bottle. Grizzard had been chatting with him online for thirteen months. "You switch it on and off. Sometimes a week or two might go by and you'd explain it online as saying you've been grounded," Grizzard said. The disk jockey, who had a prior arrest in Texas for soliciting sex online, was sentenced to seven and a half years.

Remarkably, Massillon's task force costs next to nothing to run and could be replicated in other communities. The secret to keeping it low cost is that the five police officers—three men and two women—who are part of the task force do this work in conjunction with their other activities. The mayor donated office space for the small unit and the FBI pays for their supplies, the phone bill, and computer costs. The room is large enough for the computers and a big TV. With a radio, CD player, and a doorbell chime it is easy to establish the illusion of normal teenage background noise. The department is hoping soon to get a six-hundred-dollar transformer, which has the capacity to make an adult male voice sound like a credible female one. "That will make us much more efficient," says Grizzard.

Grizzard is not the hard-bitten detective who turns up so often in prime-time TV series. He's a former college football player, married, with three kids, and he worships regularly at a local Pentecostal church. His Spider-Man memorabilia fill a bookcase in his office. He's proud of his work and the fact that there are so few local arrests now because the word is out that this task force means business and jail time.

"About eighty percent of our arrests are 'travelers,' guys who come here from out of town," he says. An engineer from Tennessee, who was recently sentenced to five and a half years, chatted with Grizzard, who was playing a teen, for three months. The man made arrangements to meet the supposed girl in Ohio after dropping his son off at college in Illinois.

Grizzard catches predators the same way we do in the *Dateline* stings—with persistent work and patience.

A chat room named "Seventh Grade Hotties" proved to be the undoing for SIBERSWEDE, one of Grizzard's recent arrests. The forty-eight-year-old man behind the screen name owned a business and coached girls' hockey at the local high school in a northern Minnesota town with a population of just 1,670.

When SIBERSWEDE logged in to the "Hotties" chat room in mid-July he started talking with Grizzard, who was posing as a fourteen-year-old girl. "That's the hot age now," said the detective. "I have no idea why."

Grizzard was just back from vacation and hadn't been online for several weeks. He logged on as fourteen-year-old TIFFANY. (The real name he used is still an active profile so we won't use it here.) Within minutes, SIBERSWEDE was chatting.

"We start this conversation at 5:36 P.M. At 5:46, which is ten minutes later, he's asking if you know Rocky River, are you close to Cleveland, have you ever heard of Lakewood?" says Grizzard. "He was online, looking for a child, because he knew he was coming here." Just like the men in the *Dateline* stings, SIBERSWEDE was shopping the aisles of the Internet for a kid.

"Hockey or hooky?" was how the chat began. When TIFFANY typed in "hockey," SIBERSWEDE told her he was a coach. TIFFANY said she'd be a sophomore and was into sports. SIBERSWEDE told her at one time or another he'd seen all the girls on the hockey team nude or partially dressed and they hadn't minded it. "That's part of the grooming process," says Grizzard. "It's also a way to lower a child's inhibition and get a reaction." If the child isn't revolted, the grooming moves to another, more explicit, level.

The two sent pictures of themselves back and forth. TIFFANY—whose picture was actually that of a detective when she was younger—looked blond and shining in her innocence. In his photo, SIBERSWEDE was smiling in the back of a boat, looking casual and middle-aged. "He said her picture gave him a hard-on," said Grizzard, who responded as TIFFANY by saying, "Cool." SIBERSWEDE quickly moved on. "He talked about the girl giving him oral sex, oral sex with ice cubes, bubble baths, and massage," recalls Grizzard.

Like the predators in our stings, SIBERSWEDE wanted to arrange a phone call to make sure he was actually communicating with a real kid. It happened that the police officer connected to the unit who does phone calls posing as a young girl was available. So, remarkably, twenty minutes after their first online encounter, SIBERSWEDE was listening to a young girl's voice that was shy, giggly, and sweet. He seemed convinced that she was not only fourteen, but interested in meeting him.

When Grizzard realized SIBERSWEDE was traveling to Ohio, he made it a point for TIFFANY to talk to him online nearly every day. "It's not the number of hours you spend online," says Grizzard, "it's how often."

Grizzard says that, like many of the predators he nets, SIBERSWEDE never talked to TIFFANY from home—he only went online at the office. It is one of the ways husbands hide their deviant behavior from their wives. SIBERSWEDE wanted to talk to TIFFANY as soon as he got to work, which was at six A.M. No problem for Grizzard, whose day starts early. "I'm on duty at seven A.M., six o'clock his time, so it was easy for me get online for an hour." The first time they talked for nearly an hour and a half.

But SIBERSWEDE made it easy for Grizzard. He called from his office and the moment he did, caller ID revealed the name of the business he owned. A quick Google check of his company revealed SIBERSWEDE's real name. With that, Grizzard was able to get more information from his driver's license. "The majority of these guys are businesspeople with careers and no arrest records. Often defense attorneys try to use that in court—he's never done this before—but we say he's never been caught before. After his arrest, this guy said he had been talking to young girls online for quite a while. He knows he has a problem with it. He has a fifteen-year-old daughter and an eighteen-year-old son."

On the day that would end his life as he knew it, SIBERSWEDE got up at three A.M. for the first leg of the thousand-mile journey from Minnesota to Ohio. He drove nearly three hours to Minneapolis for his early morning flight. After landing in Cleveland, he checked into a hotel and drove in a rental car to Lakewood to meet TIFFANY at the food court at the Belden Village mall. SIBERSWEDE had promised to take her shopping at Victoria's Secret before dinner and then they'd talked about checking into a motel.

Grizzard said SIBERSWEDE had that "pep in his step," as he entered the food court looking for TIFFANY, who had said she'd be sitting near Cinnabon wearing a dark green shirt, white shorts, and a visor. Indeed, the police decoy was.

But as SIBERSWEDE approached her, he heard the words that would divide his life into a before and after: "Excuse me, sir—police—what's your name?" He told the officers who he was, then said, "I'm here on business."

While he was being booked, SIBERSWEDE told Grizzard that he never suspected he was talking to someone who wasn't a fourteen-year-old girl. Like the *Dateline* predators, he didn't blame himself for his behavior, but something else, in this case drinking. He said he was intoxicated when he said what he did online. Grizzard pointed out that many of his chats started at six A.M. Within days, police determined that the business meetings in Ohio were a ruse. He had none. His sole purpose in coming was to have sex with a child. To cover his tracks a bit, he told several businessmen he knew that he was coming for a class reunion and might stop in to look at equipment they had for sale.

Bobby Grizzard is no stranger to predators and their scaffolding of lies. He is dogged in his pursuit of them and has talked to thousands of them in the four years the task force has been operational. In 2003, he logged 1,143 online chats.

Grizzard started doing sex crime work in 1994. But the cases he dealt with were primarily assaults, rapes, and molestations. The wake-up call for him and the local police department came with two big cases. The first was in 1999, when a local teen got involved with a man she met online in a satanic chat room. She was using a computer in the Massillon Public Library. "We had no idea that teens were using the Internet at that point as much as they were to have contact with adult men. We thought kids were communicating with other kids. We didn't know it extended to adult men in other states," says Grizzard.

"I think his screen name was LUCIFER_666," says Grizzard. The Pennsylvania man, Leonard Roth, was thirty-two, and came to Massillon and took the fourteen-year-old to motels, and tried to convince her to assist him in murder. "He wanted her to help murder a coworker of his, assume her identity, get married, and dump her body down a mine shaft in Pennsylvania," recalls Grizzard. "She is lucky to be alive."

Police were called into the case after the teen's mother, concerned about her daughter's long hours online and her secretive behavior, found a diary of hers. The diary revealed that the teen was sexually involved with a man she met on the Internet.

"We found out that he had come here and was living in the girl's bedroom." Grizzard said the man would hide under the girl's bed when her mother came in the room. "Her mother worked mornings and they had the run of the house during the day. In the evenings, they hung out around town. When her mother went to sleep, they would come back into the house. They would push the bed against the door of the room so Mom could not just walk in. It was the classic case where her mom decided her daughter's room was her haven."

During the investigation, the teen fled to Pennsylvania. Concerned that the two of them might commit murder, the FBI got involved and brought the girl back and arrested the man. Leonard Roth served a combined total of five years on state and federal charges and was released from prison in 2005.

Grizzard was drawn deeper into the ugly world of online sex predators in 2000 when he posed as SHARON, a grandmother who was going to help a local man have sex with toddlers.

SHARON was actually the screen name used by a fifty-nine-year-old grandmother who took her computer in to be repaired. When the repair shop found child pornography on it that included men raping babies, police were alerted. SHARON was arrested when she came to pick up the computer.

"The computer was a new toy for her," Grizzard said. "She stayed up late at night while her husband slept and eventually started meeting these guys." One of the men she started seeing was Craig Limbach, a forty-four-year-old factory employee. "I think she was primarily giving blow jobs to this guy. She was a retired grandmother and babysitter with a lot of time on her hands."

After SHARON's arrest, Grizzard convinced her to cooperate with authorities and he interviewed her extensively before taking over her online identity. "What he wanted her to do was babysit kids and then call him and they would meet and he would do things to the baby while she photographed it." SHARON had no prior arrest record or known interest in child pornography until she hooked up with Limbach. At her trial, she maintained that after Limbach sent her baby-rape photos she told him to stop.

"But I think it did become an interest to her," Grizzard said. "She wasn't revolted by what she saw." SHARON was sentenced to eleven months in prison for possessing child pornography. Grizzard believes

SHARON had the potential to be a sexual predator. "In the right circumstances she would have allowed a man to have access to children. She just let the conversation come up. She didn't say to him, 'No.'"

While the idea of a woman making children available to a man to molest seems unfathomable to most people, it's not to those who work with female sexual offenders. Dr. Susan Strickland is a forensic social worker in Atlanta who has treated and studied both male and female sexual deviancy for twenty years. "These women aren't bonding with men to molest children. What happens is that they pick badly. These women are so wounded themselves and have so many inadequacies socially, economically, and educationally, that they end up being easy targets for predatory men. They associate with men who are sex offenders who begin to molest their children. They may also get involved in molesting the children."

But the actual molestation of children never happened in the SHARON case because she took her computer in to be repaired and, after the pornography was found, cooperated with police. Once Grizzard assumed SHARON's online identity he began chatting with Limbach about the possibility of coming to her house to engage in toddler sex. Limbach was wary at first because he'd heard that an unnamed woman was arrested with child porn in her computer.

After nearly a month of online chats, Grizzard lured Limbach into thinking that he was going to rape a one-year-old and two-year-old at SHARON's house. When he arrested him on April 20, 2001, in a parking lot, Craig Limbach had lubricating jelly and napkins in his pocket and a digital camera on the front seat of his truck.

"He was classic in that he was married, with kids, was employed and went to work every day. He was organized, meticulous, and he was a collector," Grizzard said.

Police found 328 disks of child pornography in Limbach's home in the hollowed-out center of a model train set. The disks contained fifteen thousand images—among them 872 rape photos and more than four thousand photos of nude children. "He had a variety of interests. It was all categorized: toddlers, five- to ten-year-olds, ten-, eleven-, twelve-, thirteen-year-olds. He had things on bestiality, sex with midgets, limbless lovers, and daughters and dads." After he was arrested, Grizzard said that Limbach "blamed his wife for his problems because they weren't having sex anymore." I have heard that line over and over in the *Dateline* stings. "If my wife were this, if my wife would do that . . ." These guys will do anything to blame someone other than themselves.

At his trial, Limbach said, "It was all role playing. I would never go there to hurt kids."

The judge was unconvinced. Craig Limbach was sentenced to forty-four years and eleven months on two counts of attempted rape and for the thousands of images he had of child pornography. It's the longest sentence for any of the predators Grizzard has worked.

Grizzard scrolls through a "special interest" section of chat rooms to show just how graphic and specific they are. Any member of an Internet service provider like AOL or Yahoo! can set up a chat room. Free speech protects the right to talk about anything—even behavior that is repugnant to most. It's *acting* on it that breaks laws.

There are plenty of chat rooms that push the boundaries. With a few strokes on the keyboard, Grizzard starts pointing them out. UWATCHMEWITHURDAAU underscores his point—this is someone who wants to have sex with a woman's daughter. "DatrPicsforYours" he says is shorthand for "daughter pictures for yours," and is an offer to trade child pornography. " 'Stranger BJ' is guys looking for young girls to do blow jobs." " 'Smellyggirlsodor'—that's a guy who wants underwear sent to him that's never been washed." Grizzard points out another chat room he's visited before, "DpushesitinD." "Dad pushes it in daughter. They are talking about sex with young girls."

"You can distinguish the real from the pretenders pretty fast," says Grizzard, who, once he starts chatting, can juggle as many as fifteen chats online at a time, with quick, cryptic comments that fly back and forth until he sets his hook. He's quick to decode what people are after. "If a guy says, 'What are you wearing,' then he is just interested in cybersex. They want to talk and masturbate and Web cam it and talk dirty on the phone."

Grizzard kept one online relationship going for three years, and just recently cut it off. A West Virginia man who was in his sixties was waiting for Grizzard's decoy teen to turn sixteen, the legal age in Ohio, so he could arrange a meeting. "Next year we could have sex and not get arrested," he said. Grizzard knew that he was a dead end and it was time to terminate.

Engaging a mother and daughter for sex has real predatory appeal. In 2005, Grizzard and the task force made seven arrests based on one mother/daughter profile. The two female officers would assume the identities of a woman and her child in the phone conversations with the predator, leading up to the arrests. One of the men they nabbed worked for a federal agency in Uniontown, Ohio, as an administrator and was sentenced to three and a half years.

Grizzard plays a tape recording of one of their phone calls from their mother/daughter sting. MOM giggles in a seductive voice and tells the potential predator on the other end of the line, "Let me hear you growl." He makes a strange, throaty rumbling sound and both of them begin to laugh.

In a similar profile in 2003, one of the men arrested turned out to be a corporate lawyer in Atlanta. Grizzard shared his online chats showing how carefully he pursued his goal. The profile was slugged CANDEENAPRIL. CANDEE was forty-three, her decoy daughter twelve. The attorney said he was fifty-three. His screen name was CITATIONJOCK:

> CITATIONJOCK: I am a gentleman and also a professional with a lot to lose if things turn out badly.
> CITATIONJOCK: So are you close with your daughter or just beginning to think about things she might be interested in and desiring?

CITATIONJOCK: I would imagine your profile sparks a lot of interest from men with similar thoughts as mine.

CANDEENAPRIL: we are close

CANDEENAPRIL: well just maybe but I don't really no what you like yet

CITATIONJOCK: Has she been with anyone other than you?

CITATIONJOCK: Well I would very much enjoy finding a woman with a daughter both ready and desirous of finding a man to join them

CANDEENAPRIL: i see

CITATIONJOCK: Do you ever share a picture?

CANDEENAPRIL: yes when I am sure it is cool

CITATIONJOCK: Well it is cool but I understand lol

The conversation proceeded a bit further, but still tentatively.

CITATIONJOCK: It is difficult to reach a level of trust which allows for free and open discussion.

CANDEENAPRIL: i understand have to be careful

CANDEENAPRIL: real careful

CITATIONJOCK: I talked with a "woman" for weeks once who said she had a daughter

CANDEENAPRIL: and

CITATIONJOCK: It turned out to be some guy who just liked to talk about that sort of thing.

CITATIONJOCK: I do not understand the allure of that but it was a disappointment and reinforced my distrust until I can really know who I am talking to.

Within several days of their initial contact, CANDEE and CITATION-JOCK were making plans to meet and agreed to talk by phone.

CANDEENAPRIL: I mean, this is my child and I mean, I'm risking a lot on this end.

CITATIONJOCK: Right.

CANDEENAPRI: So, I mean I—I fully understand the risk involved and that's why there's certain things I just don't talk about.

CITATIONJOCK: Well, I understand that. I mean, why is that you want this for her? Just want her to experience this in a wonderful way. Or . . .

CANDEENAPRIL: Pretty much. Um, I want to make sure ya know her experience is good, and it's sort of a business decision.

CITATIONJOCK: Why is that?

CANDEENAPRIL: Kind of hard to explain. Um, oh, let me think here how I want to put it. . . .

CITATIONJOCK: (laugh)

CANDEENAPRIL: You know every parent wants to see their child go to college.

CITATIONJOCK: Right.

CANDEENAPRIL: Do you really think on a salary from working at a bank I'm going to be able to do this?

CITATIONJOCK: Well, probably not.

CANDEENAPRIL: Bingo.

The two talked about making these encounters regular—perhaps once a month—and the Atlanta attorney indicated that he'd be willing to pay. The telephone conversation then became more vulgar and candid.

CITATIONJOCK: Well, it is exciting that she wants to do this. I mean, does she, does she have orgasms? Well, I mean, does she—

CANDEENAPRIL: Well, what do you think?

CITATIONJOCK: I don't know, I have never, ya know, how old is she exactly?

CANDEENAPRIL: She's twelve.

CITATIONJOCK: Yeah, so I mean, I don't know whether twelve-year-olds do or not. (laugh)

But that was not the only sexually explicit question CITATION-JOCK had.

CITATIONJOCK: Has she ever been penetrated? I mean, does she have a whatever they—a hymen?

Other questions soon followed. He wanted to know if April's body was maturing, if she was developing breasts, and if she was on the pill or another form of birth control. As an attorney, he was especially aware of the risks he was taking.

CANDEENAPRIL: I mean, my daughter's future life, everything is at risk here and our future together. As well as I understand you're risking things too.

CITATIONJOCK: Yeah, I mean I don't wanna be—

CANDEENAPRIL: Okay.

CITATIONJOCK: I don't want to get there and have the FBI meet me at the airport, ya know?

CANDEENAPRIL: Oh, right. (laugh) Okay. I don't want 'em to meet me either, so how's that.

CITATIONJOCK: Well, I—

CANDEENAPRIL: Do you really think I would do that to you?

CITATIONJOCK: No, not you. I mean I don't know y— I mean, ya know, ya hear about all these operations where somebody does something like this and it's ya know, really just a fake, it's a police sting operation. I don't know. (laugh) And I have not been involved in this, but I mean, there is just so many risks involved.

CANDEENAPRIL: Well, then you can understand me bein' reserved, correct?

CITATIONJOCK: Sure, but we have to eventually just say okay, I trust the other person totally.

CANDEENAPRIL: Okay, and I am beginning to trust you.

Within about a month, the corporate attorney flew from Atlanta to Ohio in pursuit of his mother/daughter rendezvous, surrendering to the desires that would undermine every aspect of his life. He was met and arrested by police at the Akron-Canton Airport. He pleaded guilty in lieu of going to trial and was sentenced to four and a half years in prison in Georgia.

The arrest of a respectable, attractive, corporate attorney seeking sex with a twelve-year-old girl points to something positive and important about Internet stings: upscale men are being caught who were rarely caught and convicted before.

"While it looks like a new class of people is showing up in the sex offender population, I doubt very much that is the case," says Dr. David Finkelhor, director of the Crimes against Children Research Center at the University of New Hampshire. "I think that we have a tool for catching that segment that we didn't have before. That's a real boon.

"Upstanding men have been hitting on teenagers forever, the babysitter, when they drive her home, the friend of their daughter," he continues, "but the big thing that has changed is that law enforcement can go online and impersonate teens now. They can catch people without having to get the cooperation of a child."

Men who come from the upper strata of society usually have the power and means to defend themselves, and their prominence makes a victim less likely to take them on. "That's exactly the kind of person that a child doesn't feel they have a chance against. So to people who say, 'the Internet is putting our kids at risk,' I say the Internet is also providing a dramatic new tool for protecting them as well. That may counterbalance the risk it is creating. I think that is an important new development."

It also helps explain what we have seen in our *Dateline* sting operations—predators from the esteemed professions like doctors, rabbis, and educators. These men had such professional credibility pre-Internet that they were much harder to catch and convict because a child, and the child's family, had to be willing to stand up against them and their reputations knowing that the odds of success were not great. The cases were tough to prosecute, too, because victims didn't know how to collect evidence like professionals and the cases were usually driven by their testimony only.

While the overwhelming majority of Grizzard's chats and arrests are with men, he is no stranger to the lurid world of female sexual predators and feels that society minimizes their risk. "We have to reverse the thinking process when it comes to women as offenders and not say that when a boy who is fourteen years of age has sex with an adult woman he had gotten lucky. That's not the truth," Grizzard says. "It still destroys their innocence and is something that they will never get back."

Julie Ann Welborn, thirty-nine, was married with two children and living in Washington State when she became involved in June 2005 with a local fourteen-year-old boy. According to Grizzard, she met him through her daughter's online role-playing chat game, Runescape. She began instant messaging him and over the next six months developed a relationship that included frequent phone calls and cybersex.

Welborn provided the boy with her credit card so he could buy prepaid minutes for his cell phone without arousing suspicions at home. Although his parents were divorced, he was on close terms with both and doing well in school.

Welborn flew to Ohio in October 2005, using her daughter as the pretext to meet the boy. Her daughter knew about their relationship. But Welborn didn't need her after the introductions were made. "She left her daughter at the hotel and drove to his house in the early morning hours. It was about one A.M. He snuck out of the house," according to Grizzard, and they had oral sex behind or in the garage.

When the boy's mother noticed something on his computer that aroused her suspicions, she contacted police. Grizzard and the other detectives did not engage in online chats with Welborn because she and the boy had set up a code system to protect themselves. "From the chat records that we had, she would ask him when getting online, 'What was the last thing we talked about?' We weren't privy to those phone calls.

We were pretty sure that he would have tipped her off. He truly believed that she was in love with him. You have to be careful. Kids have some alliance to these people."

Welborn decided to divorce her husband and move to Ohio with her children and buy a house to be near the boy she loved. She was arrested in November 2005 outside a Red Roof Inn with her two teenagers and their pets with all their belongings in a truck. According to police, Welborn said she and the fourteen-year-old boy were planning to marry as soon as he was old enough.

Grizzard said that while it was unusual for Welborn to use her daughter as an excuse to see the teen, the grooming process and manipulation were common predatory behavior. "She isn't different, other than that she's a female. She's the typical predator who preys on a child's innocence."

Female sexual predators are rare in number. But their numbers are increasing, according to Dr. Susan Strickland. "It used to be from Department of Justice statistics that ninety-nine percent of all sex offenders were male and only one percent female. In the last five years, that number has jumped to seven percent," Strickland says. This parallels what others have found. Dr. David Finkelhor has studied female sex offenders as director of the Crimes against Children Research Center at the University of New Hampshire. He believes they account for about 2 to 5 percent of the offender population.

"There are four or five major types: there are women who act in concert with men, like a woman who makes her daughter or kid available to her boyfriend. There are the women who fall in love and seduce teenagers, the Mrs. Robinsons. There are a fair number of teenage girls who molest younger kids they babysit or know—sometimes they have been abused or are trying to get sexual experiences they can't get in other ways or they are dealing with sexual conflicts. Then you have some mothers who are abusing their own kids. They tend to be socially isolated and very depressed."

Good data are hard to track on the issue of female sexual predators because the crimes are woefully underreported—since boys are less likely to tell and most female predators, like Julie Ann Welborn, are more likely to molest boys rather than girls.

Dr. Susan Strickland is a forensic social worker in Atlanta who has treated sexual deviancy—in both men and women—for twenty years. "One of the ways that they are different, male and female sex offenders, is that females tend to have more severe sexual abuse histories than the male sex offenders. In male sex offenders, we really only find about a third have experienced sexual abuse as a child. When we are dealing with females, we are dealing with people who have incredible, incredible trauma histories. With female sexual offenders, in about every category, you are looking at about seventy to ninety percent and it's severe sexual abuse—many times before the age of ten—young children—and multiple perpetrators involving penetration."

Julie Ann Welborn told police that she had been molested. "Female sexual offenders, due to severe overall childhood trauma and deprivation, including severe sexual abuse, have few skills to negotiate their social and sexual contacts," says Strickland. Women with backgrounds like Welborn's, according to Strickland, are at risk because of their distorted sexual beliefs, values, and knowledge. They are usually emotionally needy and lack the skills to create healthy relationships with consensual adults—so they turn to younger kids and teens.

"When you can't get it on with appropriate partners but you still want to get it on and do sex because it's a pleasurable and wonderful thing," says Strickland, "you look for partners that you are able to get it on with. That would be a teenager who would be impressionable and able to be manipulated and gullible."

Based on the research he's done at the Crimes against Children Research Center, Dr. David Finkelhor explains that female offenders "do not tend to be repetitive child molesters the same way men do for the most part." Women, like men, will use sex for mood regulation of anxiety and depression. "You have blockage in their ability to get their needs met in other ways; you have the rationalization," says Finkelhor, "that is common to men and women, 'I'm in love, I can really help this child,' it's only harmful if you use force."

Strickland has seen this played out in the women she treats. "Women's sexual arousal and interest is different from men. Men have certain things that they are aroused to or that turn them on. Women are very different. They are aroused to contextual factors, like feeling safe, feeling loved, feeling wanted, feeling liked, those kinds of things. Surely there are lots of women chatting with teenage boys online who are chatting in those kinds of ways—'Oh, I love to take care of my woman,' and she's saying, 'Oh, good, because I love to be taken care of,' and he says, 'What is it that you like?' There might be banter like that going on. Women tend to be seeking some kind of love attraction and love relationship—some emotional connection with the victim."

Even though Welborn traveled from out of state, the FBI did not file federal charges against her because she did not come solely to meet the boy; she was in the process of moving and trying to find a house to buy.

In court, Welborn was apologetic. "I'm really sorry," she said. "I'm sorry how I hurt and let down so many people."

Judge Charles Brown Jr., who sentenced her, called her behavior "reprehensible" and classified her as a sexual predator. Welborn was sentenced to four years in prison, which she is now serving in Ohio.

Grizzard knows he's barely making a dent in the overall problem by arresting predators. Prevention is the way the real inroads will be made on the problem. "Parents don't realize how susceptible their kids are. Parents think that if their kids are home, they are safe from these guys, but it's an open door policy. Every time they sign on to the computer, they walk someone into their home. Parents don't realize how much information their kids give out."

To demonstrate how vulnerable kids are, Grizzard frequently does PowerPoint presentations in schools. In March 2006 he spoke at Massillon's Tuflaw High School and told the parents, "If things go right to-day, during this presentation we'll jump online and I'm going to show you that under the right circumstances, you will have a predator that will latch onto your kids in a matter of minutes."

Grizzard led parents through the steps involved in getting into a chat room. He pointed out the ones that he felt were clearly for pe-dophiles. He clicked into a room and moments later, he had an instant message from a man. "Within one minute he wanted to do a phone call." Grizzard asked for a parent in the audience who thought she could sound childish. "I'll whisper in your ear what I want you to tell this guy."

He gave the potential predator his office cell phone number and when he called, he put him on speakerphone with a roomful of parents listening. He told the mom he thought was BREE that he lived in Columbus and really wanted to meet her. She was answering simply—yes, no, sure—and when Grizzard felt it had gone on long enough, he gave the teacher a cue to yell, "Hey, Bree, I'm home." The mom quickly said, "I got to go, I got to go."

The next day, Grizzard continued the online conversation and two weeks later arrested the predator who had proved to parents just how easy the Internet makes it to connect with underage teens. The man was sentenced to prison in Ohio for eighteen months.

It never stops for Bobby Grizzard, but that's just the way he likes it. Another arrest has just gone down successfully. "A guy drove five hun-dred seventy-two miles from Connecticut yesterday. He has a master's degree in education and was working as a supervisor at a hospital for abused and chemically dependent kids." Leaving Connecticut at mid-night, he drove straight through to Ohio in ten hours and got to the meeting place—the YMCA—two hours ahead of schedule.

Grizzard had met him in an AOL chat room for older men seeking adolescent females: OLDERMAL4ADOLF. It took just twenty days from the time Grizzard started chatting with him as a fourteen-year-old girl until the balding, five-foot-nine-inch and 320-pound suspect was under arrest in Ohio. As is by now classic in our *Dateline* stings, the guy told Grizzard when he was arrested, "I had no intention of doing anything wrong. I was just going to take her shopping at Victoria's Secret."

But just in case, he had brought along a digital camera, leg irons, and handcuffs. Grizzard hopes and expects he'll be sentenced to ten years in prison. "A guy like this is fairly serious."

Keeping a sense of humor helps Bobby Grizzard keep perspective and stay so resolutely committed to the tough and emotionally grinding work he's doing. With a smile he says that whenever a potential predator asks TIFFANY what it is she wants to do to him when they actually meet, he says, "Grab hold of you and never let you go." He means it.

Chapter 9

Treatment and Offenders

Y ou never forget the first patient—the one who sets your life on its distinct path. Dr. Fred Berlin is a psychiatrist and one of the nation's foremost authorities on the treatment of sexual disorders and sexual offenders.

It was during his residency at Johns Hopkins University in Baltimore that he met a patient unlike any other he'd ever known. "There was a man who came in with his wife, and he actually had made a wooden club with a chain on it and he was having these fantasies about striking his wife with it. As it turned out, it was sexual sadism; he was aroused sexually by suffering or degrading somebody else. Intellectually he knew he didn't want to do this but he was being driven to do this."

Berlin said he was able to help the patient resolve his conflicts and get his life back on track. But as Berlin talked to people who were on the medical school faculty at Johns Hopkins at the time, he realized how little doctors understood about patients like his who were sexually deviant. "My introduction to this was certainly an extreme case. I think he made a hole in the door and was thinking of putting her head through it almost in a guillotine fashion."

That was 1975. The Internet was nearly two decades away and the phenomenon of online sexual predators unimaginable. What has remained unchanged is Fred Berlin's passion and dedication to helping sexually disordered individuals manage their sexual drives in ways that harm neither themselves nor others.

Berlin has been affiliated with Johns Hopkins for his entire career. He founded and directed the Sexual Disorders Clinic there from 1980 to 1992. He then went on to create the National Institute for the Study, Prevention and Treatment of Sexual Trauma. It's become one of the most highly regarded treatment programs in the country.

Berlin's worth listening to for a lot of reasons, but one of the biggest is that the recidivism rate in his program is in the single digits. "Our original study, in 1991, was a five-year study on six hundred men, over four hundred of whom had a diagnosis of pedophilia. In that five-year follow-up, less than eight percent recidivated. If we looked at people who were fully compliant with treatment it was less than three percent. I'm sure we missed some things but that is still a far cry from the common public misconception that most people will quickly get back into trouble. That simply isn't the case." Berlin is now working on a fifteen-year follow-up on the same group of individuals and points out that data from the Department of Justice indicate sexual offenders have a lower rate of recidivism than any other criminals except murderers.

I checked this out and it's true. According to data from the DOJ, "Child molesters had a thirteen percent reconviction rate for sexual offenses and a thirty-seven percent reconviction rate for new, non-sex offenses over a five-year period; and rapists had a nineteen percent reconviction rate for sexual offenses and a forty-six percent reconviction rate for new, non-sexual offenses over a five-year period based on statistics from 1995." (But the DOJ points out a crucial point: only about one out of three sex crimes are ever reported.) The recidivism in the overall criminal population according to the DOJ is 63 percent based on data from 1983.

Berlin, big, burly, and intense, is not only a psychiatrist, but he also has a Ph.D. in psychology. "I'm fascinated by the relationship between the brain as a biological organ and the mind as subjective experience. The area of human sexuality is a very good area to be working in if you have that interest. It's been intrinsically interesting."

I interviewed Berlin for one of our early "To Catch a Predator" broadcasts. He's followed the series and raises some fair points about its limitations and the need to go further. "There is not depth of understanding of either what these disorders are about, or these psychiatric conditions, and there's no depth of appreciation of the humanity of the people who are afflicted with them. We just see the deer in the headlight, we see the public humiliation."

My intention, then, in this chapter, is to flesh out some of this issue from his perspective. I want to be clear from the outset—Berlin feels that protecting children is priority number one and he believes there are some men who should be in prison for the rest of their lives, period. "But if in the context of protecting youngsters and society we can also salvage the lives of some of these folks, I certainly believe that is not a bad thing to do."

Berlin, who by now has treated several thousand sexually disordered individuals in his career, said that his patients have taught him about the humanity that is beyond their diagnosis. "I haven't seen the whole *Dateline* series but there were some military people who were fighting for their country who clearly made very positive contributions to society. When you are working in treatment you see that over and over again and are forced to get by the stereotypes and the stigma around sex offenders. The reality is these are complex problems deeply rooted in human nature and sexuality."

What we haven't shown in the "To Catch a Predator" series are the men who never act on their impulses, have recognized the dangerous disorder they have, and are trying valiantly to overcome it. Berlin has a patient just like that.

"This is a wonderfully successful man, he teaches and has various other professional involvements, yet he's been struggling with not down-loading images of child pornography from the Internet. He has never abused a child sexually, but if he gets caught doing this [viewing child pornography] he will be a registered sex offender and he will go to jail for a long time. It's been a poignant struggle. He has been on the verge of sui-cide," Berlin says. "For a period of time, he had his sister program his computer so she would have the access code so he could only get onto the computer if he would call her and she would get him on and that would help structure it so he wouldn't be doing things he shouldn't be doing. He's in many ways a wonderful man and yet periodically he has this urge, and again, it's so easy because the pictures are there. He's a tortured soul." What Berlin has seen in his long career is the tremendous spectrum of people who are sexually disordered. "Asking what the typical pedophile is like is akin to asking what the typical heterosexual is like."

He stresses that "none of us sit around and *decide* the sorts of part-ners we are attracted to. In growing up we *discover* the sorts of partners we're attracted to. Of men I have known over the years who are attracted only to children in no way would they have wanted to have that kind of sexual orientation. No one in the right mind would decide, if we have that choice, which we do not, to grow up sexually attracted to children."

That said, what happens when someone recognizes his urges? That's one issue Berlin sees in absolute terms. "Let me be really clear—while it is not someone's fault that he's a pedophile, it is his *responsi-bility* to do something about it. But doing something about it, like alcoholism or severe drug addiction, might mean getting access to pro-fessional help because this is not the kind of disorder someone can walk away from on their own."

That help is not easy to get. Berlin hopes that society will move in the same direction it did with alcoholism. Not too long ago alcoholism was seen as a sign of moral weakness and shamefully stigmatized. When First Lady Betty Ford went into treatment for alcoholism in 1978, a seismic cultural shift began to take place in our understanding of alcoholism as a disease. Now we accept that alcoholics are people deserving of treatment and help. "When it comes to sexual disorders, I think we are still in the pre–Betty Ford era. We are still seeing only the moral issues, and certainly there are important moral issues. But we are failing to appreciate the role that needs to be played by science and medicine."

Berlin has done research on the brains of sexually disordered individuals and thinks that's the next big area where a breakthrough might come. "My bias is biological. We did some studies with PET scans that actually look at brain chemistry during sexual arousal. Of the many things that happen when people get sexually aroused, we found that the brain releases its own internally produced opiates called endorphins. Some people describe their sexual difficulties as almost like an addiction. Maybe in a sense it is. Are some people producing more of these internally produced opiates? Is that why some of them are having a more difficult time being in control of themselves? If that is the case we can learn more about it, maybe being able to prevent it or treat it."

Before Maryland adopted a mandatory reporting statute in 1989, which was then made more stringent in 2003, Berlin said his center had seventy cases of individuals who had come in voluntarily seeking help with issues around sexual disorders. But the law changed and now a psychiatrist like Berlin or any other therapist is legally required to report a patient to authorities if either in the course of taking his history or treating him the patient admits that he's ever acted on any of his urges. "Before we had this in Maryland, and we published on this, we had seventy cases of people who were not detected, came in entirely on their own, and we got them out of certain situations, i.e., the teacher we got out of schools so he wouldn't be around children. These people needed help and sought it."

But the law has apparently made people more fearful about seeking help. "The irony is that these mandatory reporting statutes deter people from coming forward to get help which makes communities safer. So you have a law intended to protect children that's actually deterring people from getting the very help that might make them less of a threat to a child." When a *victim* comes forward Berlin feels there should be a full court press to find the perpetrator.

His point is that when people are deterred from coming forward to seek help, the problem is driven further underground, which makes everyone less safe. Radio and television are full of ads encouraging people to seek treatment for depression, drug and alcohol dependency, eating disorders, schizophrenia. Why don't we offer the same help to people with sexual disorders? "When was the last time you heard anyone on radio or television say, 'If you are having these kinds of problems, for God's sake come in before the fact rather than after the problem. We'll try to understand, we want to help you'? What they are going to see instead is, and I don't mean to be cynical, *Dateline NBC* arresting somebody, publicly humiliating them, having them thrown on the ground with people talking about the kind of sentences they deserve."

Yet in the "us against them" mentality that Berlin feels has taken hold of this issue, there are few politicians who are going to advocate for increased funding for treatment or research into the causes of sexual disorders. There is much more political gain for punitive measures that Berlin characterizes as "Let's catch a predator and put them in prison."

Berlin continues animatedly. "The whole title, 'To Catch a Predator,' creates a starting point that, in my judgment, is not where the story should begin." His point is that when an actual victim is involved, by the time a predator is caught, it's too late. I agree.

"I would argue that the best favor we can do a potential victim is to prevent him or her from being victimized in the first place. And one of the most important things we can do to make that happen is to learn how conditions like pedophilia develop and how to intercede before that becomes part of the person's long-term makeup. The issue of prevention is key."

Berlin says that he believes pedophiliacs make up about 2 percent of the population. No one knows what the exact percentage is because the research has never been done. He feels that his profession, psychiatry, has not progressed very far in understanding what gives rise to pedophilia. "One of the problems is that we really haven't asked those questions. And they are critical!"

Berlin says, in pedophilia, as in other sexual disorders, "sometimes you can identify factors in nurturing. Sometimes we can identify factors in nature, such as chromosomes, brain damage, or hormones. But in terms of etiology, what a sexual disorder is not caused by, what it is *not* due to is voluntary choice."

What the Internet has done, says Berlin, is accelerate temptation in drastic ways. "Again, I'll make this analogy to alcoholism. There are people who might become alcoholics. But they stay away from the bars and don't go where people are drinking heavily. But if someone were to every day bring a keg of alcohol into their home and sit it next to their bed, they might."

The Internet brings temptations right into the home that in the old days a predator would have to seek out. Berlin points to our "Predator" series as illustrating how people easily lose their inhibitions when they have the illusion of anonymity. People, often within minutes, say and do things that they otherwise might not do once social constraints have been removed.

Here's a perfect example from one of our California stings: His screen name was m4pixeleen. He was a fifty-six-year-old executive in the biotech industry and songwriter who sold his music from his own Web site. He was married with a grown son. Like the ER doctor in Virginia, this was a respected man with a reputation to uphold. But online, m4pixeleen was negotiating with a PJ decoy he thought was a thirteen-year-old virgin. He said that maybe they should have oral sex because intercourse is such a big step. Then he added, "Sometimes people just do anal sex first . . . then you're still a virgin."

I've seen men like this in every "Predator" shoot—guys who talk about the need to be discreet so their families don't find out. Yet something overrides all their instincts and good judgment and there they are, walking through the kitchen door.

Berlin points out that for many men the Internet initially blurs the distinction between fantasy and reality. Inhibitions melt. "What starts out as a harmless fantasy crosses the line into reality, and then people are out there in the bright light of day doing things that they might never have done had it not been for the insidious way the Internet can contribute to this kind of problem."

The treatment center he runs—which sees about 120 individuals largely on an outpatient basis—is set up along tried and true techniques. Berlin is adamant about the fact that there is "no magic bullet" with regard to treatment. Sometimes he uses what's become known as "chemical castration," injections of Depo-Lupron to regulate testosterone, the hormone that fuels the sex drive. He says it's effective with men who have testosterone levels that are inordinately high or in men who subjectively report having repeated behavioral patterns and trouble controlling their sexual drives. But not everyone who needs it can afford it. Berlin manages to provide it for his patients through a nonprofit foundation he created that helps people get drugs they can't otherwise afford. Yet it certainly points to a larger societal issue: "We have states that want to impose so-called chemical castration on unwilling people who don't want it or may not need it and we have states where people want it and can't get it."

The treatment model that works best is not based on cure. "This isn't like TB, where we give you medicine and you get cured. This is like alcoholism and drug addiction, where the real focus is on the behavior. You have an ongoing vulnerability and every day you must do what is necessary to keep you from succumbing to unacceptable temptations. Every day you have to be mindful and maintain vigilance."

So on the psychological side, group therapy is a core component to the work done at Berlin's National Institute for the Study, Prevention and Treatment of Sexual Trauma. The goal at this level of treatment is to get an individual to take responsibility and move past their self-deception and rationalization to see the implications of their behavior.

The second dynamic that happens in group therapy is creating an environment of support. Treatment works when people feel understood and supported by others like them. "You can't take a person who is having a sexual desire for children and put them in a group with people having depression or marriage problems and go around the room and they are supposed to say, 'Jeez, I see that eight-year-old and I start feeling sexual.'" But in a group therapy environment they can be supported and made to feel accountable.

The third component goes by names like "relapse prevention." It's what behavioral changes a person has to make to resist giving in to unacceptable sexual temptations. "You're an alcoholic; you don't work in a bar. If you're a pedophiliac, you don't live next to a school yard. It's that kind of common-sense counseling," Berlin says.

The fourth component involves working with an individual's support system that will help him in monitoring his behavior—be that a family member or a parole or probation officer. "The families were not part of the problem, but maybe they can be part of the solution," Berlin says.

As we've seen in the chapter on "Other Victims," families are often the last to know about a secret life. This is shocking to those involved, but not to someone like Fred Berlin, who has several decades' worth of experience in treatment with people and their secrets. "People worked with Jeffrey Dahmer, people sat next to him day in and day out. His problem wasn't due to things that had to do with the observable aspects of his character and behavior." Sex, Berlin reminds us, is often an incredibly secret aspect of our lives. "I can tell you that these people can and do keep this secret. They are on the computer at work, their spouse has gone to bed, and they are down in the basement. It's like masturbation. People masturbate and their spouses don't know about it. It's too private and personal to be discussed."

As a psychiatrist, Berlin fully appreciates how sexual predators (which he points out is a term, not a diagnosis) symbolize our worst and darkest fears. The anger and outrage toward this behavior is totally understandable to him. But he rightly points out that anger and upset don't lead to effective solutions. Emotions, when institutionalized, can lead to bad public policy. Berlin feels strongly that public policy now is being driven by the exception rather than the rule.

"Almost all public perception and all public policy are being formulated in the context of a horrible situation in which some child has been kidnapped, sexually assaulted, and murdered. That's a fraction of one percent of the number of adults who become involved with children. If we are going to have public policy based on the exception rather than the rule, it demands the question, 'Is that likely to be the most effective public policy that we as a society can formulate?' "

Berlin feels the minimum level of treatment he needs to manage sexual offenders is two years of active treatment and at least five years of follow-up. Some people need lifetime treatment and supervision. Others need and deserve lifetime incarceration. But he feels, as a society, we have to find the balance between what is fair and just.

If we locked up every alcoholic, there would never be a situation in which someone relapses, drinks too much, and then kills someone while driving drunk. What price zero tolerance, is the question. How, in a free society, do we find the balance?

Berlin remains optimistic, despite a career that has taken him into the darkest corners in the human psyche. He is optimistic that his view of a better world is one day going to become a reality. "I think there will come a time where we will have enabled children and others to be safe because we can prevent problems like pedophilia and we have a society where people who have the problems will come forward *before* they act, rather than after," he says. "We can't punish this away, we can't legislate this away. These are human beings and we do need Betty Ford clinics for sexually disordered people the same way we need them for people with drug and alcohol problems."

• • •

"Hugo" asked that I shield his identity because he feels he's caused his mother enough pain already. He's on the sexual offender registry in the Pacific Northwest. There are 560,000 others on registries across the country, according to data from the National Center of Missing and Exploited Children. (A hundred thousand others are not registered or do not have up-to-date registrations.)

Hugo was convicted in the early nineties for the rape of a fourteen-year-old boy and served seven months. He was twenty-one at the time and said he believed the boy was nineteen. Life stayed on track for Hugo until four years ago when he was convicted on child pornography charges and for the attempted rape of a minor. The thirteen-year-old boy Hugo thought he was talking to and had plans to meet turned out to be a detective. The judge gave him a one-year suspended sentence and ordered him into treatment.

"The judge believed I felt guilt for what I had done and felt I could really benefit from the treatment program," Hugo said. Hugo is thirty-seven and has been diagnosed as a pedophile. He does, in fact, have quite a list of diagnoses: bipolar disorder, congestive heart failure, rheumatoid and osteoarthritis, diabetes, chronic obstructive pulmonary disease, morbid obesity, and posttraumatic stress disorder (PTSD) from his childhood sexual abuse. He's in a wheelchair and living on disability.

Hugo was willing to speak candidly with the hope that some good might come from his anguished past. While he hasn't been part of the *Dateline* stings, he feels he recognizes those he's seen in the broadcasts. He relates to the "deer in the headlights look, almost a scared-straight look." Hugo feels that if he had been able to afford treatment after his first offenses, "I would have had a better chance of not getting caught in the web of debauchery that I did."

Hugo didn't end up being confronted by me in a kitchen somewhere. But he is an example of the kind of complicated lives that play out before someone stumbles into the viewfinder of a *Dateline* camera.

"I want people to say, 'He learned something,' not that he is just pulling the wool over our eyes; pedophiles and sexual predators are good at weaving the truth to look in their direction and make them look better. That's not my point," Hugo says. "My point is there is something we're missing, instead of treating people we are throwing them away. Throwing away people has never done any good."

He has some experience with being thrown away. Hugo spent the first seven years in the foster care system with his brother, who is now in prison for drug trafficking. They were shuttled between foster homes, on average, every three months. His biological mother lost custody of him. Hugo says he thinks, although it's never been confirmed, that he was conceived in a rape. He said he was routinely molested in his foster families. There were several failed adoptions. Hugo and his brother were hard to manage and some families sent them back.

"Life was pretty hellish. I remember as young as five or six during the abuse and stuff, they would hold our arms down and give us heroin or something. They were injecting us as well as making us smoke stuff. I started smoking cigarettes at eight or nine," he says.

But there was a glimmer of stability. He and his brother were adopted when Hugo was seven and it stuck. He had his first birthday cake and party when he turned eight. It's one of the happiest memories in all of his thirty-seven years. "My mom made me a car cake. A bunch of friends came over. I have pictures, the first birthday pictures I ever had. I was still feeling I could be returned as damaged goods because I had several failed adoptions. So at the time there was an apprehension, but I remember having a good time. I giggled, I laughed, I felt something."

But it was hard to build on his foothold of security. By ten or eleven he was doing pot, his drug of choice. He found he liked codeine and in high school got into cocaine by hanging out with kids who went to wealthier schools. Hugo got good grades in school initially. He had learning disabilities and some of his problems at school were linked to fetal alcohol syndrome. His adopted mother, whom he calls "mom," stood by him, although he said the two of them argued a lot.

At seventeen, he started turning tricks with men he met at the adult bookstore. "I wasn't really interested in the sexual act; I was interested in the money. I was highly addicted to pornography." He graduated from high school and came out to his mother as gay.

He completed a correspondence course in airline travel and customer service hoping to become a flight attendant. But it didn't work out.

His first encounter with the law was at twenty-one. Hugo said he had sex with a teen he met in a homeless shelter and whom he thought was nineteen. When he found out the teen was fourteen, he was so upset he went to the police and turned himself in. "I felt really guilty. I felt really bad, like this monster. That was the one thing I was scared of being, the abused becoming the abuser. As a result, I turned myself in and finally they arrested me. I was sentenced to three years." Hugo was sentenced to an alternative program where he would be in treatment for three years instead of jail. But he was required to pay for part of it and when he couldn't afford the payments, he was incarcerated just before Thanksgiving of 1992.

He wasn't getting the medication he needed in jail and said he tried to commit suicide. "I was bouncing off the walls, manic one moment, depressed another. It was then that I tried to physically hurt myself by sticking things in my ear to make me deaf. Anything I could do to make me physically pay for what I had done to Carl."

After he tried to scratch out his veins, he was handcuffed. "I could only lie on my side or my stomach. That's when I had my spiritual awakening. I was told that only one person had given me life and only one person could take it away and that was the Almighty. It didn't say God, just the Almighty."

The encounter was deeply moving for Hugo, and for a time it seemed to help anchor his life. Seven months later he was released from prison for good behavior and went into treatment. "I was doing really good, reporting to my community corrections officer," he said. "Then someone found out I had a record and posted my name all over the neighborhood. I lost my job at a local food bank."

But he held himself together and life stayed on track for the next seven years. He got his first computer in 1997 and started viewing pornography online but said it was not an obsession. He said he did things like pay $4.95 a month to watch a gay couple in Germany have real-time Web camera sex.

By 2000 he was taking courses at a community college. For a class on child and family services, he decided to do a final project on the Internet and kids. He posted queries on a few bulletin boards saying he was interested in communicating with people between the ages of fifteen and forty-five who are sexually active and currently involved with someone much older or younger.

"Within two months, I was inundated. I naïvely thought I might meet one or two people on the Internet." Hugo said he had invitations to travel and meet boys for sex that he did not act upon. "I was invited to places like Mexico, Puerto Rico, to meet 'stalk.' They refer to kids as 'stalk.' This is where I got to feel very embarrassed and uncomfortable. I was invited to a party in Florida. It was billed basically as teen gang rape," he says. "There were a group of guys in their forties and fifties. One of them invited me to go along. He was willing to pay my airfare. I said no. He told me 'It's my grandson. He's ready and willing and basically, we are all going to take turns filling him up.'"

His addiction to pornography accelerated exponentially, he said, once he started doing his research paper. "I got into these weird trips like S and M, bestiality, the nasty more adultish stuff," he says. At his peak, Hugo says he was on the Internet up to five hours a day. There came a point when he began to look at child pornography. "I didn't pay attention to the red flags that told me to get out earlier, I just kept going and kept going. I have to admit I did look at the pictures but I did not masturbate at the children being abused. I kept seeing my past, flashbacks of my past. I kept feeling guilty, because as a kid sometimes I enjoyed it, sometimes I didn't," Hugo says. "Then when I went to sexual deviancy therapy, I learned you can get confusing physical and mental responses to sexual abuse. It may feel good physically, but it is creating a psychological trauma in the process."

When he describes his addiction to pornography, he said it had a numbing effect on him. "At first it was intrigue, that's pleasurable in some aspects, but it wore off quick. When you're an addict, I don't know how else to explain it. I felt like there was an urge to look at it . . . I wanted to see how far it would go . . . and people do go pretty far."

Late in October 2001, Hugo was arrested. He had been talking to a detective online who posed as an underage teenage boy. He claims he didn't want to have sex with him, but he does say that his instant messaging that he was shown with his screen name attached were quite graphic. "I was talking really nasty to this kid. I thought, 'Oh, my God, how did I do this?' It was fingering your butt hole, that kind of stuff. I really wondered if I did this at all. I think I tried to block it out. I was so beyond what I believed or perceived myself to be." Pornography was confiscated from his apartment. There were eighty videos, pictures, and magazines.

He was charged with attempted rape of a minor and given a suspended sentence and sent to treatment. "This was the first time I had been in therapy for sexual deviancy." He said he worked hard and progressed well. He was in two groups a week and met with a therapist twice a week. "I'm considered a sexual deviant. I believe pornography is a deviant behavior. If I would have kept going I could have easily become a physical predator."

His treatment ended after four months because the program went bankrupt. But Hugo found another therapist and continued to grapple with his dark urges and sexual addiction. "I learned I don't need to masturbate on a daily basis, don't need pornography on a daily basis. I did a forty-five-day stint without looking at one dirty picture or masturbating once. I felt so good after forty-five days."

Over the years, he had to drop out of two support groups when his criminal record became known. One was for social anxiety and the other for male survivors of sexual abuse. It was frustrating for him because he felt the groups were a help.

"I think the Internet was very enticing," he says. "It was the forbidden fruit I was afraid to touch. I didn't want to physically do anything with anybody. It allowed me to reach out. I never really had these feelings before. But that doesn't mean they didn't exist. I watch myself and keep myself on a very tight leash. I am afraid I could become something I don't want to be."

He struggles with obesity and relies on a wheelchair. The antidepressant Paxil has decreased his libido, he says, by 90 percent. A female hormone he takes to help with his breathing issues also thwarts his sexual drive. He said he lives like a recluse, rarely leaving his apartment. He'll do grocery shopping at three A.M. so he doesn't have to see people. Hugo no longer has a computer and spends a lot of time watching TV. He no longer has sex.

"I always feel self-loathing and guilt. But I do pretty good as long as I'm on my medication, as long as I have my therapy going on and have someone to talk to." It isn't always easy but he wants to try to break the cycle of abuse that his own life has known. "I believe I am ninety percent there. I think I am in good control. I know where to turn to if I have problems. I'm in regular mental health therapy. I'm still registered as a pedophile. That title keeps me in check."

"Dave" lives on the opposite coast and has a story that in many ways is the opposite of Hugo's. He had a stable upbringing, a good job in image technology, a wife and two children. If you looked at his life a few years ago when he was in his early fifties and said, "What's wrong with this picture?" you'd be hard pressed to come up with an answer.

Dave started chatting online in 1993, and continued for nearly eight years, until his arrest. He never went to meet a teenager in person but frequented AOL chat rooms with names like "I love older men."

"I got sexual stimulation from the chats. There was just a lot of fantasy talk, a lot of imagination." He said he was also stimulated by pictures that were traded online, but they were of teenagers. "I find girls upward from the age of thirteen to fourteen attractive. I wanted to know how their attitudes matched up with how they dressed. I wanted to know what their purpose was when they dressed in suggestive ways."

Over the years, Dave developed ongoing Internet relationships with two teens he never met and said they were not sexual. "I began talking with one when she was sixteen and it lasted until I was arrested when she was twenty-three or twenty-four. The other was seventeen when we started chatting. She was in some kind of treatment center and we talked mostly around issues of alcohol and alcoholism."

Three years ago police came to his suburban home just after dawn. "The police came to my house about six A.M. When I went to open the door they served me with an arrest warrant and a warrant to search the premises. The police were very sensitive, very polite," Dave says. "They were not in any way abusive. I think they recognized that they were destroying my life and were satisfied to have done that."

Dave had been chatting online with a police decoy he believed initially to be a fourteen-year-old girl. After four months, Dave became suspicious that "she" might be a decoy when she suggested a meeting. "I knew that was not something a normal fourteen-year-old girl would do. I said I'd like to call her up and hear her voice. She said her mother would kill her if she knew she had taken a call from an Internet stranger. I said to myself, 'Wait a minute, you are willing to have sex with me but you won't take a phone call?' It didn't compute." Too suspicious, he cut off the conversation.

He was arrested a week later. Dave said that he did not realize talking online about sex with a minor was a crime. He felt as long as he didn't try to actually meet her nothing illegal was happening.

Police found one disk of pornography in his home. He spent the day in jail until his wife came and posted twenty-five thousand dollars in bail. Dave pleaded guilty to attempting to disseminate indecent material to a minor although he had not sent the decoy pornography. "I was arrested for text." Subsequently, the law he pleaded guilty to was invalidated, but he was unable to retract his guilty plea. "Essentially I ended up pleading guilty to noncriminal conduct because the law under which I was arrested was misapplied."

Dave was placed on probation for ten years, which requires him to notify the police before he leaves the county he lives in for any reason—even something as routine as a doctor's appointment, a sporting event, or a trip to a museum. If he does get permission to travel beyond the county, he must then check in with local police as soon as he gets there and notify them of his presence.

Ken Lau is a clinical social worker in the New York area who has worked with sexual offenders and victims for over twenty years. He's the president of the New York state chapter of the Association for the Treatment of Sexual Abusers. Men like Dave are part of a new population he's been seeing in treatment since the nineties: white, upper-middle-class men who are arrested for Internet crimes. "We don't know how many people with pedophile and other tendencies never acted out, never had the opportunity to act out. The Internet provided what they thought was a safe place to do that," Lau says. "Once you get caught up into a behavior and the more it is reinforced, the more difficult it is going to be to control. Guys will convince themselves that they are not doing anything the child does not want to engage in so it's let's go meet. At some level, they want to believe they are not going to go through with it, but all of a sudden the person seems interested and they build up all these thoughts and fantasies."

Dave said in his chats with the decoy the talk escalated into the possibility of meeting. "I said I'll take you shopping, that kind of thing, but I said if we ever met, there wouldn't be any sex." The decoy then introduced another "teen" into the mix. "There was a second persona, a fifteen-year-old girl who was introduced to me as someone with a lot of experience with sex who was eager to meet an older guy. So the trap was broadened. We talked about when we would meet. I was nuts."

Dave felt he had managed his attraction to young teenage girls well until the Internet. "I didn't like being attracted to fourteen-year-olds. It was as much frustrating as it was about anything else. I didn't see it as a crime against humanity; it was more a pain in the butt."

Dave's wife and family have stood beside him since his arrest although it has not been easy. "My wife was incredibly supportive but very, very pissed off. But she was prepared to take the steps to go forward. I don't want to paint it as a rosy picture. She has tremendous personal strength and that allowed her to eventually forgive me for the incredible mistake I made. But this was a long process."

Three years later, Dave and his wife are still in therapy twice a week. Dave meets weekly for group therapy with other offenders. His two grown children, while initially furious, remained supportive. "My daughter said she knew this would happen to me because I spent too much time online. My son was angry, yelling, screaming, but supportive while not pretending everything was sweetness and light. It's invaluable, this kind of catastrophe. It's never without a bright side. I learned my kids would stick beside me however stupid I acted and that my wife was there, no matter what. I had friends I could count on, too."

Dave knows now what he did was wrong and feels remorse. Ken Lau says rationalizing behavior is common to men who get in trouble on the Internet. He thinks that is why people talk to me in the kitchens of the *Dateline* hidden camera houses. "They are chatting away like it's a Sunday afternoon brunch. That did surprise me. I think one of the reasons they talk to *Dateline* is because they don't really think that what they are doing is wrong. It's like when you get pulled over for speeding, you think you can talk the cop out of the ticket sometimes."

Lau sees in treatment what I heard a lot in talking to predators: "Some of them have this rescue fantasy, not that I buy it, but they want to believe that they are going to help a kid. They want to believe that they are not hurting the child or doing anything that the child doesn't want them to do. They are thinking they will come and have sex with a teenager that wanted to have sex with them."

What Dave shares in common with patients Lau has treated over the years is that he developed a relationship with the teenagers he met online—two of which lasted for years. While the length of those friendships is somewhat atypical, Lau said that the fact that men build relationships with teenagers is not. "It seems that the media is pushing the 'stranger danger.' I realize that guys on the Internet are strangers in the sense of physically knowing the person, but by the time they reach out to actually connect they are no longer strangers. These guys aren't just tapping onto someone they met on the Internet and running out to meet there. They are developing that relationship over a period of time and parents need to be aware of that."

Dave said that he was financially destroyed by his behavior. "I made ten times more money than I'm making now, so everything in my life in terms of the external elements changed." That's been a tough adjustment for everyone in the family. In time, he feels like he's getting stronger in the broken places. But in one respect, his healing has a long way to go.

"I haven't forgiven myself. I don't expect to. I don't expect to wallow in self-pity. But I don't expect to forgive myself. It's not where I need to be focused going forward. I guess if you're not looking back you're sort of forgiving yourself. But I'm very angry at what I did."

Chapter 10

Georgia and Northern California Investigations

F or our sixth investigation we headed south to Fortson, Georgia, which is about a ninety-minute drive south of Atlanta. It's rural, but just minutes from a major interstate highway. The house was set back from the road on about five acres of land. It had been vacant and for sale. Spiders, ticks, and ants were everywhere. We've dealt with a lot of challenges on these investigations, but Georgia was difficult on many levels.

Things got off to a good start. I arrived on a Thursday in late July. The Wagenbergs were finishing up wiring the house. The Harris County Sheriff's Department had set up a task force with federal agents in a garage apartment. Frag and Del told me that quite a few potential predators from the area had already taken part in sexually charged chats with decoys and made plans to visit. Emily once again joined us to pose as a teenage girl who was home alone. Everything looked good to go.

It has become somewhat of a signature of our show to have a snack or beverage waiting for the men who visit. We've offered chips and pretzels. In Florida it was chocolate chip cookies fresh from the oven. Here in Georgia we had a pitcher of sweet tea. The plan was to have Emily invite the man in, tell him to have a seat at the counter, offer him some tea, and then say she had to throw some clothes in the dryer. She would then try to keep the man talking from the next room in an effort to draw out his intent. This dialogue is often compelling. Then, when I thought the moment was right, I would come out for the confrontation.

We were all rehearsed and secured at eleven thirty on Friday morning when our first man came in the door. marriedbutlookingforfun31313 was a thirty-three-year-old army sergeant who had done two tours of combat duty in Iraq. He had been chatting online for three weeks with BEDHEADRED, a decoy posing as a fourteen-year-old virgin named Whitney. He starts off, "You like older guys? Damn, you're very sexy. Do u you have a boyfriend?" The decoy tells the sergeant that she's in ninth grade. He said he was getting his master's degree in education and planned on becoming a teacher once he left the army. He said that he had been separated from his wife for six months, that she cheated on him and that he had twin sons.

"Can I ask you something?" he typed. "Ya," said the decoy. "You shave?" "Ya cuz I wear a bathing suit lol." He asked her if she masturbates, if she's seen a man naked before, and when her period began that month. Eventually he said that when he visits they can take a shower together: "I will undress you and you will undress me, OK?" Then he says, "I will have to get some lubricant, too . . . for a virgin to have sex it hurts, so is better if I put in some extra lubricant."

marriedbutlookingforfun31313 warns the girl that she can't tell anyone, including her dad, about their relationship, because he could be accused of statutory rape. But he does try to show some consideration toward the girl's father. After talking about having sex with the fourteen-year-old in her father's bed he wrote, "Now remember sex is a little nasty, I don't want him to find stuff in his bed lol." The decoy said: "We can put something there . . . like towels or something."

"That will be kool," he replies.

marriedbutlookingforfun31313 also promised to bring the girl beer, sexy lingerie, and a Web cam. But as he walked into our home he appeared to be empty-handed. Emily invited him into the kitchen for some sweet tea. "Having a little iced tea?" I asked as I walked into the room.

"Oh, hi, sir," said the clearly startled man.

"What are you doing here today?" I asked.

"Sir, I wasn't about to do anything," he said.

"Well, who were you here to see?" I pressed.

"I was going to meet her," he said.

"Meet who?"

"Your daughter."

"My daughter . . . what makes you think it's my daughter?"

He never answered that question. Instead he started to plead with me. "Sir, please I don't want you to destroy my life." I reminded him that he made the decision to come to our house. "I know sir, but I wasn't going to do anything, I swear," he said. Then I started to read to him from his own chat log. He stood up and started to move toward me. He's not physically menacing, about five foot seven, medium build, but his time in the military has made him fit. He was still refusing to sit down.

I wanted to make sure we had the right man. I said: "marriedbut-lookingforfun31313, that's you, right?" He admitted it was. Then the army sergeant did something I had never seen before in any of our investigations. He got down on his knees and put his hands behind his head. It was almost as if he was assuming the prisoner of war position. He continued to plead: "I would not, never do it again, I swear . . . but, just don't destroy my career. I will get counseling, I swear."

On his knees, you could almost feel sorry for the guy, but remember this is the same man who typed more than fifty pages of often explicit chats to a girl he thought was fourteen years old. I asked him what he thought should happen to him. "Don't you see something wrong with a grown adult, a sergeant in the army coming to meet a fourteen-year-old girl?" I said.

"I will get counseling sir, I swear."

I asked marriedbutlookingforfun31313 if he had ever seen *Dateline NBC* before. He said that he had. "Did you ever see one of the 'To Catch a Predator' shows?" I asked.

"Yes, but I am not a predator," he claimed. Then came the six words none of these guys want to hear: "I'm Chris Hansen with *Dateline NBC* . . . and we're doing a story on . . ." He cut me off before I finished. "Oh my God." I told him that if he had anything else to say, we'd like to hear it, if not, he was free to leave. But he remained kneeling on the floor, perhaps because he knew what was going to happen next. Finally, he got up on his feet, and with his head hanging low, headed for the front door. He wasn't on his feet for long.

He was arrested and charged with criminal attempt of child molestation, a felony that carries a sentence of between one and twenty years. In the soldier's car police found Astroglide, a sexual lubricant. They also found condoms, panties, and a camisole he had apparently purchased for the girl. They also found a Web cam.

In Georgia, we meet a lot of men who have seen or heard about some of our previous shows. We always have a handful of guys who try to make a run for it as soon as they see me, but the men in Georgia seemed especially skittish. Such was the case with a thirty-two-year-old man using the screen name zavior01. He was a media director at his church, a volunteer position that involved working with young teens, which made his sexually explicit online chat with a decoy posing as a fifteen-year-old girl all the more disturbing.

"Have you f—d yet?" he asked the girl in the chat room. "No not yet," she replied.

"Have you ever played with your p—y?"

"Not really . . . it's kind of embarrassing," she wrote back. He asked if she'd ever had an orgasm. She said: "I don't think so."

zavior01 said, "Good." Then he asked her, "Do you want to be on top or bottom?"

"I'm not sure, which is better?" the girl asked.

"We'll have to see where you fit best . . . or we could do dawgy style."

When zavior01 showed up he immediately asked to use the restroom. This is always a problem for us because if he were to go into the bathroom, we'd lose sight of him. We wouldn't know what he was doing in there and we'd lose control of the situation. I stepped out into the kitchen right away. "Why don't you have a seat real quick right over there." He instantly knew what he'd walked into. "I know what this is," he said. "I just wanted to test it out, that's all." With that, zavior01 bolted for the door and was arrested by the deputies waiting outside.

In all, five men showed up that first day in Georgia. One of them gave me among the creepiest interviews I had ever experienced during these investigations. He was a twenty-year-old man who used the screen name perfect_buddy_ga. He had been chatting online with a decoy posing as a thirteen-year-old girl named maddiegurl192. The girl told him she's never had sex. perfect_buddy_ga said: "Awesome, I'd definitely appreciate being your first." The decoy asked, "Really, you don't mind if I'm a virgin?" perfect_buddy_ga said: "If you don't mind me taking it from you, I actually would love it and never have been with a virgin."

He told the girl he couldn't come over until later in the evening because he had to visit his parole officer. He said he'd had a drunk driving ticket and a hit and run accident. Then he typed that he'd bring condoms for regular sex. He asked if he could have oral sex with the girl and eventually: "So may I ask a naughty?" He continued, "Would you let me stick my dick in your behind also?" When the decoy asked if that would hurt, he said: "That is something you will have to grow accustomed to." What a gentleman. He also sent eight pictures of his penis. A lot of guys who turn up in our investigations do this, probably about half. It amazes me that anyone has that much time in their day.

It was about eleven thirty at night when he pulled into our driveway in a silver Cadillac Escalade and walked through our door. "I made some tea, it's on the table," Emily said as she scooted into the other room. He tried to follow her, but instead ran right into me. "Please sir, I drove this

far for no reason," he said. perfect_buddy_ga said he was really just looking for a friend, nothing more. But then his story started to change. "I
really, I swear sir, I'm a desperate person, I need a girl in my life . . . and
if she really wanted to be my friend that would be all I needed from her."

I reminded him that the girl told him online that she was only thirteen and that his actions that night violated Georgia law. He said he understood. And then I read back to him some of his chat: "'Are you ready
to have my thang in your mouth?' What did you mean by that?" I
asked. He translated for me: "Are you ready to have my dick in your
mouth? Because she was going with it."

I asked him if he thought that made it her fault. He said it didn't
and then admitted to me that, had a thirteen-year-old girl been willing,
he would have had sex with her. He went on to explain: "I'm sorry, I
know you think it's bad, but that's what it is and that would be probably the cleanest, best pleasure." It's hard to imagine someone thinking
that, much less admitting it—another stark reminder about who is trolling the Internet.

The next day confirmed that no matter how well we plan one of
these shoots, there are things that can go wrong that are out of our control. This is one of them. You may recall that in July 2006 there was a
heat wave in northern California. On Saturday, July 22, it caused a
massive power outage. The blackout impacted Yahoo!, whose chat
rooms several PJ contributors were using in this investigation. Yahoo!
chat rooms were down for nearly nine hours that day. That meant for
nine hours it was not only difficult to track and communicate with the
potential predators who wanted to come to our house, it was also nearly
impossible for decoys to meet anyone who might show up the next day.

Normally, in a situation like this, we'd simply extend the shoot an
extra day. We always make sure everyone's available to stay just in case.
The problem was that I had to get out of Georgia on Sunday for the funeral of two very dear friends of mine who had just died in a tragic accident, leaving behind their three children.

It was a little difficult for me to focus on the shoot with that awful event as a backdrop. Everybody on the "Predator" team was extremely supportive helping me cope and we pushed on. In spite of the difficulties, six men showed up on the second day of our investigation. There was another military man, a three-hundred-pound thirty-eight-year-old, who came over after a sexually explicit chat with a decoy posing as a fourteen-year-old boy, and a guy who went by the screen name truesweetguy69. The twenty-four-year-old chatted about oral sex with a decoy posing as a fourteen-year-old girl. He also sent a picture of his genitals. A few hours later he was at our house. When I asked him what his plans were all he could say was, "Whatever was gonna happen was gonna happen."

Then he made a startling statement: "I've seen this show about three times on TV already."

"So you know exactly what's going on here?" I asked.

"Yeah," said truesweetguy69.

"You know who I am?" I asked.

"Mm-hm. You're the . . . I forgot your name, but you're on the *Dateline* show."

"I'm Chris Hansen," I said.

A lightbulb went on for truesweetguy69: "Yeah, Chris, there we go, yeah." It was convenient that he knew the routine. It made it easier for the police to arrest him.

The next day, Sunday, was one of the slowest days we've ever had during one of our investigations, mostly due to the blackout and Internet outage on Saturday. Only one man showed up and he was a classic example of some of the split personalities you'll find online. He had two different screen names: centgaguy04 and talmatt. He also had two very different lives on the Internet. The clean-cut, all-American-looking twenty-two-year-old had a MySpace site that said "Jesus Rocks" and listed God as his number-one hero, but when he was in a Yahoo! chat room talking to a decoy posing as a fourteen-year-old girl, it was a whole different story.

"You deepthroat any?" he asked.

"What's that?" typed the decoy.

"It's where you take the guy's entire dick in your mouth where it goes to the back of your throat." And he wanted to know: "When it comes to us having fun, what will be off limits? I know some people don't like to be open-minded about sex and all like anal and stuff." The decoy said she had a hot tub outside and there were no neighbors close by. The twenty-two-year-old guy said, "So you can moan and squeal all you want." When talmatt arrived at our hidden camera house, I asked him to have a seat. Right away he said: "I had a feeling this was going to happen . . . is this the national news thing, all that stuff." I told him that in fact it was and asked him how he could square his religious declaration on his MySpace with his lurid chat. talmatt said that he had been in a struggle with himself over what he wanted. He told me that he was a virgin and it was stupid that he did this. Not as stupid as he probably felt spending the night in jail waiting for a bond hearing.

That night I flew into Detroit for the funeral on Monday. I went home Tuesday to get a few things done around the house and in the office. I flew back to Georgia on Wednesday to finish our investigation. We were all back in place, with the exception of Emily. She had to go back to college. We needed another young-looking woman to play the role of the teen. Fortunately, Lynn had a sister in Atlanta whose son had a friend who fit the bill. Lynn picked her up and drove her to Fortson. Del and Frag briefed her and she was ready to go.

We worked through Thursday and by the end of the investigation, twenty men showed up for sex after chatting online with someone they thought was a thirteen-, fourteen-, or fifteen-year-old boy or girl. And before it was over there was another "To Catch a Predator" first. A thirty-five-year-old with the screen name swgamaleyess told a decoy posing as a fifteen-year-old girl that he and his girlfriend both wanted to have sex with her.

It was one of the most graphic chats we had yet seen. First he offered the decoy two hundred fifty dollars in exchange for sex. Then he told her about another girl he met online. "She was fifteen like you. Her mom was at work. She invited me over . . . had never had sex . . . her and her friend." swgamaleyess then apparently put his girlfriend Phyllis online to talk to our decoy: "He would have sex with both of us . . . as he's doing one of us, he would want us to play with each other." Phyllis never showed up at our house, but swgamaleyess sure did. He walked in and immediately went into hot pursuit of our decoy, saying: "Any chance I can get a hug?" Almost right away, though, he spotted one of our camera crews and ran. He refused a sheriff's deputy's order to stop. Finally an officer's Taser knocked him to the ground.

Suddenly he wasn't so tough. He was in tears, saying he was married and was worried his wife would find out, and he was telling the deputies that he was a Baptist minister and didn't want to go to jail. But jail, as it would turn out, would be his next stop.

One of the first big stories that I covered for NBC was the 1993 kidnapping and murder of twelve-year-old Polly Klass. It was an awful crime. Polly was having a slumber party with her friends at her mother's home in Petaluma, California, about an hour north of San Francisco. In the middle of the night a sex predator came in through a window and kidnapped her. Because of that crime Petaluma police are acutely aware of the dangers posed by predators and contacted Perverted Justice to help set up a sting operation.

Sergeant Matthew Stapleton explained that "we wanted to make sure that people around us got the message crystal clear that we have resources dedicated to this and that we will continue to dedicate resources to this as much as we can."

While the Georgia investigation was one complication after the next, Petaluma could not have been smoother or more successful. Each time we set out to do one of these stories I wonder if maybe we've gotten so much exposure that no one will show up. I imagine ending up with nothing more than hours of hidden camera video of me pacing around the house. Based on what I've seen, I don't think that day is coming any time soon.

In Petaluma, we set up in a luxurious home in a wealthy neighborhood. Instead of a kitchen, the Wagenberg team set up a bar and hot tub on the back patio. It was an intricate set. A virtual tent had to be hung overhead to diffuse the sun and keep the lighting moderate. Decorative lamps were put in to control the lighting at night, and thank God it didn't rain. Fourteen hidden cameras were ready to capture everything. We had a new actress posing as the young girl. And we added a young-looking male actor, Danny, to pose as a boy. Both learned their roles quickly and were very convincing.

The goal was for the actors to ask the potential predators to have a seat at the bar and pour themselves a frozen drink from the pitcher already in place. The decoy would then say he or she was going to get changed to go in the hot tub and disappear behind a wall, all the while trying to keep a conversation going with the man. For the most part it worked very well, but a few times the visitors followed the decoy around the wall, where a camera crew and I were waiting. On a few occasions, the man would run as soon as he got a peek at us.

The first day, August 25, 2006, was wild. Twelve men showed up. Once again we saw some "To Catch a Predator" firsts. Among the first through the door was a twenty-three-year-old who went by the screen name strega_num_7. He had been chatting online with a decoy posing as a thirteen-year-old girl. First he apologized for chatting up someone so young, but in less than twenty minutes he was asking questions like: "Would you ever suck dick?" He also asked: "Would you ever let me fuck you? How big are your tits?" and "Is your p—y shaved?" The last one is a question we have heard dozens of times and seems to be a common curiosity among predators.

He said he was an amateur pilot and was in school studying security—specifically how to protect dignitaries. Then he said something to the decoy that made us all very anxious: "I carry a gun everywhere I go." We quickly decided that it was not worth the risk of letting him inside the house. The police arrested him as he was walking from his car to the house. Because the arrest went down that way, I was not able to interview the man, but our cameras were rolling when the police did.

It turns out that he was a Marine Corps sniper who'd done a tour of duty in Iraq. He said his surveillance training initially tipped him off that something might have been up. He told officers: "I noticed a couple of vehicles that looked out of place, so I left the first time. I had seen this on TV before and never thought I'd be a part of it . . . I didn't listen to my sixth sense that kept me alive in Iraq."

strega_num_7 looked upset. "I let the other head get the best of me," he told police. "And I'm pretty regretful right about now 'cause my wife comes back in three days from the army and I'm not gonna know how to tell her this." Later police searched his car and confiscated his loaded shotgun. He said it "pretty much goes anywhere with me." At least his wife wouldn't be able to get her hands on it.

We saw a number of other men in the military, including a guy in the air force who said he wanted to perform oral sex on a thirteen-year-old virgin. He told the decoy he had been married for two months. And he said something else online that we continue to hear time and time again: "I watched *Dateline* the other night about guys going to meet a younger girl and they all went to jail."

The reason we saw so many military men is because there are many military bases near northern California. We also had a handful of software designers and computer executives show up since we were within two hours of Silicon Valley. These men come from all walks of life, but the professional guys usually come from the industries that are nearby. We also saw some men who worked in agriculture because there was a lot of that in the area.

What continues to surprise me in these investigations is how some men will reveal their deepest, darkest secrets once they're caught. A thirty-four-year-old cabinetmaker with the screen name jefe6 was just that sort of guy. He spent hours chatting online with someone he thought was a thirteen-year-old girl named Ava. After saying he should know better than to hit on a thirteen-year-old, he pointed out that he was older than Ava's mom. He told the decoy that she should have a hot tub party because her mom was out of town and that she should invite him.

He offered to bring wine and Thai food and the conversation turned overtly sexual. "Are you thinking you might want to have sex with me this weekend?" he asked. Then he typed: "What would you say if I told you that I am laying in bed completely naked right now? I have a huge erection that I got from chatting with you." jefe6 asked the girl if she's ever had oral sex and then says, "Would you like to?"

He drove his motorcycle an hour to get here and when he sees our actress he says: "You even look better in person." jefe6 says: "I thought you would be in the hot tub already."

"Oh, I'm just getting dressed. I've got a surprise for you," she said.

It's then that I come out. "I guess I'm probably not the surprise you expected," I tell him. He said he suspected that he might be walking into some sort of a sting operation. Then he admitted he had an addiction. "I'll tell you I spent a lot of time online in the last ten years developing the stupid fantasies. I knew I had a problem and then the other day I got back online." He told me he never sought professional help, trying instead to deal with it himself.

He admitted he brought wine and that the only reason he didn't bring condoms was because he was running late and didn't want to miss his date. He seems almost relieved to be caught and to deal with his online issues. But then I asked him if there was a part of him that really wished there had been a young girl at the house. He laughed nervously as he said, "If there were really a thirteen-year-old girl who looked like your friend there, then I don't know."

What happened next was not so funny. After our interview, jefe6 was arrested and made another admission to police. He said that he might have saved sexually explicit pictures of children on his computer.

"I thought I might regret deleting them. I thought maybe I might want to masturbate to them at some point."

It seems that in virtually every one of our investigations there is a man of such stature that it is hard to imagine he'd be taking part in this kind of behavior. In Petaluma it was a forty-eight-year-old physician using the screen name talldreamy_doc. He was married, with two daughters, and worked for a company that made drugs for treating cancer. Online he told a decoy posing as a thirteen-year-old girl that he was twenty-nine, drove a Mercedes convertible, and knew how to treat a girlfriend.

The conversation spanned three days. "I like to make out slowly," he typed, "and other things."

The decoy asked, "Like what?"

"Touching, kissing, making each other feel good," he says, adding, "I wouldn't stop until you came over and over." He told the decoy, "You are under eighteen, I am over . . . we would have to be soooo careful." He asked what bra size she wore and then started talking about his visit. He wanted to know what she'd wear and if she'd take off his pants. He wrote, "I want to first lick you down there. You can also do things to me." Later in the chat he again said he was nervous because of her age, but in almost the same breath told her, "I mean you are very smart and mature." Later he said, "I'm horny for you," asking her to masturbate while thinking of him.

talldreamy_doc showed up at our house on a sunny Saturday afternoon, but he didn't stay long. He was visibly anxious; the actress told him to pour himself some frozen lemonade at the bar. As he did this, he knocked over the glass and spilled his drink all over the place. He asked for something to clean up his mess. He walked to the hot tub to grab a towel and spotted a member of our camera crew. "Okay, I gotta take off," he said as he tried to leave. There was no way at this point he was going to stay and talk to me. He could not, however, get by the police.

As they put handcuffs on the doctor, it was as though he was in excruciating pain. "My life is over," he winced. "But I didn't do anything."

He was taken away to be booked and then questioned by detectives. He said he was scared and that the worst thing he'd ever done before was get a traffic ticket. He said he came to the house because he was curious. "I chatted with someone online. She had asked me to meet on several occasions. I declined. And today again she asked. I had a little bit of time, not very much. And so I thought I'd come out and meet her and nothing more."

When detectives confronted him with some of the online chat, he said: "I was playing with her." He claimed he didn't know the girl was thirteen, but when a detective read back the chat where talldreamy_doc refers to the age difference he said: "I don't remember saying that. But, I told her that she needed to be—I was concerned about her. She needed to be careful." The detective seemed skeptical, asking why he would drive forty minutes to meet someone who was thirteen so that nothing would happen. "That's right," answered the doctor. "You expect me to believe that?" asked the detective. "It's true," he said.

Moments later the interview was over and talldreamy_doc was on the phone with his wife. "Honey, I'm in big trouble—I'll explain. You have to bail me out of the Sonoma County Jail. Bring a thirty-thousand-dollar check. It was a sting operation. I'll explain it to you later. Don't bring the girls."

The doctor was among twenty-nine men who came to our house over a three-day period to meet a young teen after a sexually charged online chat. All were charged under California law with attempted lewd or lascivious behavior with a child.

*Georgia: marriedbutlookingforfun31313, zavior01, perfect_buddy_ga, true-sweetguy69, talmatt, swgamaleyess, and straga_um_7—as of this writing, all are awaiting trial. At this stage the Georgia court system assumes a plea of not guilty.

*Petaluma: As of this writing, jefe6 and talldreamy_doc have both pleaded not guilty.

Chapter 11

Keeping Kids Safe

I'll never forget one afternoon I spent with a group of about a dozen kids between the ages of eleven and thirteen. I interviewed them as part of our first "To Catch a Predator" investigation. All of them were smart kids from good families. Some were children of NBC News employees.

Basically I wanted to show the kids some of the video from our hidden camera house and get their reaction to the way potential predators could go from the chat room to the living room, sometimes in a matter of hours.

We rolled the tape and the kids were glued to the screen. But the interesting thing was that some of them automatically assumed the men were actors and that the tape was demonstrating what could happen instead of what did happen.

When I made it clear to them that all of this happened in real life they were wide-eyed. (I suppose I was, too, as it was happening in front of my eyes.) But as much as this might have been a scared-straight moment, the answers to my next questions really got my attention not only as a journalist, but as a parent as well.

"Show of hands," I said, "how many of you have been approached online by someone in a sexual way that made you feel uncomfortable?" Virtually all the kids raised their hands. "Okay," I said, "how many of you told your parents?" The answer: none. The kids were looking down at their feet acting antsy. "Why not?" I asked. The response was that they were afraid their parents would take their computers away or cut off their Internet access.

You can't kill the messenger. My father was famous for creating a huge noisy stink any time my sisters or I stepped out of line or did something that displeased him. Our solution was not to tell him anything. Kids will take the path of least resistance. If you take away their Internet access, they will go to a friend's house, the public library, or just about any coffeehouse in the world.

Parents need to have an open, honest conversation with their children about the dangers online. They need to explain it in age-appropriate terms and not be afraid to share with them a scary story or two (I've provided some good examples in this book) about what can happen when kids are taken advantage of online.

I have always found it helpful to share with my sons a real-life story that exemplifies the potential dangers online. Many times it's something I have come across while reporting, traveling, or simply something I've read in a newspaper. Here is one that really got their attention. It comes from Katie Tarbox, a young woman who at thirteen was lured to a meeting by an online predator and later wrote a book about her experience and online safety called *A Girl's Life Online*. She now hears from other predator victims through a forum she operates. It's a story I think is appropriate to share with kids who are thirteen and older.

The story goes like this: A teenage boy had been talking to a girl his own age in a regional chat room. She had a picture in her profile that was very attractive. She was very nice and shared his taste in music. They talked about innocent things like homework and after-school activities. Eventually they decided to meet. The boy thought he was doing everything right. He had spent time getting to know the girl. He was going to meet her in a public place, a local mall. What could go wrong? A lot, as it turned out. The boy was waiting at the appointed meeting spot in the mall when he was approached by a man who looked to be in his early twenties.

He said he was the girl's older brother and that she had sent him in to check out the boy and make sure he wasn't creepy. With that task accomplished, the "older brother" said his sister was waiting out in the family van and invited the boy to come meet her, which he did. As it turned out, there was no sister. It had been a setup. The man in his twenties was a predator who sexually assaulted the teenager. Now, here's a kid who thought he was doing everything right and still was taken advantage of.

What I often do after sharing a story like that is ask my kids to identify what mistakes were made. You need to make them think. Too often we assume that everybody is who they say they are and that they are being honest about their motives. That is not always the case in the cyber world. You don't have to be a news reporter to have access to this sort of information. Go to Google News and enter a few key phrases and you'll find recent stories about kids getting victimized online.

For children younger than thirteen, I really believe there is no good reason to be talking to anyone online whom they don't already know in person. But you can't make that rule without explaining why it's necessary. Here's one way to start a discussion: "You know not everyone on the Internet is who they say they are. There are adults who use the Internet to trick people into doing all sorts of things. Some try to use their computers to steal money. Some try to take advantage of children, try to trick them into doing things they shouldn't do. If a strange man were walking down the street, you wouldn't call out to him and invite him into our house. You don't know anything about him or what he might do once he's inside. It's the same reason you shouldn't talk to anyone you don't know online. It's the same thing as inviting that stranger into our home."

There are a number of organizations devoted to online safety in this country. To try to name them all will only invite angry correspondences from those I omit. They all are extremely committed to protecting kids, but they are also extremely competitive with each other for funding and occasionally accuse each other of stealing the other's ideas and copying the other's programs.

The organizations I've dealt with most are the National Center for Missing and Exploited Children, i-SAFE, and Wired Safety.org. I've learned important things from each group. All three have very helpful Web sites that offer online safety tutorials for parents and kids.

One of the most commonsense approaches comes from Teri Schroeder of i-SAFE. Schroeder says, and I agree, that too many parents are intimidated by the Internet, chat rooms, and social networking sites. The reality is you don't have to be a Web master to be a good parent. You don't even have to know how to download a photo from your digital camera.

The conversation you need to have with your kids about online safety starts the same way as the conversation our parents had with us about talking to strangers in the park or at the movie theater or not accepting rides from strangers. You just have to apply it to Internet behavior. As kids get older the conversation, though, has to evolve. They will have access to chat rooms and they will be tempted to talk to those whom they've not met in person.

You must stress that no matter how long they've been chatting with someone, you never really know who they are. It is very easy to fake a profile. Someone who says they're a sixteen-year-old high school student could be a fifty-year-old sitting in his underwear in a basement surrounded by empty pizza boxes and God knows what else. That's why there are certain things that must be off limits in the chat rooms. It's okay to say you like baseball; you can even say who your favorite team is. It's not okay to say what school's team you play on or what Little

League field your team uses. To give that information to a stranger is an invitation for him to visit you.

It's okay to tell someone what kind of music you like. It's not a good idea to share what music store you go to after school. It's all right to say that you like Mustang convertibles, but never tell someone what kind of car you or your parents drive. And although it would seem obvious, you need to tell your children that they should never give out information like cell phone numbers or home addresses.

The incredibly good news for parents is that there is no magic way a predator can come through the high-speed line and materialize in your house. Your child has to provide the information the predator is seeking. If that information isn't provided, you're pretty darn safe.

But as you've read in this book, predators can be crafty and seductive. Children who fall prey to them can come from good homes just as easily as they can come from broken ones.

One of the problems is that kids who are between the ages of twelve and fifteen are not as smart as they think they are when it comes to their online activities. My sons have both sat on the couch with me and watched the "To Catch a Predator" shows. If any kids should know the dangers posed by computer predators it should be those two. I regularly call home and tell them about some of the more memorable and menacing characters who have visited us right after I have confronted them.

Even after all that, when my oldest son recently wanted to join a social networking site, I once again went over the rules. No chatting with people you don't already know. Don't post cell phone numbers, home addresses, or any other personal information about your family. And even if someone tries to contact you, saying they were referred by a friend, don't accept the message.

When I reminded my son of those rules, he looked at me with all the angst a teen could muster and said: "Dad, I'm not stupid." My response: "If I thought you were stupid, I wouldn't have let you use the social networking site in the first place." Half the battle, I think, is keeping a dialogue going and reminding them of what can happen if they don't follow the rules. In this case my son told me that you had to have a student identification number to access the site and that made it perfectly safe. I suggested that it wouldn't be too awfully difficult for an adult predator to get his hands on such a number.

The other thing I have learned is that instead of demanding to see your child's Web site or looking at it when they're not around, ask them to show it to you, demonstrate how it works, and have them teach you something. My fifteen-year-old was very willing to show me his site when I told him that I needed to understand how it worked so I could be knowledgeable on *Dateline* and in this book. He was teaching me something. I was not intruding into his personal business.

Internet safety discussions should start early. Parry Aftab, who founded WiredSafety.org, says that children ten or younger should definitely have parental controls governing their Internet access. That means the computer will only allow them to chat with people who are on their approved buddy list. Aftab also says that a filtered search engine is a must. "If they do a search on turtles you want to make sure they get information on turtles, not a list of pornographic sites," Aftab said.

For older kids Aftab says you need to stress that "what you post online stays there forever. It matters. It's real." It will be there when you apply to colleges and when you apply for jobs. And when it comes to meeting other people online, Aftab says: "The person you think is a fourteen-year-old boy may not be cute or fourteen and there is no way to know."

You also need to consistently monitor your high school–aged kid's social networking site. Here Aftab suggests a two-tiered approach. First, let them know a day ahead of time that you want to review their My-Space, Xanga, or Facebook site. That way they know they are going to be held accountable, but it gives them a day to look it over and change or delete anything questionable on their own. It gives them a chance to show some responsibility before a confrontation occurs.

Second, trust but verify. One way to see if your child's private information has gone public is to run a Google search on him or her. Put in your child's name and cell phone number and see what pops up. If nothing does, you should be pretty safe.

There are plenty of reasons for teenagers to have a social networking site and during her many presentations at schools across the country, Aftab hears from students why they feel they need them. To become better known locally, to communicate with kids from summer camp, to promote a band, raise awareness about a cause, or share expertise are the most popular reasons given.

WiredSafety.org has developed a program called Safer Spacers that will help teens create safer social networking sites and limit their exposure to potential predators. It basically provides a template so that, for instance, if you're promoting your band, your site will have the name of the band, photos, bios, and a schedule of appearances. But for contact information a Hotmail account will be used that has no connection to the band members' home addresses or other personal information.

If for instance your child wanted to set up a site to keep in contact with kids from summer camp, he could click on that template and just fill in the blanks. He could post a photo from the summer and list his first name. But there would be no mention of his school and a disposable e-mail address would be used for other campers to contact him. It's another way to filter out predators who prowl these sites.

There is no reason for hysteria, but these are conversations you cannot afford to delay. Statistics on how many children are solicited for sex online vary. The National Center for Missing and Exploited Children often cites a study that says one out of five children online is solicited for sex.

Part of the problem with some of these surveys is that the survey sample is so small and the number of kids online is so large. Parry Aftab says she speaks to between five thousand and ten thousand kids a month. Based on her face-to-face polling of the students she estimates that 60 percent of them over the age of thirteen who have unfiltered access to the Internet have been solicited or approached for sexual purposes by someone they didn't know.

Twenty-five percent of the fourteen- to sixteen-year-olds Aftab has met have told her that they have actually met people offline whom they first met online. As a parent I would always suggest to my kids that they never go meet someone in person they've only met online. Aftab likened that to telling young people to abstain from sex until marriage and not to drink until they're twenty-one. Aftab tries to teach students how to meet someone safely: always meet in a public place like a shopping mall. Movie theaters are bad because they are dark. Amusement parks are unwise because they are loud: if you had to scream for help no one may hear you. Aftab advises teens to tell their parents before going to any meeting. If a parent won't accompany you, take some friends along. You should step back and watch the meeting place, see that the person you are going to meet is who they said they were. If anything looks suspicious, go to a phone and dial 911. Stay in a public place; don't go anywhere in a car.

And there's something else that Aftab says kids are reporting more frequently now: suspected predators are asking kids to either remove the hard drives from their computers or bring their laptops to a rendezvous location. That is a definite sign that the person you're meeting wants to get rid of incriminating information and they are obviously to be avoided.

Virtually everyone involved in online safety, from police to counselors to advocacy groups, agrees incidents of online sexual solicitation are vastly underreported. It goes back to what I talked about at the beginning of this chapter. Kids are sometimes afraid or embarrassed to tell their parents when this sort of thing happens.

Every expert I've interviewed in the course of preparing the *Dateline NBC* programs stresses how important it is for parents to keep the lines of communication open with their children. It sounds so obvious, but in our increasingly frenetic lives what often gets shortchanged is the opportunity for parents to really talk and listen to their children. Children also need to be encouraged to come to their parents regardless of how scared or ashamed they might be from something that has happened online. Kids need to know that handling these situations on their own can backfire in ways that are unpredictable and dangerous.

You need to tell your kids that if they are approached by someone online in an inappropriate way they can come and tell you about it. Together, you can contact the Internet service provider and law enforcement and get something done.

I have come face-to-face with more than two hundred suspected predators and interviewed dozens of law enforcement officers, computer safety experts, and watchdogs. That has given me a unique perspective and allowed me to come up with what I call a top twenty list kids and parents should consider online:

1. Limit the amount of time children have interactive access to the computer to two hours a day. WiredSafety.org says that based upon its research, the risk of a child being exposed to predators, pornography, or cyber bullying goes up dramatically beyond that daily exposure. The more time a kid has to wander around chat rooms and social networking sites, the more time he or she has to find trouble. If a teen knows they only have two hours, they get down to the business of downloading music, searching for concert tickets, and chatting with friends first, and have less time to talk to strangers. (Parents also need to lead by example here. Experts tell us that if a child sees Mom or Dad spending excessive time on the computer or meeting other people in chat rooms or in person, the child will more likely engage in similar behavior.)

2. The computer should always be in an open area of the house. Wireless laptops being used in bedrooms is an invitation for trouble for most kids. You should be able to look in from time to time and see what your child is doing, what he or she is look-

ing at, and know who they are talking to. Even if they type in the dreaded "POS" (parent over shoulder) to their pal as a signal you're watching, it's good to let them know you're paying attention. It helps them learn they will be held accountable.

3. Remind children that online, people aren't always who they say that are and that there are real-life consequences should they give away personal information that could allow a predator to find them and take advantage of them.

4. What you post online stays online forever. In this digital age, it's easy to snap a quick picture that could be viewed by millions of people. Perry Aftab has a great line about this: "Don't post anything you wouldn't want to be seen by your parents, a principal, police, or predators."

5. Beware of the cell phone, digital camera, or Web cam showing up that you as a parent didn't buy. If you see one of these items, it could mean your child bought it without your permission or that someone else, possibly a potential predator, provided it to ensure he will get photos. This is very common. We had a predator show up at one of our homes who wouldn't come in, but instead wanted the girl to come to his vehicle so he could hand over the Web cam he bought for her. He wanted her to perform naked for him.

6. Guard your passwords. Nothing good can come from fellow students being able to access your child's personal information or their social networking site. A person who may be your friend today may not be next month.

7. Set up any social networking site so that only people you invite and approve can enter. For a teen to have an open site is like putting up an advertisement for predators.

8.   There is a fine line between spying on your kid and respecting his or her privacy, but I think it's okay to take a look at their computer now and again. Ask your son or daughter to show you their buddy list. Just as you should know the first and last names of the friends they hang out with in real life, you should know the identities of those they are talking to online.

9.   Know the chat rooms your child is visiting. Is it a regional room or a topic room? Is the topic age-appropriate for your child? Remember that when we shoot one of our "To Catch a Predator" investigations, it only takes minutes in some cases for our decoys to be hit on.

10.   Is your child forming an addiction or obsession to the Internet? Is he or she getting up in the middle of the night and spending time online? You can check the archive of who your teen has been talking to. If there is an unusual amount of time spent talking to one person, especially a person you don't know, you need to pursue this.

11.   Develop trust. Your child has to know that if he or she is approached in an inappropriate way online, they can come to you as a parent and confide in you what has happened. The child needs to know that they won't be punished. Remember, if this happens, the kid is the victim and in most cases is not to be blamed.

12.   Know where to go if a predator has approached your child. Yahoo! and AOL have mechanisms to report suspicious activity. You should never be shy about calling an Internet service provider to report something. Also, many police departments have youth officers who specialize in this area. Most are eager to pursue this sort of thing.

13. Don't delay reporting a predator incident. Remember, it probably isn't the first time the guy has tried to solicit a teen. If you don't do anything, you're only giving him the opportunity to go after another innocent kid.

14. It's never about the technology. It's about communication. Parry Aftab stresses this over and over again and I think she's right. Don't blame the Internet or be intimidated because your kid is more tech-savvy than you are. Your job is to be a parent and help your children make the right choices.

15. There are certain things that you should tell your kids are off limits for online discussions with non-family members. If they feel they can come to you for advice on emotional issues, they are less likely to seek answers on the Internet from strangers.

16. Make sure you have antivirus and other protective programs. A lot of children are exposed to inappropriate material because of spam on the family computer. With the software available today, there is no excuse for that to happen.

17. Don't ever allow your child to use their real name as a screen name. CHRISHANSEN4U for instance is a bad idea and gives a potential predator enough information to check for a home address.

18. Interactive games like World of Warcraft, Xbox 360 Live, and other games allow players to communicate with each other in real time, without a reliable way of logging those conversations. This creates the potential for predators to use these games to groom or meet teenagers. These games have an addictive quality to begin with, so if your kid is staying up until all hours playing he could be exposed to conversations with people from all over the world. This is another area

where a little parental interest goes a long way. We're beyond World of Warcraft in our house now, but when my sons were playing, it could dominate their lives for hours at a time. I asked my boys to show me how it worked and explain how they communicated with other players and they were more than happy to do so. They were flattered that I showed interest in their current activity.

19. Computer contracts work for some families. Essentially the parents agree that the child will be guaranteed a certain amount of time on the Internet and computer per week and in return the child signs a document promising to abide by certain behavior. No talking to strangers in chat rooms, for instance. It's not a bad way to go, especially because you can have your child actually draft the agreement, which could be a healthy exercise in itself.

20. If they still don't understand what kind of people are cruising through chat rooms, go to the *Dateline NBC* Web site via msnbc.com and you can show them streaming video of men who are willing to show up at a home where they think a young teen is alone.

It is also not a bad idea to initiate a discussion with your kids about their friends' online habits. Ask them if their pals are on MySpace, Facebook, or Xanga and if they restrict the people who can visit their sites. Ask if they are worried that any of their friends might be engaging in risky behavior. Is anyone talking to adults? Explain that it's not tattling to say so and that you will be careful about handling the information so that it does not come back to embarrass your child. It's okay, I think, to promise limited immunity in exchange for information that could protect one of your kid's friends.

I've had to read more than my fair share of chat logs between potential predators and decoys while working the "To Catch a Predator" series and I can tell you that there is a grooming pattern among these guys that parents and kids should be aware of and look out for.

We are aware of a number of cases where predators pretend to be teens when they're not. They will go so far as to get a teenager's picture and use it to build a fictitious profile. The adult posing as a teen will then try to build online relationships with kids. Sometimes a man in a situation like that will simply derive his satisfaction from the online chat itself and there is no intent to meet physically. But in the majority of cases I've seen, the predator doesn't hide the fact that he is an adult and the goal is to meet the teen in person for a sexual liaison.

First off, I can't imagine why any adult would think it's appropriate to strike up a conversation online with a child he's never met. But, as we've seen in state after state through ten investigations, there is no shortage of men who will seek out these conversations and relationships.

It's a grooming process and parents and kids need to be aware of how it works. In our investigations, we've seen men continue online chats for four weeks with a child who he is trying to seduce. The conversation often starts innocently with the potential predator saying things like: "Hey what's up? What brings you into the chat room tonight? What are you looking for?" The guy will often try to find some common ground.

He'll ask about homework, pets, music, or sports. He'll try to determine the relationship between the child and his or her parents. There will be questions about siblings. If he senses there is any friction in the home, he'll take the child's side. If the child says their parents are too strict, the predator will say he had strict parents and knows how difficult that can be.

If the parents are divorced or widowed, the predator will want to know if the parent the child lives with has a significant other. He'll want to know if the child gets along with that person. If not, he can capitalize on that by empathizing with the child's difficult situation. Often the first few conversations don't even involve sex or meeting in person.

They end almost politely with lines like, "Bye, good luck with your test tomorrow" or "Hope you score a goal in the soccer game."

The next phase we often see in the grooming process is the stroking phase. The predator will offer the child nice words, compliments, and praise. He'll ask for a picture and then tell the child how handsome or beautiful they are and how mature they act. This can obviously be very flattering to an adolescent who may be having a rough go of it in the rest of their life. Then there may be an offer to buy clothes, an invite for dinner, or a meeting at a mall.

If the child is still involved in the conversation at this point, there's a very good chance that the predator's questions will become more personal. He'll ask about the child's dating habits, what he or she has done sexually. Oddly, we've seen lots of these men ask girls if they are ticklish.

The next conversations usually are more sexually graphic and sometimes very specific about what sex acts the predator wants to perform. We had one man in Georgia tell the decoy he was going to bring a wedding dress for her to wear as he took her virginity. Men have offered lingerie, boots, and motorcycle jackets.

In our investigations, by the time all this happens the guy is ready and more than willing to pay a visit to our undercover house to consummate the relationship. In those cases, of course, they end up being confronted by me and ultimately arrested by police. But remember, these predators don't go into the chat room just because we're doing an investigation. They are in there every day looking for kids.

You must teach your children to recognize this questionable behavior and this grooming pattern. Just because it's flattering doesn't make it appropriate. You need to remind them over and over that if they sense an adult is trying to solicit them they must tell you. So much of this activity goes unreported because of embarrassment or shame on the part of the kids. The environment in your home must be one where they feel comfortable telling you about an incident like this.

The other thing to remember is that in some ways these are not crimes being committed by strangers. The predator and his intended victim may not know each other in person but so much time has been spent grooming that the child could start to feel like he or she actually knows the man. They might even start to feel they have something invested in the relationship. So when warning your kids about not talking to strangers on the Internet, remember your definition of a stranger and theirs might be two different things. That's why it's so critical to teach your kids to recognize the grooming process.

We as parents also have a responsibility beyond keeping the lines of communication open. We are ultimately responsible for the technology we put in our children's hands. We are quick to purchase the latest cell phone or handheld portable video game and let our kids walk around towns that have wireless Internet connections on virtually every block. Do you know if your son or daughter has unmonitored Internet access through one of those devices? Do you know how much time they spend in communication on them and with whom? We should all know the answers to those questions.

Virtually every Internet service provider has parental controls to block pornography, spam, and pop-ups, but those are the basics. There is also highly sophisticated software that can track what a child is doing on the Internet so it may be monitored by parents. The danger in recommending any single software security program is that there are many great products available and you can't name them all. However, when it comes to key logging software, SpectorSoft is one of the most highly regarded on the market and is even used by the CIA. Key logging software essentially records everything typed into your computer. Every e-mail that's typed, every instant message sent, and every Web site visited can all be replayed as if it were videotape.

The software can also record MySpace activity so you can know what your children are posting on their sites as well as what other children are posting about them. It will also give you the ability to see every search that's been conducted on Google, Yahoo!, AOL, and MSN. It can also analyze what your children are doing on the computer and if a threat is sensed, the program can notify you via e-mail. There are options to block specific Web sites or Internet access altogether. It costs about a hundred dollars and is available at www.SpectorSoft.com.

Perverted Justice has reviewed several filter software programs and says Content Protect is at the top of its list. Content Protect is also protective filtering software that allows you to track what your children have been doing online. It also has a remote function that allows you to check the logs of computer activities from anywhere around the world. The product uses dynamic filtering, which means a Web site might be blocked one morning because there was a particularly violent story being shown, but unblocked in the afternoon after that story was removed from the site. It costs about thirty-five dollars. You can learn more at www.contentwatch.com.

Those are examples of add-ons, some of the dozens of security software programs currently available, but there is also new technology available when it comes to the operating systems. One example is the new Windows Vista platform that came out in January 2007. This system is designed for one-stop shopping when it comes to parental controls. All you have to do is go to Family Safety Settings and everything is right there. You can set limits on Web sites and Web games for your children. You can set time limits for Internet access and restrict the applications your children use. The platform also allows you to click on an icon for Activity Reporting which will give you a history of what each user has been doing on the computer. Vista also lets users add on other more advanced security programs should they be necessary.

Each family has to set its own policy when it comes to the computer. All the protective software is impressive, but one day your kids will have access to another computer, whether it's at a friend's house, an Internet café, or when they go off to college. That computer may not be as well protected, and the only protection they'll have is what you as a parent taught them.

Afterword

We've now finished and broadcast our eleventh To Catch a Predator investigation. I keep thinking that at some point, all the notoriety of these investigations would keep men from showing up at our hidden cameras houses. Not so. Recently in Ocean County, New Jersey, in a four million dollar home situated on a beautiful beach on the Atlantic Ocean, twenty-eight men showed up in four days, apparently hoping to have a sexual liaison with a young teenage boy or girl.

I always say that each time we conduct one of these investigations I go into it thinking that I've seen it all. But, in New Jersey, once again I was wrong. What was stunning there was not only that so many men would show up after three and a half years of To Catch a Predator investigations, but that so many would almost instantly recognize what he had walked into.

Take the case of twenty-five-year old Michael Lubrano. Online using the screen name icetruckkiller103, he chats with a Perverted Just decoy posing as a fourteen-year old girl calling herself viking_pride92. At first he doesn't get very specific about sex, leaving the subject open. Icetruckkiller103 says he wants to "get high and watch *Family Guy*, then see where that takes us."

But later icetruckkiller103 gets more specific about sex in a phone call with the decoy. She asks him if he was serious about all the hardcore sex and he says: "we'll see what happens" and "I'm definitely interested. What about you?" The next thing I knew he was walking into our house in New Jersey. He brought marijuana and was anxious to show our on-site decoy his stash.

In New Jersey we had the incredible fortune to find a nineteen-year old college student named Casey to pose as the young teen home alone. She may have been a college student but she easily passed as thirteen or fourteen, and she was sharp. Casey was not afraid to engage the visitors in a conversation that would end up being revealing and showing intent. We saw the grooming process many of these potential predators use online, in real life, and in real time. It was eye opening.

Michael Lubrano seemed right at home as he laid out his marijuana on a bar counter for Casey to smell. "Smells good" she said before she went to get something to drink from the kitchen. It seemed something about the kitchen line got Lubrano thinking. As I watched from the next room on a TV monitor, I could see that suddenly he got suspicious. I knew it was time to walk out and confront him. Before I could get the third question out of my mouth, he looked at me and said: "You're Chris Hansen." I said: "I am. Have you seen this show before?" He then told me I was "real funny" on Opie and Anthony, a syndicated morning radio program on which I had recently been a guest.

Lubrano confided that his life had been "shit" lately and that he was having a hard time finding girls his own age. He confides that even when he was chatting with the decoy online he was nervous about running into me. He then said something that boggled the minds of the entire crew. "I'm a religious watcher," he says. Lubrano goes on to tell me that he watches To Catch a Predator whenever he can and that he even hunts for clips of the show on the Internet. Like many of the other men who surfaced in the New Jersey investigation, Lubrano knew the routine. He walked out the door suspecting he'd be arrested by police who were conducting a parallel investigation. He was. As of this writing Lubrano has pleaded not guilty and is awaiting trial. Lubrano was not alone. There were plenty of other men who showed up in our eleventh investigation who had seen our previous investigations, were suspicious of being caught trying to hook up with a young teen, but showed up anyway. It continues to astonish me that in spite of all the attention our investigations have gotten, in spite of all the investigaitons the FBI and local law enforcement agencies conduct virtually every day across the country, men are willing to take big risks to go online, meet young teens, and try to set up dates for sex.

It's a reminder that as parents our best defense is what we do at home. It's what we teach our kids and how we warn them that will ultimately be our best defense against online predators. That's why it's important to update you on what some of the most vigilant child advocacy groups are offering you as parents in an attempt to educate and protect both you and your kids.

With that in mind I thought it would be helpful to go back to some of the experts in this field to see what has developed since this book was first published. There'd been a lot as it turned out. Parry Aftab of wiredsafety.org told me recently that she's grown concerned that parents often are not aware of the latest ways predators can reach kids. "Handheld game risks are deeply underappreciated," Aftab says. "Many permit the kids to connect via Wi-Fi to the Internet and communicate with anyone else with the same handheld system in a mall. Parents are totally clueless here."

Aftab also told me that her teenangels and tweenangels, her young recruits who go into schools to try to educate their peers about online risks, report that predators are using cell phones more and more, even getting kids to text them and send photos. Aftab points to the case of some thirteen-year old girls in New Jersey who took nakes pictures of themselves using their cell phones and sent them to some senior boys to impress them. "Lack of judgement," Aftab says, is a "serious and grow-ing problem. They do not understand the consequences."

One of Aftab's new initiatives involves creating a cyberarmy of moms, helping each other to get up to speed on these things, creating the first mom-to-mom social network, called WiredMoms.com.

In the near future, Aftab believes the goal is to "professionalize the Web2.0 industry, including social networks, mobile networks, video networks and online gaming, we are setting up the first center devoted to the industry." It's to be called The Wired Trust and The Wired Trust Institute. Housed in Canada, Aftabs envisions that it will "operate in multiple languages worldwide. It will certify practices, technologies, provide outsourcing for moderation and risk management and handle law enforcement liaison work for the industry." Another goal Aftab says is to train industry executives. The bottom line: professionalize safety.

Teri Schroeder of i-SAFE recently reminded me that "a child living in a statistically low-crime area is just as vulnerable to online crimes and criminals as is a child living anywhere. Location doesn't matter! All criminals, including predators, use the same strategies and tactics on the Internet."

i-SAFE offers a number of online initiatives designed to help par-ents and educators protect children on the Inernet. One of them is called Operation i-SHIELD. It's a growing nationwide network of in-dependent i-SHIELD task forces that pursue the common goal of In-ternet crime prevention. Schroeder says that "members of i-SHIELD task forces share ideas, information, and contacts." Each i-SHIELD task force acts independently, aligning its Internet safety education goals and strategies with the unique needs of its geographic area, but each i-SHIELD task force is also a part of the entire national network.

i-SHIELD is a cyber spot for federal and local law enforcement as well as prosecutors to interact and get educated. Schroeder says: "it's a powerful forum." And the i-SAFE website continues to be a powerful learning tool for for parents, educators, and children as well. The cur-lum now offers more than 150 lessons addressing all aspects of Internet safety topics. Schroeder says that "lesson plans and student activities provide educators with materials that are aligned to educational standards in a variety of academic subjects, making them easy to include with existing curricula."

The truly great thing about the websites designed by these child advocacy groups is that the vital information parents can use to protect their children online is easily accessible, straightforward, and really solid advice. Recently I gave a presentation about online predators in Washington, DC, and had the chance to catch up with Ernie Allen, the president of the National Center For Missing and Exploited Children. NCMEC is a federally funded organization mandated by Congress to assist parents and law enforcement find missing children and prevent the exploitation of children. Along the way NCMEC has developed a website that educates parents, children and law enforcement on the problem of online predators and the many ways children can be protected from them. NCMEC recently re-launched its NetSmartz411 site and it's really easy to use.

The site lists several questions frequently asked by parents, like: "How do I access my child's MySpace profile?" "What do online abbreviations/acronyms mean?" "Is it unsafe to post family pictures of children online?" "How can my child be safe while using a social networking site?" and "How do I select the right monitoring software for my family?" among many others.

The NetSmartz411 page also deals with technology your child may be using to communicate with others that you might not even know about. If your child was using Skype to chat, would you know it? What is IRC? XD? These questions are all answered with a click of your mouse. NetSmartz411 also has a "search for answers" section where you can ask your own questions and have them answered by a panel of experts. The bottom line here is that if you as a parent take advantage of resources like these and absorb the information, research, and advice in this book, your child will be infinitely more safe online.

Del Harvey of Perverted Justice, the online watchdog group we hired as consultants, has now launched a website called howtodeal withcreepypeople.com. It is straightforward, appealing to teens, and provides real life scenarios where teens are approached by either predators, stalkers, or bullies. It's broken up into three categories: it happened to me, how do I deal with it, and predators in the news. It also has a blog component.

I also wanted to take a moment and update you on one of our To Catch a Predator investigations that has stirred up controversy. In November of 2006 we launched an operation in Murphy, Texas, a bedroom community outside Dallas. Some politicians including the local district attorney took issue with civilians and a television network conducting this kind of an investigation. In fact, the prosecutor has, as of this writing declined to prosecute any of the men who surfaced in our investigation. This is the first case where this has happened when law enforcement has conducted a parallel operation to ours.

As you may recall and as you'll read about shortly, a fifty-six-year-old assistant district attorney from a neighboring county surfaced in our investigation. Louis William Conradt Jr. never showed up at our house, but in Texas an online solicitation itself can constitute a felony. Based on his sexually explicit online chat with the decoy and a sexually graphic phone conversation, Murphy police sought an arrest warrant for Conradt and a search warrant for his home. Two different judges signed the warrants and police went to the prosecutor's home in Terrell, Texas, to arrest him and search for evidence. As officers entered the home they encountered Conradt in a hallway; he put a pistol to his head and killed himself.

In the months following Conradt's suicide his sister filed a wrongful death lawsuit against NBC News. NBC lawyers have reviewed the suit and have said the claims are completely without merit. NBC will vigorously defend itself in the matter.

There have been allegations in Texas that *Dateline* somehow pressured the Murphy police to seek warrants against Conradt. Let me be absolutely clear on this. It just didn't happen. Had the police decided to apprehend Conradt a day later, a week later, or a month later we would have covered the story. Timing wasn't an issue for us.

We may never know what was going on in Conradt's mind the day he took his own life, but we do now know more about what was in his home and on his computer the day police tried to arrest him. Recently I obtained the forensic report detailing some of what was on the assistant district attorney's laptop. The list included child pornography. As someone intimately familiar with Texas law, Conradt had to know that if those images were ever discovered, he faced years in prison.

Counting the New Jersey investigation, 286 men have surfaced since we began our To Catch a Predator investigations. As of this writing 256 have been arrested and 128 men have been convicted by a judge or jury or have pleaded guilty. The sentences have ranged from probation and having to register as a sex offender all the way up to thirteen years in prison. That sentence was given to thirty-six-year-old Marvin Harrison Smith, who surfaced in our Georgia investigation. Smith was convicted of attempted child molestation, attempted enticing a child for indecent purposes, and obstructing or hindering law enforcement officers. Called "the worst of the worst" by Harris County Chief Assistant District Attorney Mark Post, Smith was the man who tried to run from police and was finally subdued with a taser.

Acknowledgments

I get credit for being the creator of "To Catch a Predator" because I originally pitched the idea and because I am the one who appears on camera to tell it. But an investigative proposal would never make it on television without some tremendously smart and creative people. Lynn Keller has been my producer from the start. She is indefatigable, bright, pleasant to work with, and a fountain of clever ideas. Allan Maraynes has been invaluable from the very beginning as my senior investigative producer. He was instrumental, along with Lynn, in designing our hidden camera operations and coming up with great input to make each investigation more compelling than the previous one. Mitchell Wagenberg is nothing short of a genius. His brother, Eric, and the rest of his team come up with ways to rig cameras and microphones that would make James Bond envious.

David Corvo, our executive producer at *Dateline*, has been supportive of my team's efforts and wise when it comes to structuring these shows for television. I would not even want to think about shooting one of these shows without Donna "D.J." Johnson and Loren Burlando. From the smallest detail to the biggest challenge, they get the job done every time. As we expanded our investigations our team grew. Producer Meade Jorgensen joined us and has done superb work. The editors and production folks here at 30 Rock are all incredibly talented. Ron Knight, who works with NBC security, makes sure that we are all kept safe. I would not shoot one of these stories without him.

NBC lawyer Craig Bloom and NBC Standards executives Lisa Green and David McCormick have been there for me through it all. I respect their keen legal minds and their advice. They have made all of our investigations better.

There are countless child advocates who have helped in our investigations and have given me important advice in researching and writing this book. Parry Aftab of WiredSafety.org, Teri Schroeder of i-SAFE, and Michelle Collins of the National Center for Missing and Exploited Children have all been extremely helpful to me on this issue over the years.

This book would not have happened without the steady hand and experience of Laura Palmer and the ever patient and exceedingly bright editor in chief at Dutton, Trena Keating.

Many people guided me in many ways while writing this book and I would like to thank Dr. Leslie A. Coleman, Gregg Schwarz, Dan Dietz, Kevin Dietz, Jay Manning, Suzanne Bates, Neal Shapiro, Tim Uehlinger, and Polly Denham. Helen Shabason and Sloan Harris at ICM are great people to have on your team and were critical in framing this project early on.

This kind of investigative work requires a lot of time and travel. It also requires a steady stream of support from loved ones. I owe a huge debt of gratitude to my wife, Mary Jo, and my sons, who probably know me best and love me anyway. I am often asked if my wife "works" and my answer is yes and way harder than when she was a fashion and communications executive. The Hansen ship would not float without her. I could not do my job the way I do without her loving commitment to our family. While I am invigorated by the adventure and travel my job requires, there is no better feeling than coming home.

And finally, I would like to thank my folks, Big Bill and Pat, and the two best sisters a man could have, Karen and Amy. All of them, since the very beginning, showed unwavering support for a son and brother who did not show early promise.